Agent Molière

Agent Molière

The Life of John Cairncross, the Fifth
Man of the Cambridge Spy Circle

Geoff Andrews

BLOOMSBURY ACADEMIC
LONDON · NEW YORK · OXFORD · NEW DELHI · SYDNEY

BLOOMSBURY ACADEMIC
Bloomsbury Publishing Plc
50 Bedford Square, London, WC1B 3DP, UK
1385 Broadway, New York, NY 10018, USA
29 Earlsfort Terrace, Dublin 2, Ireland

BLOOMSBURY, BLOOMSBURY ACADEMIC and the Diana logo are
trademarks of Bloomsbury Publishing Plc

First published in Great Britain 2020
Paperback edition published 2023

A catalogue record for this book is available from the British Library.

A catalog record for this book is available from the Library of Congress

ISBN: PB: 978-1-3503-8486-6
ePDF: 978-1-8386-0675-6
eBook: 978-1-8386-0676-3

Printed and bound in Great Britain

To find out more about our authors and books visit www.bloomsbury.com
and sign up for our newsletters.

Contents

Acknowledgements

Following the publication of my previous book, *The Shadow Man*, a biography of James Klugmann, the Cambridge communist who recruited John Cairncross to work for the Soviets, I met Gayle Brinkerhoff, Cairncross's widow, who told me about her life with him. I was intrigued and decided to look more into his background. It seemed to me that existing accounts, particularly those from journalists and so-called molehunters, did not really 'get' John Cairncross at all: they often misunderstood or misrepresented his motivations, distorted his Scottish background and attributed to him political ideas that he did not hold. Above all, he suffered in comparison to the other four members of the Cambridge spy circle. Assumptions made about them were inevitably applied to him, but in doing so often obscured the important facts of his life before, during and after his period as a Soviet agent. As I researched his life, Gayle was always supportive, providing access to papers as well as contacts and contributing ideas and reflections, but never obstructive; we agreed early on that I would do the biography entirely in my own way. Gayle and David Gow have been very generous with their time throughout the writing of the book, and I'm very grateful to them for suggestions and pointers along the way.

Similar gratitude is due to the Cairncross family, who provided me with further insight, reflections and permission to use family correspondence and papers. I am particularly grateful to David Cairncross for clarifying points and reading over sections and Frances Cairncross for permission to use her father's papers and for passing on miscellaneous correspondence. Philip Cairncross and Sandy Cairncross made helpful suggestions on later drafts.

Former friends and colleagues of John Cairncross were invaluable during the research for this book, and I am particularly grateful to David

Rubin for reflecting on his friendship with Cairncross (including his estimation of him as a scholar) and for sharing some of his expertise of French literature. Thanks are due to Allan Evans for sending me his memoir of John Cairncross in Rome and telling me of Cairncross's connection with Frances Keene. Declan and Jeannette Walton were excellent hosts and generous in reminiscing about their time with John and Gabi Cairncross in Rome and Geneva, and I benefited from their constant interest and encouragement.

They also set me on the trail of other former FAO colleagues in Rome, Kay Killingsworth and Silvia Balit, who recounted not only her memories of John but also the earlier friendship between him and her parents. While in Rome, I was fortunate to meet Fiorenzo Niccoli, one of Cairncross's old friends in Parioli, who spoke of their times together, including their unofficial membership of the Parioli dog-walking circle. It was a pleasure to collaborate with Marco Zatterin of *La Stampa*, who was generous with his time and contacts. Nick Parmée told me more about his father, Douglas Parmée, Cairncross's best friend at Cambridge, over a convivial lunch at the French House in Soho.

Richard Norton-Taylor has been supportive and encouraging from the start of this project. I am grateful to Richard Davenport-Hines for advice and suggestions; he continues to set a formidable example for any historian and biographer. I enjoyed meeting and exchanging ideas about John Cairncross and Donald Maclean with Roland Philipps. In addition, I would like to thank the following who helped in various ways: David Broadhead, Secretary of the Travellers Club, Andy Young, my old friend from Ruskin, for taking me to Lesmahagow, Jonathan Byrne of the Bletchley Park Trust, David Cahn, David Farrell of Cleveland, Ohio, Caroline Moorehead, Andrew Lownie, Ann Lawson Lucas, Anita Sandhu, Tom Buchanan and Richard Heffernan and colleagues in the Politics and International Studies Department of the Open University.

I am indebted to staff from several libraries and archives, including Glasgow University Library; John Wells and colleagues in the Manuscripts Department of Cambridge University Library; Jonathan Smith and colleagues at the Wren Library, Trinity College, Cambridge; Emily Patterson and James Cox at Gonville and Caius College Archives; and Meirian Jump at the Marx Memorial Library. I am also grateful to librarians and archivists at the BBC Written Archives at Caversham for permission to use correspondence related to John Cairncross's broadcasting work, the National Archives in Kew, the Imperial War Museum, the Anglo-Jewish Association, the John J. Burns Library of Rare Books and Special Collections at Boston College, Massachusetts (for permission to use the correspondence of Graham Greene), the Fondazione Biblioteca Benedetto Croce in Naples, the Bodleian Library, Oxford, and the London Library.

Jo Godfrey, my editor at I.B. Tauris, encouraged the book from the start and once again provided insightful comment and support throughout. I'm grateful to her colleagues, notably Olivia Dellow, for help at various stages of the book's progress.

Geoff Andrews

Note on sources

This book draws on John Cairncross's personal papers and correspondence provided by his widow and now maintained in the Special Collections section of Cambridge University Library (MS Add.10042). Alec Cairncross's papers – vast in range and content – are held in the University of Glasgow Archives. The Cairncross family and friends of John Cairncross also provided me with items of private correspondence and related material. While John Cairncross's own MI5 files have still to be released, transcripts of his interviews with the security services and their impressions of him can be found in the MI5 files of others (notably Guy Burgess), held at the National Archives, which also holds the relevant Cabinet Office and Foreign Office material. The KGB and Soviet Intelligence archive in Moscow is no longer widely available to researchers, and for the most part I have relied on the earlier work of Nigel West in making public material relevant to John Cairncross's recruitment, espionage and relations with his Soviet controllers. Details of John Cairncross's work for the BBC are held in the BBC Written Archives at Caversham. The extensive correspondence between Graham Greene and John Cairncross is held in the John Burns Library of Rare Books and Special Collections, Boston College, Massachusetts. The book draws on interviews with John Cairncross's friends, former colleagues and family members.

Prologue: The chase

On Friday 16 November 1979, Britain's prime minister, Margaret Thatcher, confirmed that Sir Anthony Blunt was the 'fourth man' of the Cambridge spy circle. Andrew Boyle's recently published book, *The Climate of Treason*, drawn from his interviews with leading intelligence figures, had identified 'Maurice', who was later uncovered as Blunt with the help of *Private Eye* magazine. Blunt's public exposure came fifteen years after he had confessed to spying for the Russians in return for immunity from prosecution. His identity as the fourth man, following the earlier defection to the Soviet Union of Foreign Office (FO) diplomats Donald Maclean and Guy Burgess and MI6's Kim Philby, was already being discussed in political circles by the time of Thatcher's announcement. The search was now on for others.

Two days after Thatcher's statement to the House of Commons, the *Sunday Times* revealed that another FO official had been a Soviet agent, without naming him. In a race to beat their competitors to the scoop, they put two of their investigative journalists on the case. The following month Barrie Penrose and David Leitch pounded the streets of Parioli, an affluent, elegant and hilly suburb of Rome, hot on the trail of a 'Fifth Man'. Penrose later detailed his account of their *Sunday Times* scoop, which carries triumphant echoes of Carl Bernstein's and Bob Woodward's reporting of the Watergate conspiracy of a few years before. Determined to beat rivals to the story, they acted on information provided by Sir John Colville, Winston Churchill's former aide and an old FO official. With Colville's cooperation and aided by a last-minute dash to the civil service library and their rigorous scrutiny of the pages of a Lanarkshire telephone directory for the name 'Cairncross', their discoveries had finally taken them to Italy, though they had agreed to keep their destination 'secret' from the readers.

Unsurprisingly perhaps, their first visit to John Cairncross's fourth floor apartment at 1.00 am was unanswered: he was a heavy sleeper and deaf in one ear. Their return at 7.30 am was more successful in rousing 'The Spy Who Lives Alone'. 'This time', they revealed to the *Sunday Times* readers, 'an elderly man, wearing sandals, grey flannels and an old cardigan, answered the door.' Cairncross had just finished breakfast and invited the two men into his small home, where they were impressed by his books and his intellect, while at the same time noting his frugality and 'almost hermitic' life, later embellished by Penrose's own photographs. The scoop with which they now proposed to allure their readers was Cairncross's admission that in the late 1930s he had discussed FO views on appeasement with notorious Soviet spy Guy Burgess. Other admissions by Cairncross that he had been a member of the student communist group at Cambridge and had known members of the spy circle were also misleadingly repackaged in the following day's headlines.

In 'I Was Spy for Soviets', Leitch and Penrose reported that Cairncross admitted passing to Burgess 'an up-to-the-minute account of Britain's diplomatic strategy and "inside" top level political options during the volatile spring of 1939 and he continued to do so at least until the outbreak of the Second World War in September'. In fact, Cairncross was unaware at the time that Burgess or any of the other four were Soviet agents (membership of a 'ring' has always been an unhelpful description of Cairncross's role). The 'diplomatic and political material' he admitted to passing were handwritten summaries of lunch conversations with FO colleagues at the Travellers Club. His two interrogators now shifted to a more empathetic style, eliciting (they claimed) not only a 'confession' but also 'a sense of relief' and even 'relaxation', as he sought refuge in a 'secluded' and 'scholarly' existence.[1]

'I am so glad that you have survived events!' Graham Greene, Cairncross's friend, wrote from Antibes shortly after seeing the newspaper article. 'I was a bit puzzled because none of the photographs looked in the least like you and only the address tallied.'[2] Greene also wondered, in the same letter, how the front page scoop had managed to miss the fact that he and Cairncross were both MI6 colleagues of Kim Philby, the most prominent and damaging Cambridge spy.

Leitch would later claim that his *Sunday Times* story had 'ended [Cairncross's] life in Rome'.[3] In fact, Cairncross would stay in the Eternal City for another ten years, during which time he published his third book on the seventeenth-century French playwright Molière, completed a translation of La Fontaine's Fables, contributed to Italy's arts TV channel, translated several Racine plays for dramatization in London and Edinburgh theatres and carried on working as a consultant for the Food and Agriculture Organization of the United Nations (FAO).

Shortly after Penrose's and Leitch's early morning interview, another *Sunday Times* journalist, Marjorie Wallace, attempted to get a little closer to an understanding of Cairncross the man. She contacted Cairncross, who had still not read the original *Sunday Times* article, and after he reluctantly agreed to discuss 'his side' of the story, she encountered a 'down at heel don', whose surroundings were suggestive of 'an air of impermanence: a suitable place for a man on the run, without the paraphernalia of relationships, comfort or security'. Initially cautious over the purpose of the interview, Cairncross opened up and impressed her with his collections of rare books and ornaments, and charmed her by showing his renowned translations of French drama and poetry. That evening he took her out to a local trattoria and over dinner told her about his life and his writing ambitions.

The next day, the 'unworldly poet', as Wallace described him, took her on a bus tour of Rome, stopping off at the Vatican and other sights. They continued to argue over the purpose of the interview, with Cairncross worried that earlier 'misrepresentations' of his espionage role would be repeated. Wallace herself became exasperated as she tried to cajole Cairncross to divulge his secrets: 'Are you or are you not the "Fifth Man"', she shouted to him above the traffic and the noise of the city. 'Because if you are not I am really wasting my time.'[4]

A decade later, in October 1990, by which time John Cairncross had now retired to the village of St Antonin du Var in Provence, with his new partner Gayle Brinkerhoff, he received another visitor. Christopher Andrew was a rising academic in the field of intelligence studies and, in collaboration with the former KGB officer Oleg Gordievsky, was about to expose Cairncross as the 'Fifth Man' in their new book.[5] After keeping him under surveillance, Andrew confronted him at the entrance to his home as he returned from a shopping visit. A TV crew, which had accompanied Andrew, was filming from the nearby vineyards.

Cairncross invited Andrew in for a late morning aperitif, a habit he had long enjoyed in Italy. Over a glass of *kir*, Andrew prompted him about his role in helping the Soviets win the decisive Battle of Kursk in 1943, supposedly for the benefit of his and Gordievsky's book, though that was already completed and would be published the following month.

For a week, St Antonin, his latest escape route, became the most famous village in Provence, according to the writer Alan Coren, a part-time resident of the region.[6] From the BBC's Paris studios, Cairncross, by now seventy-seven and cutting a mysterious figure in clip-over sunglasses to protect an eye condition, procrastinated in response to requests for clarifications, confirmations or denials. Back in the *Newsnight* studio, Peter Snow turned to Andrew, Chapman Pincher and Phillip Knightley, experienced espionage hunters, for an estimation of Cairncross's importance as a spy and the validity of the 'Fifth Man' claim. They couldn't agree on either.

Fictional portraits of Cairncross have taken us no nearer an understanding of his character, or his importance as a spy. In *Cambridge Spies*, Peter Moffat's impressive four-part dramatization, uninhibited by the need for historical accuracy, Cairncross is a marginal figure, reduced to a cameo appearance as a reluctant pawn of the bullying Anthony Blunt. According to this account, Cairncross had to be pressured by Blunt on the instructions of Soviet agents to pass to the Russians details of German military manoeuvres taken from the Enigma decrypts at Bletchley Park. In *The Imitation Game*, where the lean, angular Cairncross appears as a short, chubby Scot, played by the Downton Abbey actor Allen Leech, he is even relocated from his linguist team at the Government Code and Cypher School (GC&CS) at Bletchley Park to the cryptographers' hut, as a close colleague of Alan Turing, somebody he never met. *The Imitation Game* presents Cairncross as Turing's blackmailer, an erroneous and pernicious idea which probably has its origins in John Costello's *Mask of Treachery*, in which Cairncross's ten-month stay at Bletchley Park is expanded to four years. Cairncross, according to Costello, 'was well-placed to obtain technical data from Turing, whose vulnerability to blackmail because of his homosexuality made him a security risk'.[7] Costello even has Cairncross 'helping the communist takeover of Yugoslavia'.[8]

Whereas *Cambridge Spies* had Blunt as Cairncross's master controller, *The Imitation Game* puts the British intelligence services in command: Cairncross, in this account, is utilized as a double agent for their benefit. This portrayal of an efficacious British intelligence service having Cairncross in their pocket would no doubt surprise some critics, who blame them for letting him get away. Indeed his contradictory Bletchley Park legacy only seems to confirm the wider mystery of John Cairncross's life and character. He is listed in its Roll of Honour, though not commemorated on the Codebreaker's Wall, and while the Battle of Kursk is listed in the Bletchley Park glossary of achievements, the official who did most to influence it is not mentioned by name. However, in the puzzle posed in its souvenir version of the mystery board game *Cluedo*, subtitled 'Who Killed the Bletchley Park Spy?', there is a coded reference to one of their more notorious employees: 'Yesterday security staff at Bletchley Park started an investigation following the discovery of a body of the intelligence officer, John Blackcross. Rumours about Blackcross's communist sympathies had been circulating for several months with many believing that he was a spy who was selling the park's secrets.'

There is a very fine line between fact and fiction in the life of John Cairncross. Misleading trails that emanated on account of his supposed 'working-class' background, his 'Clydeside militancy', his unyielding loyalty to the Soviet Union and his manipulation by his 'tutor' Anthony Blunt (all of which are palpably false) concluded with his depiction as the 'Fifth Man' of a *ring* of spies, despite being unaware of the activities of the other four. The refusal to release his own MI5 file has not helped. Cairncross, who died in 1995, had intended to write a full account of the events leading up to the Munich crisis of 1938 that would revisit the political choices he made at that time, when the British government appeased fascism. It was a task that went unfulfilled, and many questions about his motivations remain unanswered. Wrongly caricatured as a class conscious working-class agitator at odds with capitalist rulers, his politics were driven by a combination of a European anti-fascism borne from cycling around Germany and Austria at the age of nineteen and supplemented through meetings with Italian exiles in Paris; a Scottish disdain for the inertia, elitism and conservatism of English governing institutions; and from Molière (rather than Marx) a contempt for the *précieuses* as they paraded their follies and privileges.

Regarded as an obfuscator, even to those in his own family, his single-mindedness and refusal of orthodoxy or convention often worked to his disadvantage. His own autobiography, published posthumously and derived from different versions of his memoirs, went some way to challenging accounts of his life and espionage, but also carried significant omissions and evasions.

In reality, his life had been one of escape. His early move from Glasgow to Paris and his first-hand discovery of Europe's culture (and its fascism) was a search for freedom, intellectual curiosity and principles to live by. His move from the civil service to Italy was not merely an expedient one but a journey which he believed would free him to be a scholar and a writer. Italy's art and culture also offered a means of escape, while regular travel brought new freedoms. It freed him to a degree, while he never got away from the past; its memories, loyalties and judgements caught up with him.

But what was he escaping *from*? And who was the real John Cairncross?

Chapter 1
A Scottish education

Lesmahagow is a small town situated on high ground in the Clyde Valley, 25 miles southwest from Glasgow, in South Lanarkshire, on the road to England. Its name is derived from a sixth-century Welsh saint Machutus or Mahagw, and in Gaelic it means an enclosed or walled area. The arrival of Benedictine monks in the twelfth century provides the early origins of the village settlement, with its community formed around the church of St. Machutus. It was they who both bequeathed the village's name and planted the fruit trees in the surrounding fertile land that was ideal for farming. Lesmahagow subsequently became a useful coach stop on the way to Glasgow, but it was the coal industry that brought people to the area in the period of Victorian prosperity. The growth of the Coalburn collieries, a short distance away, had implications for the character of the village and its relationship to the fast expanding port of Glasgow, whose rapid development was crucial in driving wealth in the Victorian era. By the time John Cairncross was born in 1913, 'The Gow' had contributed to the prosperity of Glasgow's economy, in an area increasingly defined socially and economically by the mines at Coalburn.

However, Lesmahagow's place in history had already been partly shaped by the religious dissent of its inhabitants, including the seventeenth-century Covenanters who were imprisoned for their beliefs. Later, Lesmagahow's nonconformist religious convictions were manifested in variants of Presbyterianism, and in the nineteenth century its temperance hall was the meeting place for many of the village's social activities and gatherings, including concerts and talks, which gave it a distinctive social cohesion. A poem written in 1914 by Thomas Thomson, a former resident of Lesmahagow by then living in the United States, reflected on the 'worthies' of his village as he had left it fifty years previously. Partly written in Old Lowland Scots dialect, the first four verses give a flavour of the village, its characters and its sense of community.

---

(1) There leeved langsyne, in Lesmahagow toon,
Some gie droll worthies, an' the country roon;
In hamely verse, their names I'll try to tell,
So I'll begin at the fit wi' Guy Dalzell.

(2) He was the inventor o' the Wooden Horse, **(1)**
An' on its back he carried claith and tea;
While o'er the road leeved Andrew Wilson,
If onybody owed him, he cried pay, pay.

(3) But I manna forget the Weavers' hooses,
Where the Auld Baillie wove the waft to tartan;
Dan Haddow, his twa dochters, an Guy Cooper,
Auld King Carwell an' Bauldy Martin.

(4) There was Tam McCartney an' Leezie Steele,
Tailor Brown an' Sanny McKie;
Morris Harrison an' Geordie Scott,
Doctor Slimon an' Jock o' the eye.

The 'Tam' or Tom McCartney of the fourth verse had, at the time of Thomson's departure in 1864, owned a draper's shop cum general store in the village's main street. In that same year, Andrew Cairncross, John's grandfather, a chief buyer at Arthur and Company in Glasgow, came to live in Lesmahagow after marrying Tom McCartney's daughter, Margaret. He helped his father-in-law run the village shop which they turned into an ironmongery. It was this shop that John Cairncross's father would inherit, though little else came his way from his own grandfather. The nephew of a Chartist martyr from Strathaven hanged for leading a demonstration, Tom McCartney had accumulated some of his own wealth and property, though he later caused a family rift by marrying his housekeeper in his early eighties and making her the sole beneficiary of his estate. John Cairncross's father, Alexander, as the eldest son, took on the responsibility of looking after the family ironmonger business, Cairncross and Menzies, to which he devoted his life, establishing himself in his own generation as a notable Lesmahagow 'worthy'.

The status of the Cairncross family as well-regarded stalwarts of the local community was thus well established by the time John Cairncross was born. It was a solidly lower-middle-class background; he was not an 'impoverished militant, working-class' son of Red Clydeside, as he has sometimes been depicted by molehunters and espionage writers; he also did not, as some lazy Marxist discourse might put it, have a typically 'petit-bourgeois' upbringing. Social classes mixed and the Cairncrosses could count farmers and miners alike as friendly neighbours. His Presbyterian inheritance would leave its mark on the seriousness he and his family attached to education and the benefits a good schooling would bring: the importance of working hard, getting on in life and aspirations to achieve were ingrained at an early age. The dissenting traditions were there too, and perhaps his lifelong nonconformism had its roots in an ambivalence towards established authorities first aired along its rural lanes and moorlands. On the other hand, the closeness of the community, its seclusion from the city and broader cosmopolitan cultures would stimulate in him a restlessness for travel and exploration. In later life he would attribute his 'argumentative temperament' to an indirect consequence of 'Presbyterian fervour',[1] and believed also that it helped him acquire the doctrinal clarity he brought to his translations and editing work. However, there were other significant roots for what became an impressively highbrow family.

Though Alexander Cairncross's own ambitions were constrained by the realities of running a business, his younger brother Tom became a Church of Scotland minister and, as T. S. Cairncross, met with some success as a poet and author. Between 1901 and 1907 he was a minister of Langholm South United Free Church, located just 8 miles from the English border, where he became an early mentor of the renowned poet Hugh MacDiarmid (then known as Christopher Grieve), imbibing in his young protégé, who attended his church, borrowed from his library and taught at his Sunday school, a strong sense of Scots border identity. Along with the certificates for bible knowledge, MacDiarmid, by his own admission, owed a debt to the Reverend Cairncross for introducing him to modernist verse, notably his own poetry on Langholm and the borders. This influence was at its height when MacDiarmid was in his early teens but was also evident in some of his later poetry, and he remained in touch with T. S. Cairncross until after the First World War; he included some of the latter's poetry in his Northern Numbers annual of 1920.[2]

Their paths would diverge radically in later years, as T. S. Cairncross made clear his ideological opposition to socialism, while MacDiarmid, whose politics evolved from Scottish nationalism to communism, later renounced the religious doctrines of his former mentor, seeing in his work both a sentimentality and an implied superiority of the Covenanters, who held the key to knowledge and wisdom. T. S. Cairncross produced, in addition to poetry, books on the mission and role of ministers, the elements of a good sermon and the task of reviving religion in a secular and 'commercial' world. Along the way, he researched his own family history, discovering links between his ancestors and Walter Scott and uncovering what he took to be a 'Cairncross motto', with which he prefaced some of his ideas and values: 'Recte faciendo neminem timeo', or 'I fear none in doing right.' It might be said that John Cairncross adopted a similar principle in later life when explaining why, on anti-fascist grounds, he had decided to pass confidential material to the Soviets at the time of appeasement and during the Second World War.

Alexander Cairncross may have relinquished any academic interests in order to keep the family business going, but he clearly held such ambitions for his children and recognized the virtues of higher education for Scottish lower-middle-class families. He married a local schoolteacher, Elizabeth Wishart, whom he had met at a mutual improvement class, and her conviction that education was the key to advancement made an early impression on him. 'It has been mutual improvement ever since,' Alexander Cairncross later recounted to his family.[3] Indeed, John Cairncross's mother was the primary parental influence on his early development, and his memories of childhood centred on her as the source of intimacy and contentment. Like many women of her generation, she invested a lot of her own hopes and aspirations in the prospects of her children. Formerly a teacher at the village upper school, she encouraged a love of learning in sons and daughters alike, which was maintained in later generations. Two of Cairncross's sisters, Margaret and Elsie, took university degrees and became schoolteachers; two of his brothers became university professors, a post he would briefly hold himself. Academic ambitions were clearly nurtured and expanded over subsequent generations. It was 'quite an intellectual family'.[4] His mother's efforts were the more commendable given the burden of bringing up a large family – a task relieved by their live-in maid. In addition to encouraging her children with their studies, it was left to his mother to supply what he later called the 'special feeling of harmony' in his early life.[5]

By contrast, he acknowledged that he never enjoyed a close relationship with his father, partly a consequence of the age difference between them.

> As my father married late, by the time I was born he was old enough to be my grandfather. This, coupled with a Scots restraint, made for a lack of intimacy between us. … My trouble was that, being the youngest, I never got to know him well and had little knowledge of his many virtues which I would have appreciated had I been in closer contact with him.[6]

He felt his father was constrained by the values of an earlier generation and was not in any sense a role model or significant influence on his youngest son. Nor was he a particularly good communicator. Cairncross senior, in the recollections of his children, was not given to unnecessary fraternizing. After a hastily murmured grace, conversations at mealtimes were often discouraged, curtailed abruptly, or ended prematurely with an unexplained proverb, a habit which irritated his youngest son. At mealtimes, at least, possible horizons were left unexplored. Aside from his interest in bowls – he was the president of the Lanarkshire Bowling Club – he remained immersed in his business and its accounts. His aptitude for figures meant he was a reliable consultant on tax affairs, which enhanced his esteem in the village.[7] Alexander's religious observance, in a village which had maintained its nonconformist inclinations by accommodating three different Presbyterian congregations, included taking the family on its weekly church visit, where he would record the attendance and make notes of the sermon, perhaps out of deference to his younger brother.

The infant school, which John Cairncross entered at the age of five, was at Turfholm, situated at the poorer side of the village beyond the River Nethan. It retained some Victorian features in the period after the First World War when Cairncross first became a pupil. With one main room accommodating up to seventy or so pupils, some discipline was inevitable and the 'tawse', a long leather strap, was still in use for punishing misdemeanours. Nevertheless, in these early classes, consisting of large numbers of boys and girls, there was, he recalled, 'an egalitarian spirit', unimpaired by any serious social divisions.[8] Despite differing economic circumstances, friendships developed between children of farmers, miners and shopkeepers. Resources were limited (classwork was still conducted by chalking answers on slates), but educational success was widely valued as the main route to social mobility. As the youngest in a family of eight children (four boys and four girls), whose nearest brother Alec was only two years his senior, John Cairncross felt that he was sometimes compared unfavourably to his siblings. Nevertheless, he impressed in his early schooling, with his retentive memory constantly earning good marks and a sound basis for his proficiency in languages.

In his early years he developed a strong interest in the history of Christianity, stimulated by Bible lessons and reinforced by the local environment of nonconformism. A prominent picture on the wall in the Cairncross dining room which portrayed a congregation abandoning the official church was a daily reminder of this. His brother Alec had been a very early convert to religious principles, who between the ages of five and eight studiously followed the commandments, obeying authority and seeking the rewards for good behaviour.

> Heaven was a reality to be played for and that meant keeping commandments, 'being good' and doing as you were told. So I went through at an early age phases of religious experience not unlike those of the lower orders in earlier centuries, following a subservient moral code in the expectation of future but unknown benefits.[9]

Alec joined the Lesmahagow Boys Brigade which, like the scouts, had a religious side as well as an ethos of authority, organization and discipline. Through the Boys Brigade he was taken to camps, went on drilling exercises and marched with its band. Sunday school outings were other occasions where religion played a part in fostering notions of community and commitment.

John Cairncross, who on his own admission was in awe of his older brother – and, to a degree, remained so throughout his life – developed a more sceptical view of religion from an early age, notwithstanding his keen interest in its history and contribution to language and culture. This early scepticism suggested a wider search for greater intellectual freedom and an escape from narrow conventions and moral constraints.

I felt at odds early on with the inhibitions of a Calvinist society, and my aspirations were generally out of line with standard Scottish patterns. Strengthened by the pagan tradition which in Scotland flows just below the surface, I developed strong reservations about the prevailing Puritan morality.[10]

As they grew up together, he and Alec became more critical of religious doctrines, and in their own ways impatient with orthodoxies and prevailing dogmas. They welcomed emerging modern innovations, even if newspapers and the wireless were largely absent from home life. Their academic interests embraced the newer disciplines of political economy, English literature and modern languages. Yet there were some significant differences which originated in their early life. Alec, after outgrowing his early religious beliefs, was the more practical and rational of the two in the clarity and elucidation of his arguments and his problem-solving approach to study – an early example being his willingness to offer solutions to *The Glasgow Herald*'s chess queries.[11] He quickly won the respect of teachers as an impressive thinker with a good future ahead of him, even if his ambitions prior to university had been limited to chartered accountancy.

His younger brother 'Johnny', slight in build, redheaded, impulsive and, at times, impractical, presented a more challenging proposition for his teachers. Inquisitive, like his brother, he was less cautious and conservative and more likely to rebel. He was precocious, even poetical in some of his ideas and occasionally musical, filling some of his spare hours with piano lessons while his brother was absorbed in chess. These early interests eventually lead him down a different path to the one taken by his brother. The brothers both excelled at school, and it must have been to their mutual benefit that being so close in age they could share experiences, discuss their teachers and compare their grades.

When John Cairncross was born, the family lived in Pine Cottage in the village, which could barely accommodate the large family of eight children, two adults and a maid. In 1922, they bought Helenslea, a bigger house situated on a small slope, winding down to the main street of the village and Alexander's Ironmongers. Space was still limited, with John and Alec sharing a bedroom and the maid sleeping in the kitchen. At home the Cairncrosses, like other village families, often adopted the local dialect, Old Lowland Scots, or Lallans. T. S. Cairncross, in his poetry, drew much from Lallans in his comments on Scottish identity and in articulating the predicament facing the people of the borders. In John Cairncross's own estimation, the dialect was ideal preparation for his career as a linguist as it enabled him to appreciate different vocabularies and intonations, while loosening any inhibitions in speaking foreign languages. He was first introduced to formal French in the upper school by the formidable Miss Williamson, who combined rigorous testing of French verbs with Friday afternoon sewing lessons for the boys (while the girls did gym). More significantly, Miss Williamson's class first opened his horizons to European culture, which from his teens became a growing obsession and the source of early aspirations to travel.

The school's English teacher, Robin Macintyre, stimulated a lifelong passion for Shakespeare with the chance to act out scenes and explore the world of English literature, though the school buildings could hardly accommodate any theatre productions. The Cairncrosses had already made their mark in that subject. Andrew Cairncross, the elder of the four Cairncross brothers, was by the late 1920s already an English teacher at a neighbouring school. He would become a distinguished Shakespearean scholar, which he combined with teaching duties in Scottish secondary schools until later moving to the United States as a university professor.

John Cairncross's early schooling had the wider benefit of exciting in him an interest in books and the habit of reading. Reading for him, as for others, was in its own way an escape, and the future bibliophile was already hooked by the time he purchased his first book (on the Arabian Nights) at the age of six. The seeds of what he called his 'roving spirit' had been sown by his early experiences, which also suggested that he was comfortable when left to his own initiative or to find his own entertainment. In addition to family walks and outings, he often took off on his own, ending up at the other end of the village or brought back home by kindly neighbours. At that time Lesmahagow was relatively self-contained and far from the commuter town it became. The Cairncrosses' occasional outings of any distance were either by bus or by train (from Brocketsbrae, a mile and a half from their home) to Glasgow; the most common form of transport in the village was the 'Clydesdale', the horse and cart that delivered the milk and other provisions. Cars were virtually unheard of, and though one of the Cairncross uncles possessed a Jowett, travelling any distance was reserved for a special occasion, to watch a football match at New Year or to visit relatives, and usually accomplished by train or motor coach. Family holidays, Alec Cairncross recalled, 'involved quite a feat of organisation, since so much in the way of sheets, towels, clothes and other requirements had to be carefully packed and forwarded to the holiday address'.[12]

Recreation and entertainment were largely confined to the village, which, allowing for evident differences of wealth, was devoid of serious social divisions. The threat of illness was always present, exemplified by the regular appearance of the 'fever van', though outbreaks of measles were the most severe illnesses suffered by the children. The Cairncross brothers would help out with the milking of cows on local farms and at harvest time often enjoyed a lift on the back of carts. Since they shared a classroom and other social gatherings, it was not surprising that they mixed freely with the children of both farmers and miners. Relations between the social classes in the village must have been strained during the General Strike of 1926, when the condition of miners was desperate, but it led to no violence or sustained conflict among the villagers. Alexander, despite being a 'staunch Conservative', had empathy for the predicament of his customers, offering discounts on the production of a union card, for example.

There were no big status divisions; ostentatious demonstrations of wealth would have been unacceptable and Alexander Cairncross was not given to extravagance, and, as his youngest son recalled, there was 'never much time left over for frivolous extras in such a large family'.[13] Self-improvement and social mobility, however, were priorities and the key to a better life, and Alexander and Elizabeth took pride in the fast accumulating achievements of their children. Moreover the Scottish education system, effectively free through the availability of scholarships, was the vehicle through which talented children of less privileged backgrounds could succeed if they performed well up to the age of eleven – something still largely absent from the English education system. In addition to the success of the Cairncross siblings, earlier graduates from 'The Gow' included Alexander Sandy Lindsay, a future master of Balliol College, Oxford (and a communist-backed Popular Front candidate in the 1938 Oxford by-election), and the renowned psychoanalyst Dr Edward Glover. Alec Cairncross's direct contemporaries included Tom Fraser, who became a Labour cabinet minister, and John Inch, a future chief constable of Edinburgh.

The opportunities, shared experiences and wider social mixing experienced by the Cairncross brothers were quite different from those provided by the education system south of the border, notably that of the English public schools, which had such a significant influence on the writers, poets, public figures and future spies of their generation. Cyril Connolly, for example, even before he went to prep school, was on his own admission a pampered, lazy, sulking child, whose only encounters with his working-class contemporaries were servants' children or occasional brushes with the 'urchins' of Bath, Earls Court or the Isle of Purbeck, as he moved between relations. His experience of bullying and bedwetting at St Cyprians, followed by the rituals of Eton, helped form the basis of his classic work *The Enemies of Promise*. Graham Greene, who would later be a good friend to John Cairncross, was so convinced of the pernicious effects of (mainly) private education for the future of English literature that he edited a whole volume on the subject. There, his own attempts to escape Berkhamsted, where his father was the headmaster, were set out alongside W. H. Auden's early acquaintance of a 'fascist' mentality that he attributed to the honours system at Gresham's.[14]

Of Cairncross's fellow Cambridge spies, all had an early education in the ways of privilege. Among Guy Burgess's contemporaries at Eton, a few years after Connolly, were a future viceroy of India, a lord chancellor, the speaker of the House of Commons, the director of the National Gallery, the editor of *The Times* and numerous MPs.[15] Kim Philby, while head boy, house prefect and commander of the Drill Squad at Aldro Prep School in Eastbourne, briefly interrupted his studies to be taken by his father on a 'grand tour' of the Middle East, from Damascus to Jerusalem.[16] At the same age, John Cairncross had barely left his village. Later, a King's Scholar at Westminster School, adorned in gown and white tie, Philby was told by his grandmother not to mingle with working-class children lest he might 'catch something'.[17] A few years earlier, Anthony Blunt, son of a vicar from Bournemouth, had faced bullying, fagging, poor food and unhygienic toilets at Marlborough. This helped drive him further into the aesthetes' camp with schoolmates John Betjeman and Louis MacNeice and eventually into the arms of the Bloomsbury Group. His gradual dissent bore fruit in the critical outlook an art and culture he developed at Cambridge, though his experience of other social classes by this point was virtually non-existent. Donald Maclean, too, whose nonconformist Presbyterian Sundays were even more spartan affairs than John Cairncross's, had important formative experiences and early expectations of high office thrust upon him. His father, Sir Donald, a Cardiff solicitor who ended his days as president of the Board of Education in Ramsay MacDonald's 1931 national government, was much admired by Gresham's headmaster John Eccles, a fellow Liberal, who invited him to talk at the school. Gresham's, under Eccles, offered itself to parents as a progressive alternative to harsher regimes elsewhere. Its own regime, which had alarmed W. H. Auden and had also upset Benjamin Britten, a classmate of Maclean's, expected its alumni to go on to give enlightened civic leadership.

By contrast, John Cairncross's academic career had its roots in a Scottish education system less concerned with hierarchy, ritual and status and more focused on providing a meritocratic vehicle of social mobility which enabled the most talented pupils to get into a well-regarded secondary education system, where they would take 'Highers' (Higher Grade) with the prospect of going on to university. In the case of the Cairncross family, this meant that after school in Lesmahagow they were able to go on to Hamilton Academy, one of Scotland's most prestigious secondary schools, with a reputation for academic excellence and already boasting a growing list of notable alumni. It had a particularly close relationship with Glasgow University, to which competitive scholarships were available. Alec Cairncross had entered the school in 1925 and found the teaching 'excellent' and unsurprisingly a step up in intellectual range and endeavour, with the teaching of English literature particularly stimulating. He followed his sister Elsie in winning the dux medal, a prestigious academic school prize. His younger brother joined him in 1928, no doubt relishing the journey by motor coach and the new experiences it offered.

However, despite his achievements, he was not as stimulated by the teaching at the Academy as his brother had been. French was taught without recourse to Molière, Corneille or Racine, or any of the other literary figures who so inspired him later, and he was eager to get to university. He was also unimpressed by the prefect system, to which as one of its brightest pupils he was initially recommended. He felt that as a young-looking, red-haired nonconformist it was a role for which he was ill-suited. He attributed the prefect system to the unwelcome influence of the English faith in hierarchy and patronage, which he thought negated the ideals and principles of Scottish education. He was beginning to question authority. Despite his academic success, it appeared that his teachers were also unconvinced about his capacity to provide a leading role model to the juniors.

They could not dispute his academic talents, however, and he only needed two years – as distinct from the normal three years – to secure his place at Glasgow University. In 1930, he even outperformed his brother in coming an impressive fifth in the competition for open scholarships (Alec had come nineteenth in his year), before joining him in digs in the city. He had excelled at his academic work, an achievement which earned him a ten shilling note from his proud – if remote – father.

New horizons beckoned. He had scaled the walls of Lesmahagow.

Chapter 2

From Glasgow to Germany

John Cairncross arrived in Glasgow in October 1930. He had completed his Highers in two years and was keen not to waste any more time at Hamilton Academy. His excellent academic record had taken him to Glasgow on a grant from the Carnegie Trust, set up by Andrew Carnegie in 1901. This was one of numerous acts of philanthropy by the Scottish-American steel owner, a weaver's son from a village near Dunfermline. His grants enabled bright pupils of Scottish heritage to pay university fees and was thus an important provider for talented students from a wide range of backgrounds.

The benevolence of Carnegie and others ensured that Glasgow, Scotland's second oldest university (after St Andrews), continued to broaden its intake to reach out to the lower-middle-class children of tradesmen. Like Edinburgh, Glasgow University had played a significant role in the Scottish Enlightenment. Adam Smith was one of its most distinguished alumni, and when the Cairncross brothers were passing through its ranks, political economy was becoming an influential discipline with growing appeal among students. Moreover, it had a particular significance since Britain was entering into a serious depression on the back of the Wall Street crash of the previous year. The relevance of its theories, notably those of John Maynard Keynes, was given a new urgency. Beyond political economy, other core subjects fitted the growing professions of law, the civil service and medicine, with a sprinkling of future politicians among the alumni of Alec Cairncross's year.[1]

This meant that Glasgow had certain differences in the social composition of the students, ethos and tradition when compared to the Cambridge University that both brothers would know later in the 1930s. There was less posturing, ostentation and grandiloquence among student cohorts. Students at Glasgow, as at all universities, held high ambitions, if without the expectations of power and status held by some of their contemporaries in the old English universities. If working-class students were still largely absent from its lecture rooms, they were not as removed from wider society, and the sight of hunger marchers would not have been the life-defining spectacle it became for the generation of the left-wing Cambridge students in the mid-1930s. Nevertheless, when Alec Cairncross arrived two years before his brother in 1928, he still thought himself out of place and lacking the confidence of some of his more affluent contemporaries. This apprehension subsided, however, as his passion grew for economics and he availed himself of the extensive opportunities afforded by student life.

For the first year and a half Alec had lived at home, travelling daily on the early morning bus to attend lectures. This proved inconvenient for studying and so during his second year he took digs with a Maths student, Ian Smith, in Havelock Street, off Byres Road, a short walk from the university. It was here that John Cairncross, aged seventeen, joined his brother and his friend for his first year at the university. This was his first time away for any length of time, though he was still close enough to Lesmahagow to return most weekends and during the holidays. He relished the new freedoms and opportunities to study, while he was reassured by the knowledge that his brother was close at hand for advice.

The teaching was formal, and compulsory attendance was required for many of his classes, which for him began with weekly sessions conducted entirely in French and German. The first-year lectures at Glasgow were 'enormous, rowdy and very mixed in ability' and each lecturer was greeted by song – 'Ye Mariners of England' among them.[2] First-year teaching was taken by professors, so at least there was the excitement of being taught by experts in their field, even if he would eventually tire of their methods. Initially, he relished the new intellectual freedoms afforded by the university and the city. Aside from his main specialisms, French and German, he was required to take an additional subject each year, and so he also attended classes in political economy

(1930–1) and English literature (1931–2).[3] Both of these subjects left their mark and he was able to draw on them for some of his future endeavours. A knowledge of political economy would be vital for his later occupations at the FAO, as a correspondent with *The Economist* and as a consultant for Italian banks. It also enabled him to keep sufficiently abreast of the key theoretical developments and empirical research in that subject to maintain a lasting dialogue with Alec, who would emerge as one of Britain's leading political economists. John Cairncross's literary interests, first stimulated in depth here, sustained a whole range of research projects in later years. But it was the study of French and in particular his introduction to the ideas and plays of Molière, the seventeenth-century French dramatist, that caught the imagination of the young undergraduate.

Outside formal studies, his early perceptions of class prejudice south of the border – without at this point having any direct experience of it – had brought an early sympathy for Scottish nationalism, and he attended the odd meeting. There was little enthusiasm for conservatism, which he associated with English snobbery, and socialism was not yet a strong movement among Glasgow University students. Despite an increasing unease with religious doctrines and the puritanical morality of the church, his Presbyterian background had encouraged 'a fierce feeling of independence, a refusal to accept a feudal class structure and a confidence in personal worth and dignity'.[4] At that time, as a young undergraduate, a critical reflection on the religious dimension to his Scottish background was a more important influence in shaping his values than politics. His affinity for his own country was evident, and even after he had spent most of his life outside it, he would attribute his early 'poetic, imaginative and impractical' side to his Celtic origins. He admired the openness of Scotland's education system and its distinct legal structure and church body, while he took pride in Scotland's intellectual heritage.

Perhaps unsurprisingly therefore in his early search for principles to live by, he embraced the traditions of the Scottish Enlightenment, notably the work of David Hume. Hume's *Treatise of Human Nature* influenced Cairncross's thinking on justice, religion and the importance of backing arguments with empirical evidence and drawing on experience in explaining human conduct. Significantly, Hume and other Scottish Enlightenment thinkers provided a pathway to the wider European

Enlightenment tradition and some of its leading intellectual figures and philosophies. He was particularly taken with Hume's critique of religious orthodoxy – mindful perhaps of the constraints of his Presbyterian upbringing – and eagerly embraced his rejection of the notion that humans are driven by acts of divine inspiration. This recognition and its philosophical implications was a radical step forward in Cairncross's thinking and was the source of some of his early radicalism which centred on the concept of free speech. Hume's ideas imbibed him with a lifelong scepticism towards religious or any other orthodoxies; he would always be comfortable with the status of a heretic, even when it came at the cost of isolation or rejection.

It was French language and literature which absorbed his attention, though he had to wait a year for his introduction to Molière. In his first months he studied the works of Balzac, Flaubert and Faguet, whose essays on political ideas (including those on feminism and pacifism) would likely have appealed to a freethinking radical. From Balzac and Flaubert he gained a solid introduction to the tradition of literary realism, even if the hard-working life of the country doctor among the nineteenth-century peasantry in *Le Médecin de campagne* – the chosen text of the former – was not the most stimulating. These readings were interesting, if not enough to satisfy his thirst.

It was Molière who made the biggest impression. The main text for the second-year option was *Le Bourgeois Gentilhomme* ('The would-be Gentleman').[5] It was an ideal introduction to the French dramatist, whose work provided Cairncross with a critical outlook on the traits and tensions within his own society. *Le Bourgeois Gentilhomme* was first performed in October 1670 in Chambard Castle, Touraine. It was a five-act comedy that held many of the typical features of a Molière production: the use of irony in uncovering hypocrisy, a satire on manners and, above all, the gradual uncovering of the illusions of a pretentious social climber, M. Jourdain (played by Molière himself in its first production). M. Jourdain had a 'craze for gentility and refinement', according to his music master, as the latter waited to begin a specially composed serenade to greet Jourdain, whose eventual arrival was marked by his Indian silk dressing gown protruding from beneath a green velvet waistcoat and red velvet breeches. Molière's depiction of M. Jourdain as the archetypal aspiring self-seeker who will go to any lengths to learn the status of a gentlemen no doubt amused

Cairncross, who was developing his own critique of pretention, vanity and deference to rank.

Among the delusions and deceptions of M. Jourdain were the attempts to hide his and his wife's humble origins as children of tradespeople, something which might have irked John Cairncross, the son of an ironmonger. John Cairncross saw no need to 'learn to be a gentleman' as he might have put it, though he later believed that lacking in such status put him at a disadvantage at Cambridge, the FO and the civil service. Ironically, two of the other Cambridge spies – both supposedly orthodox communists – were among those who berated him for these particular failings and lack of respect for rank. 'He speaks with a strong Scottish accent and cannot be called a gentleman,' Guy Burgess would report back to his Soviet controller 1937, in a detailed biographical note on their potential new recruit. Donald Maclean, who shared a room in the FO with Cairncross in the same period, thought his colleague's unwillingness to conform to the gentlemanly conventions of British diplomacy could make him a liability as far as Soviet espionage was concerned.

Cairncross was taken with Molière's literary style, notably the *commedia dell'arte*, the form of theatre which had originated in Italy and was renowned for its improvised style, rich character portrayals and targeting of particular social groups. He was impressed with the quality of the language and the use of social criticism and humour in the plays. He found in Molière's humanism a rich counter to the staid theatrical conventions and the religious world views which continued to constrain art and politics of the time. In the future, his rigorous study of Molière's body of work would lead to an interrogation of his sources and an exploration of the historical context of his plays. His work in that field would establish him as one of Molière's foremost experts. At Glasgow, his study of Molière was inevitably limited and constrained by the demands of his other subjects. It was only in Paris and Cambridge that he was able to dedicate a serious amount of time to his work and consider the possibility that he might one day become a Molière scholar.

Cairncross's outlook on life had been awakened by Molière's freethinking and David Hume's critique of religion. This did not draw him to politics, and he did not follow Alec (then a Liberal) in seeking election to the Students' Representative Council of the university. Indeed, he would never be a political activist in any meaningful way, preferring smaller discussion circles and the force of intellectual argument. Ideological world views did not appeal, and he remained unsuited to the loyalties and disciplines required by political parties. Nevertheless, his studies did stimulate an interest in some of the wider philosophical debates on the themes of reason, religion, sexuality and science. At the end of his first year he joined the Glasgow district of the Rationalist Free Press Association and during the autumn of 1931 and spring 1932 attended a series of their lectures at the McLellan Galleries in Sauchiehall Street, near the university. The speakers included Dora Russell on 'The Importance of Atheism to Women'; Hyman Levy on 'Is the Universe Mysterious?'; Anthony Ludovics on 'Christianity's Influence on the Graphic Arts'; and Harold Laski addressing 'The Difficulties of Tolerance'.[6] He must have made some impression of his own in discussions and meetings outside formal lectures as his thoughts on such matters were now being sought. Ian Smith was eager for 'Johnny' to send in some 'serious to heavy stuff' for *The Critic*, a journal he had founded with Alec and others to provide a space for rigorous comment. As with many student publications, however, the journal did not outlast its first issue.[7]

Cairncross excelled in his studies, winning end-of-year prizes for both French and German. His second year was equally creditable, resulting in more French and German prizes and another one for English literature: his enthusiasm for 'Shakespeare and the Elizabethan stage' making the early morning sessions worthwhile. In his second year he was introduced to Jean Racine, another defining moment in his student days. In later years his translations of the 'untranslatable' Racine would be pioneering. In this first encounter, he studied Racine's play *Andromaque*, one that he would later bring to BBC Radio audiences.[8] Yet, his intellectual curiosity had not been entirely satisfied. Studying French and German had brought new passions and a longing for travel. Moreover, if he was stimulated by the subjects, he found the teaching rudimentary and inhibiting, a feeling he shared with one of his classmates, who disclosed to Alec that 'the infantility [sic] of the German class is distressing'. 'French, though a terrible bore, is slightly more adult.'[9]

In 1932, at the end of his second year at Glasgow University, he was required as a modern languages student to spend a year abroad. Before commencing his study in France in the autumn he planned to take a summer cycling holiday. His curiosity about Europe had been stirred by his studies. He had been saving some money for what would be his first trip outside Scotland and relished the chance to travel. As a nineteen-year-old who had not been much beyond his home and university, it was nevertheless a challenge to cycle long distances, arrange his own accommodation and manage his living costs in a foreign country. It was also notable that he was content to journey alone – an indication of his determination to pursue his own interests and ambitions without relying on his peers. In organizing his trip, he turned to the Youth Hostels Association, which in the early 1930s was a fast-growing and essential facility for those who wanted to travel on a modest budget. Prior to his departure, he joined its Scottish association and signed up to its regulations – 'I hereby promise to leave no litter ... and preserve the amenities of the countryside.' His journey through Belgium to Germany and Austria offered the chance to improve his knowledge of its languages, meet local people and appreciate the vast sites of art and culture. However, he would find, as his journey progressed, that his enjoyment of the rich culture of the continent was tempered by his encounters with 'workless' young Germans and the growth in support for Hitler. It was to be a formative moment in the development of his political ideas. His contemporaneous diary of the trip records the range of his experiences and his impressions on conditions in Germany and Austria, formed through his meetings and conversations.[10]

Travelling with the comfort of a bicycle and his Paget Poncho – a cape 'made from superfine material' – he departed at the end of July for Hull, from where he would take the boat to Ghent in Belgium. He needed his cape, as he got 'drenched' on his first day cycling. However, even before he reached the continent, the joy of escape is evident from his diary entries. He took a train from Abington to Lockerbie, finally ending his first night outside Scotland sleeping in a barn at Clifton, south of Penrith. The next day he completed a 'very stiff climb' through the Pennines, and stayed the night at Boroughbridge in North Yorkshire. With the wind now behind him on the next morning, he set off on a long fast stretch into Brough, a village in the Eden Valley, in the East Riding of Yorkshire. At Brough, an old coaching stop for travellers between Scotland and England, he lodged at an old inn where he met two 'boozers' – one 'maudlin' and the other 'decrepit'. The latter sent him on his way with words of encouragement: 'You've got a good Scots accent. My father was Scotch. ... God bless you.'

The next day, Friday, 29 July, he got as far as Pocklington, a small market town 25 miles from the port, where he put up at the Black Bull Inn.[11] Here he found a 'jovial host' who welcomed him into his family gathering, and 'was much interested in my love affairs'. 'You've a sweetheart in Scotland. How would you like to 'ave my wife?' ('I was rather taken aback,' Cairncross noted in his diary.) Finally arriving at Hull Docks on Saturday, he was pleased to make the acquaintance of another linguist: an Irishman 'who could speak half a dozen languages, and had been educated at Lisbon, London, Liverpool and Edinburgh'. With work scarce, he told Cairncross that he had only been able to find a job as an interpreter on the recommendation of his father, a manager on the line. He also met 'an exceedingly well-informed' Jewish man from Leeds who nourished Cairncross's interest in religion by telling him the story of the 'Jewish curse on York' where the Rabbi was reduced to cutting the throats of his co-religionists during a massacre.

His voyage the next day (Sunday) was 'calm' and only disturbed by the concern that he seemed to have mislaid £15 of the £25 he had saved for the trip. However, financial crisis was averted – more serious ones would follow over the years – when the missing £5 notes turned up in his belt and his pocketbook. He was amused to discover on arrival at the port of Ghent that the 'very decent old buffer at customs', in a valiant attempt to speak English, ascertained whether Scotland was a 'destreet of England'. 'I duly enlightened him.'

The delight at being in a foreign country was tempered by his first experience on Belgian roads; the cobbled streets made cycling difficult, and he narrowly avoided being knocked down by a cycle race. But he quickly adjusted and started to enjoy his first day on the continent, and happily acclimatized himself to a new country and its people. He had the impression that 'everybody owns a bicycle, smokes a cigar and drinks beer'. After an evening's rest, the next day he cycled into Brussels and stayed in the Leopold quarter, a prestigious residential area in the years before it became dominated by the buildings of the European Union. He found Brussels a 'beautiful city' and after some sightseeing that included listening to an unorthodox band playing 'ear-splitting noises', watched the arrival of riders on another cycle race and finished the evening dancing in the street 'to the best of my ability' with an elderly lady.

The next day he enjoyed a late lunch of *omelette aux crevettes*, his first real taste of Belgian food before passing the afternoon at the Palais des Beaux Arts, on the recommendation of a First World War veteran and 'ardent Fleming' who 'compared Flemish soldiers serving under French officers to Britons fighting for Germany'. This was the first time on the trip he had encountered any political discussion, and he was still more interested in the artistic attractions of the city. After admiring the 'very fine' Rubens at the Palais, he moved on to the cathedral, before an evening's entertainment in the square where he puzzled over the rules of the handball game in front of him. He was less impressed with his first taste of Belgian beer, but he had enjoyed his day in the capital: 'A fine city is Brussels, with wide streets, shady boulevards and big open spaces. The air is very pure.'

This new exposure to a foreign country and its art and culture was significant in persuading him to extend his studies abroad. His curiosity about the people and their political views had also been mildly aroused by Flemish home-rulers seeking equality for their language among the French-speaking majority. This political interest reached another level of intensity, however, after he took the train from Brussels to Cologne. Once in Germany, he encountered a range of opinion from Germans who, at the beginning of the 1930s, were still coming to terms with the aftermath of the First World War. As he travelled he was struck by the similarity between those he met and some of the characters he had read about in Erich Maria Remarque's novel *All Quiet on the Western Front*, with its vivid depiction of the plight, fears and grievances of those returning to the civilian fold after fighting on the front. He would meet many 'workless' Germans, middle-aged war veterans, students and beggars, communists and socialists and Jewish intellectuals. Above all, however, it was his conversations with Nazi supporters in the year before Hitler took power that had a lasting impact.

On arrival in Cologne, he spent the day recovering from the journey before visiting the house of Joseph Welter, a young German he had got to know slightly in Glasgow. Joseph was out when he arrived, but his father, a First World War veteran, inveigled him with stories of his wartime experiences, which had taken him to within 20 miles of Paris. Herr Welter offered unambiguous explanations of Germany's prevailing problems which were now stirring a growing unrest among the population. He attributed it all to a lack of discipline. 'Germany must have an army,' he told his young visitor, in what would become a familiar refrain for Cairncross as he travelled between towns and cities. Poland was making things difficult, Herr Welter believed, and to prepare for any future conflict he felt there must be conscription. 'Ask any old German', he told Cairncross, 'and he will tell you that his two happiest years were his two years spent in the army.' He 'bemoaned' the decline of discipline among the young, while he regarded the implications of the Versailles Treaty, which held Germany liable for the war damage and demanded reparations and disarmament as a result, as disastrous. The implied guilt on the back of defeat had created only economic hardship and burning resentment, which the 'Hitlerites' were 'exploiting by great promises'. Welter did, however, believe that 'Hitler has reached his zenith and would decline'.

This was the first of many troubling conversations Cairncross would have on the rise of Hitler, but in this first exchange with his host he was content to enjoy the hospitality and his first impressions of a new country: 'He was a most jovial old soul, with a stolid dignity, as he smoked his cigars & drank his beer and told us jokes with a rather self-conscious laugh.' Herr Welter told him that he too had enjoyed *All Quiet on the Western Front* and found it quite realistic. After his son Joseph finally arrived, they stayed up late talking with his father. The next morning Joseph took him to meet his aunt, who introduced Cairncross to ('excellent') German wine, while, in the dialect he sometimes found difficult to follow, the aunt described a recent clash between communists and Nazis.

As Joseph showed him around Cologne Cathedral, Cairncross heard more on the causes of the First World War and its aftermath: 'Germany had not violated Belgium's neutrality and France would have placed her at a disadvantage. Besides, Russia was threatening Austria, so Prussia had to support her. Etc etc.' 'Very interesting', Cairncross noted.

He found what followed more disturbing:

Joseph laid forth concerning the evils of Jews. They were atheists, immoral, dishonest in business and anti-national. I pointed out that there was much dishonesty among the native Deutsch magnates but he said all potentates were Jews. It amounted to this. All the successful personages in Germany were Jews often by somewhat shady means. This was bad for Germany. Therefore the Jews must go. Then he said, nobody kept to the Treaty of Versailles. Everybody is arming. The German minorities (in Alsace Lorraine) were oppressed. Therefore Germany should not keep to it.

'I took leave of the bold Joe,' Cairncross added after what seemed to be a prolonged disquisition, and left for Koblenz. In Koblenz he stayed at a 'cheap hostel', where he listened with interest to the political views of his fellow lodgers, which included both a communist and a Nazi. The communist argued that Hitler had won support through 'lies' and claimed the Nazis were 'mere jingoists'. The socialists were regarded by communists as 'the MacDonald type; no friends of the workers', Cairncross noted, in a reference to the bitterness towards Britain's prime minister who had been expelled from the Labour Party in 1931 after deciding to lead a national government with Conservative support.

The unemployed Nazi, 'lame' and dependent on begging for money, showed Cairncross a poem he had written, entitled 'My Fate'. Both he and the communist complimented him on his German (which they felt worthy of a professor) and, as the Belgians had before, mildly chaffed the Scots' frugal qualities, cheekily suggesting they travelled by tram in order to save on shoe leather. Despite the modesty of their surroundings – before they retired to bed, their sheets were inspected for fleas – Cairncross was provided with excellent food (the Schwarzbrot bread and local plums being particularly memorable), and even if he found the wine a bit too strong, he enjoyed the convivial company of his ideologically opposed housemates. In addition to a German 'workless', he also shared a room with three Czechs and a Slovakian who, in an argument with the Nazi, rejected the claim that his country was mistreating its German minority.

Cairncross's new surroundings had given him the feeling of an escape from routine experienced by many young travellers and he relished immersing himself in the new country. He found the people 'a fine looking set, fine physique and very decent. Nearly everyone has bare legs and there are dozens of wanderers.' The weather, too, was quite a departure from grey Glasgow skies, and the summer heat had taken him by surprise; he was becoming aware that his red hair was now complemented by the 'fine lobster colour' of the rest of his uncovered body.

Early next morning he was back on his bicycle, cycling up through the Mosel vineyards, before going down to the river. There he met another German 'workless', – 'a very decent fellow' – with whom he bathed in the river and sunbathed on its banks before parting. In the evening he crossed the Rhine and cycled back to his hostel in Koblenz where he encountered a young artist able to speak a dozen languages. The following day, Wednesday, he met an Austrian German from Heidelberg in his mid-twenties who had left his Austrian home at the age of fifteen in search of work. He told Cairncross that all German political parties were in it for money. Hitler was in politics for money and would then 'clear out'. He went on to say that the National Socialists were a tough lot who had promised everything to the German people. The Socialists, on the other hand, had 'squandered money on civil servants' wages'. Everyone in Germany was 'nuts on politics', but they considered only their own political party's interests and not that of the German people or their country as a whole. He warned Cairncross that 'there was going to be a social upheaval throughout Europe in a short time'.

Chapter 3
A political awakening

Meetings with several 'young German workless' had given John Cairncross more to think about, and he started to jot down some early comments on the situation in Germany. In that summer of 1932, a year before Hitler took power, these were to be his first recorded political observations on what he knew as 'Hitlerism'; they included some thoughts on its origins and appeal, the ideas it espoused and some tentative suggestions on how its threat might be addressed. These notes were not derived from a particular political viewpoint (he knew little of Marxism, for example); rather, they were impressions born of his conversations, encounters and observations as he travelled.

'Hitlerism', he noted in his diary,

> seems to be an exploitation of the injustice sustained by Germany after the war, combined with the dishonest business control of the Jews & anger at the former gt's [government's] incompetency; nearly all the idealistic youth & the middle classes are in it. Big business as everywhere in Germany is behind it, it seems to be distinctly reactionary & militaristic, though it has no real programme. The unemployed lad on the Mosel seemed to hit it, when he said to me: 'Believe nothing of it & belong to no party. I am a free man.'

What his temporary companion had 'hit on' was that the vested interests consuming all political parties prevented urgent, practical solutions to Germany's economic crisis. Pragmatism had lost out to ideology, and there was now a need for independent voices which espoused the national interest, free of partisan alignments. Cairncross continued to reflect on the situation as he travelled through Germany and then Austria. It must have felt mildly discomfiting – as well as exciting – to absorb the magnificent art and architecture on the one hand, while being confronted by the emerging political and economic crisis on the other. Poverty was a recurrent theme. As he stopped for food in the villages of the Rhine wine region, he was told by a shopkeeper that sardines weren't stocked because 'the people were too poor'. Another told him that 'everyone is out of work. There used to be work at the factory, but that's closed now and things are getting worse.'

As he cycled on the next morning, there were further encounters with disaffected and angry Germans. One meeting with a 'real old German Burger' brought more condemnation of the trade unions and the communists. 'Germany is Christian and national', he was told. 'The communists will never succeed.' This industrialist (and another war veteran) blamed communists for the riots that had broken out in German cities. His outburst ended with a resilient endorsement of the 'fighting' spirit of the Germans – in contrast to the French and Russians who 'might beg for grace'.

Cairncross continued to find the picturesque landscape and countryside enchanting. Cycling in the Rhine Gorge through Boppard and surrounding villages, he came across the 'magnificent' Stahleck Castle where he lodged for the night. Recently constructed by the architect Ernst Stahl, this was unlike any of the other youth hostels he had stayed in. Its palatial spaces complemented the landscape, with murals on the walls and a refurbished dining room in the ruins of the old Schloss, and he was lucky to find a place at the normally oversubscribed hostel. It would gain a notorious reputation under Nazi rule as an official propaganda training centre for young Germans, as well as an internment and re-education site for students held in occupied Luxembourg, and finally as a military training camp.

His enlightening cycling tour of Germany could not obscure its dark underbelly. Talking to his fellow (German) travellers that evening, he found once more that they 'strenuously denied the war guilt position. … France was the chief guilty party'. On another 'glorious' morning he discovered more 'idyllic' country further into the valley where, in need of refreshment, he was delighted to come across a mineral spa where the waters tasted 'deliciously'. His curiosity over German politics was provoked once more after he was warned by a wine producer that 'everything was desperate in Germany', and things would likely end in a 'civil war'. As he made his way up more steep hills the following day, he noticed a monument to the Franco–German war of 1870; it seemed to him as if the spectre of war was now a recurring theme on his travels. His final view of the Rhine, before cycling into Wiesbaden that evening, gave him much to ponder.

The next morning an old German resident of Wiesbaden escorted him on a tour of the town, taking the opportunity to quiz Cairncross on whether Britain regretted entering the First World War on the side of France. After admiring Wiesbaden's parks and old buildings, he spent the rest of the day cycling 25 miles into Frankfurt where, after resting from his journey, he took in the cathedral, the Goethe Museum and a visit to the opera in the evening. He had now covered hundreds of miles and, as well as suffering from tiredness, he was having some trouble with his bicycle, which had begun to slow him down. Finally, after some help from 'an exceptionally decent bloke' who also put him up for the night, he was able to make the next stage of his journey to nearby Bad Homburg, a spa town with a declining Jewish population, and then on to the Roman fortress and museum at Saalburg. After dinner that evening, he went into Bad Homburg with one of his fellow boarders, a young Nazi from Frankfurt, who gave him a stark outline of what Hitler needed to do after he took power. First, the *Frankfurter Zeitung*, a 'Jewish rag', would be 'printed in Yiddish'. Once the Nazis were in government, he told Cairncross over a glass of wine, 'all other parties were to be suppressed'. After this interrogation, Cairncross recalled 'staggering somewhat' back to his lodging. He attributed it to tiredness and the strength of the wine, but it could have been exacerbated by the fanatical convictions of his young companion.

He spent the next day in stifling heat, cycling uphill through old Bavarian villages with their narrow streets and ox-drawn carts, passing noisy geese, until he reached Wurzburg. Here he delighted in the stunning baroque and rococo buildings. He admired its Romanesque cathedral for its 'fine stucco work', and in particular the Franconia Fountain in front of the Wurzburger Residenz, the highlight of his visit. It was a 'magnificent baroque building', with a 'sumptuous staircase' and 'the largest ceiling fresco in the world' – the work of Giovanni Battista Tiepolo and his son, Domenico, with their paintings of the

four continents. He was captivated by the 'lavish decorations', while
the 'mirror room especially was unbelievably beautiful'. It was, he
concluded, 'altogether about the finest building I have seen yet'.

His long summer holiday – he would not see any rain until early
September – was an eye-opening experience for him. He relished the
new freedoms, and although he had started off as a solitary traveller, his
journey had been enriched by the people and places he had encountered
along the way. 'At home one is like a bird in a cage', he confided to his
diary. Among other liberations, he was enjoying a new diet, and made a
note of the memorable meals. The fruit market in Cologne and the fine
Schwarzbrot bread, plus the pancake he had eaten in Wiesbaden; all
were agreeable new tastes and detailed with satisfaction. Despite his
tight budget, he was happy with his introduction to foreign food; a chunk
of bread, supplemented with cheese, sardines, tomatoes and grapes,
was sufficient to sustain him throughout his journey. The origins of a
discerning palate and the knowledge of how to eat well on a low budget
were laid here. Despite needing some repairs, cycling had given him the
freedom to roam, while his facility for languages had inevitably enabled
him to mix freely and win the confidence of his fellow travellers and hosts.
As well as recording his daily movements, he used his diary to reflect
on earlier meetings, evaluate the respective merits of the various youth
hostels as he found them, his impressions of the food and, of course,
carry out an appraisal of the contending political viewpoints he had
encountered. It was a heady mixture of art and politics enlivened by the
input of strong-minded characters. It would have been unsurprising if,
as a teenager on his first trip abroad, he had not felt lonely occasionally.
However, this seems to have been compensated by his many meetings
and various exchanges made possible by his improving German. His
absorption in the unfolding events – his diary entries suggest the eye of
a promising journalist – surely justified his decision to visit Germany in
his own way, where moving at a leisurely pace unconstrained by others
enabled him to gather his thoughts and reflect on the political climate
around him.

In late August he took the ferry from Passau in Bavaria along the
Danube into Austria. He found Austria quieter than Germany, and his
first observations were encouraging. People on the whole appeared
good-natured. Begging was absent in public squares (he would later
discover that it was forbidden). The rolling green hills along the Danube

made it ideal for walking, and on arrival in Vienna he was struck by its 'marvellous' sunlight. Vienna was then a cosmopolitan city, regarded by many as the most civilized in Europe and renowned not only for the beauty of its palaces and architecture but also for its artistic and sexual freedoms and rich Jewish culture. He was to see it in its twilight years before the civil war in 1934 and German occupation in 1938. It stimulated his knowledge of art and culture, while its deteriorating political situation would leave a marked impression on him.

Shortly after arriving in Vienna, he had a rendezvous with an English acquaintance who introduced him to the Viennese cafes and, by way of the city tram, gave him a quick tour of the main sights of the city. But it was a meeting with an older 'Jewish gentleman', Herr Rosenberger, which over the next couple of days gave him insight into the city's art and culture. This 'lively old fellow', who was 'aged 64 but looked 40', adopting the pair as their guide, 'took us all over Vienna'. This included 'a most wonderful dinner at the Tivoli', in 'very fine open air surroundings'. On the second day, after another 'ripping feed' with their guide's sister-in-law, they visited the Burgtheater where he admired another beautiful staircase adorned with frescoes. Without his guide the next day, he found time to buy five volumes of Goethe and to attend a Wagner concert in the evening. Another full day with the guide took him to the art gallery to admire Rubens and the old German Masters, together with Italian Renaissance painters displayed in a building with more frescoes and yet another 'lavish' staircase. Later that evening he went to a performance of Faust, which he found 'exceedingly well-done'.

After a late stroll around the city he returned to his hostel at 1.00 am to find 'a wonderfully international gathering'. On his trip to date he had befriended a collection of Belgians, Germans, Austrians and the odd Czech of varying political persuasions. This group, however, was much broader. It included an Indian student from London, a journalist from Cologne en route to Constantinople, a Hungarian and a Frenchman. 'We sat up for a time and had a most uproarious evening', he recounted. The Indian was asked about Gandhi, while the group discussed with some amusement a recent edition of the *Daily Express* which had warned of a 'Red Terror' in Germany. Hilarity aside, many of the young people present that evening predicted a German civil war in the near future.

The next day he was reunited with Herr Rosenberger who took him to the opening of the Vienna Fair. Here they discussed politics for the first time. His friend told him that he was a socialist and an international pacifist and blamed the German Kaiser for the First World War. He also denounced the rise of the Nazis. With the help of Rosenberger, Cairncross quickly absorbed the wider Jewish culture. They lunched together after touring the museum, and Cairncross was warmly accepted into his family and friendship circles. One evening he was taken to the home of two Jewish ladies, in a 'very fine flat' in the city. One of his hosts spoke excellent English, even if Cairncross found it a 'little gushing' at times. ('The highlands of Scotland are said to be marvellous', etc.)They complimented him on his German and promised him a teaching job if he continued to keep in touch. More worryingly, the evening he spent with his Jewish friends had brought home the scale of the crisis engulfing Austria. They told him of their helplessness when meeting friends in dire straits, now a daily occurrence. 'Everything's getting worse, wages down. Everything is coming down', he was told. And, they added ominously, 'in these times there has to be a scapegoat & of course the Jews are always handy'.

Now engrossed in Jewish culture, he had his haircut in a Jewish barbershop and was breakfasting daily in an orthodox Jewish restaurant: a habit which, he noted, 'was continually contravening the regulations'. 'Vienna is a Jewish city', he reflected. 'The streets are crowded with real Jews wearing kaftans. Most of the shops are owned by them.' He met Herr Rosenberger one final time to visit the National Library, where they saw the oldest map in the world and the oldest German bible. On their last evening together over 'fine Viennese food', they listened to English records on the gramophone. He was even cajoled to draw on his early music lessons in Lesmahagow to 'rattle out Auf Wiedersehen on the piano'.

It was now mid-September, and the next day he started out for Passau on the last stage of his journey which would take him through Munich, Stuttgart, Heidelberg, Baden Baden, Strasbourg and finally to Paris ahead of the new academic year. More meetings with young Germans and Austrians kept the political situation and the plight of the Jews in the forefront of his mind: 'Met Frankfurt Jew who had travelled all over Europe. I asked him about the Frankfurt brawling in July and he told me that before he sat his finals he was set upon by a mob of

50 Nazis & mercilessly beaten. That happens every week, said he.' An American student he met on the way to Munich attributed blame for the Frankfurt riots to both sides. 'Jews', he was told, 'were mostly communist, forever meddling with political matters.' He thought the numbers of beggars had increased even since the last time he was in Germany and was told that soon even professors would be on the streets. At his hostel, more fears about Germany's position in the wider world was forthcoming from 'a young chap in shorts', who was 'very frightened' about future attacks on his country. He had no confidence in world opinion, which had said little when the French attacked the Saar. He and Cairncross and a 'plump Hungarian' argued about the social composition of Hitlerites. Were the supporters mainly workers, lower middle class or unemployed? The young man rejected the proposition that Hitlerites were fascists and reiterated the view that the problem was caused by Germany's post-First World War anomie. 'The same old story', Cairncross later noted in his diary. 'Germany must have an army.' It was as if the First World War had never ended.

A respite from cycling took him up to the summit of the Alps accompanied by new companions: Helmut, a follower of Nietzsche, and his friend Heinz, who carried on debating Germany's relationship to the wider world. 'Socialism has had its day', Helmut told him. 'Germany is under terrible distress. Its frontiers are being attacked', said Heinz, who also repeated another familiar story that the Jews were 'mostly communists and socialists'. According to Heinz, they had contributed to the split in the left which had occurred after 1918 and had paved the way for later problems. After a brief stop in Stuttgart, where he admired the 'magnificent parks' and 'very fine' sculpture, he entered Heidelberg under 'a leaden sky'.

Some respite from the familiar tales of the 'Jewish problem' and Germany's need for rearmament was provided at Baden Baden by Max Metzcher, a retired customs official (and another 'jovial sort'), who, while stationed at Lubeck, had been one of the first to hear of the Titanic's fate. They enjoyed a 'right good musical evening together', and Cairncross was pleased to discover that his new friend was of an internationalist persuasion, believing that 'one should be able to go anywhere on God's earth without a visa or passport'. From his diary entries, it is apparent that the glint of internationalism was now a counter to the dark forces of Hitlerism and stimulated his thinking as he made the long and sometimes monotonous train journey to Strasbourg, and then on to Paris.

He arrived in Paris on Monday, 10 October and reported to the British consul. He was now officially about to start his year abroad as part of his modern languages degree. His travelling had broadened his horizons and even after only one vacation there must have been doubts in his mind over whether he would return to Glasgow. In fact, he was to stay in Paris for two years after managing to transfer his scholarship from Glasgow in order to take the *Licence-ès-lettres*.

His eye-opening experience in Germany and Austria had aroused his political curiosity and empathy for the predicaments of the Jewish community. Shortly before he reached Paris, he had begun to set down in his diary more pronounced impressions of Hitler's Nazis, looking for similarities and differences with what he had heard about Mussolini's fascist regime in Italy, which had been in power since 1922 and had succeeded in eliminating all opposition. In a little diary section, he sketched out some ideas on a 'comparison between Hitler and Mussolini and their respective movements'. In both, he recognized a militaristic and nationalistic reaction among the youth against pacifism, internationalism and socialism. He thought there were differences too.

> In the case of Hitler, the race was stressed. It alone made the nation. The will to power, to the self-preservation of the race in the mould of the nation, was emphasised. ... In the case of Mussolini the nation was everything & it alone gave the race its validity. Mussolini was merely imprinting the old Roman idea of order on a nation which had not yet been disciplined.

These early thoughts of a nineteen-year-old student of modern languages showed some original thinking in attempting to make sense of what was an emerging international crisis. He would return to Germany in 1934 prior to going up to Cambridge, to spend another vacation teaching a German pupil. By then Hitler had come to power. In 1932 he only had knowledge of basic political theory, though he was able to draw on some of his wider reading of Nietzsche and Darwin in analysing Hitler's ideas. The details and circumstances of his own mild 'politicization' differed markedly from that of the other Cambridge spies. It was not until the following year, in March 1933, that Kim Philby, three years Cairncross's senior and already calling himself a communist, witnessed anti-Jewish protests in Germany; later that year, Philby was sent by his communist economics tutor Maurice Dobb to join comrades in the International Red Aid, a Comintern front organization. Through contacts there, Philby, in 1934, ended up fighting in the Austrian Civil War, alongside his girlfriend (and later wife) Litzi Friedmann.[1] In the summer of 1932, Donald Maclean, halfway through his Cambridge degree, was in the process of 'coming out' as a communist following the death of his father, a government minister, earlier that year.[2] Maclean's communism, influenced by his friend and Gresham's school and Cambridge contemporary James Klugmann, had initially prompted the idea of teaching in Soviet Russia, a country he was yet to visit. Guy Burgess spent the summer holidays in 1932 on the Scottish island of Eigg with his history tutor (and probable lover) Steven Runciman, whose father owned the island. Burgess, who had been attracted to communism on the back of 'intellectual and theoretical' discussions in the Trinity Historical Society and among fellow students, spent the following summer in Monte Carlo and Rome, where he persuaded his friend Anthony Blunt that the history of art had much to learn from Marxism.[3] It was in 1934 that Anthony Blunt would see the effects of Nazism at first hand, by which time, in his words, 'Marxism had hit Cambridge'.[4]

Many travellers to Germany and Austria were, like Cairncross, shocked by what they saw, but many foreign observers, journalists, students, diplomats and others who visited in a similar period held if not admiration then tolerance for Hitler during his rise to power, as many had done with Mussolini ten years before. Germany remained a very popular holiday venue for the British, and their impressions of Germany were regarded as important by their hosts. In the conclusion to her study *Travellers in the Third Reich*, Julia Boyd reflects that 'the most chilling fact to emerge from these travellers' tales is that so many perfectly decent people could return home from Hitler's Germany singing its praises'.[5]

Some fellow students were among those who came away with a different impression than Cairncross. For example, John ('Jock') Colville, later a Cambridge contemporary, civil service colleague and lunch companion of Cairncross, whose testimony was vital in his exposure as the 'Fifth Man', held quite a different view of Germany during his visit in the spring of 1933, shortly after Hitler had become chancellor. He had hoped 'to learn something of the outside world before going up to Cambridge'.[6] Before leaving for Germany his Harrow headmaster had warned that Hitler would be 'a disaster for Europe' and his mother let on that 'everything she reads about Hitler and his National Socialist Party filled her with revulsion'.[7]

Nevertheless, after a fortnight in the Black Forest, Colville decided that the warnings he had received 'showed a total misunderstanding of the youthful and infectious spirit sweeping across Germany. ... I now perceived that the older generation at home, were and doubtless always had been, hopelessly biased and out of touch with the modern world. An idyllic summer', he recorded in his diary.[8] Colville's youthful admiration of the Nazis extended to joining in some of the celebrations: 'In the towns and villages, festooned with Nazi flags and with the old black, white and red ensign of imperial Germany, there was an atmosphere of purpose and alert contentment. ... I found it impossible not to be infected by the unflagging enthusiasm. In 1933 the Nazi slogan, "strength through joy", had an evident reality.'[9] He continued to defend National Socialism on his return – 'it was mean and unrealistic to deny the benefits it offered Germany' – and encountered the wrath of Lionel de Rothschild, a family friend, who noted (not entirely tongue in cheek) to his mother: 'Your son ... comes to stay in my house, shoots my pheasants, drinks my champagne, smokes my cigars and then tells me there is a lot to be said for Hitler!'[10] His recognition of Hitler's 'selfless enthusiasm for national regeneration'[11] seemed to outlast even his Cambridge student years. It was only when cramming for his FO exam in 1936–7, enhanced by conversation classes with a young Nazi, 'that the new face of Germany became known to me'.[12]

For his part, Cairncross's perceptive observations did not drive him into the clutches of the Communist Party nor did he develop any particular interest in the superiority of the Soviet system over Germany. Moreover his political curiosity at this time was matched by an overwhelming appreciation of European art and culture, and on arrival in Paris he expected something different again in that regard. He quickly settled into his lodgings in Rue de la Bucherie, an old medieval part of the Left Bank, near Notre-Dame, which he shared with a Welsh student. He felt at home in the heart of Paris's rich culture of writers and artists and welcomed what he felt was a new 'air of freedom'.[13] He would later play down the extent of his own bohemian living – his lodgings restricted his socializing and he put his studies first – but he undoubtedly enjoyed a new student lifestyle where he could visit the second-hand bookshops and galleries, and include wine in his regular fixed price dinners in the cheap restaurants. Glasgow had been stimulating in its own way, but he felt he had little 'outside life' beyond lectures, and Paris presented a completely different proposition in that regard.

He was only a short distance from the Sorbonne where he would attend lectures. That he was at the Sorbonne at all was largely thanks to his parents who had agreed to subsidize his time there after he had requested a change from his original placement at Clermont-Ferrand ('a pleasant but unexciting city') in the Auvergne region. Once settled in Paris, he became engrossed in his work. Reading and writing in the French style was obviously a big change but one of lasting importance for his future editing and translating, and he later attributed his understanding of the intricacies of Racine to that formative experience. His reading had broadened to include Baudelaire, Nietzsche and André Gide, whose autobiographical prose poem *Les nourritures terrestres* ('The Fruits of the Earth') had a particular appeal. The constraints of Gide's religious background and his subsequent quest for intellectual and sexual freedom to embrace adventure over convention and security might at least have resonated with Cairncross's own situation. Gide, then at the peak of his influence, would, like Cairncross, flirt with communism as a fellow-traveller but would break with it following a visit to the Soviet Union. Subsequently, he became a leading critic of communism for its denials of freedom.

It was at the Sorbonne that he first met Lester Crocker, who would be a lifelong friend and sponsor of Cairncross's brief university career thirty years later. Crocker was spending a year in Paris reading for his Certificat de Littérature Française prior to completing his studies in the United States. He would become a noted expert on the French Enlightenment, and during 1933 he and Cairncross enjoyed stimulating discussions on French literature while exploring Paris together. He was now in Molière's city where Molière's theatrical performances, under Royal patronage, had amused, challenged, stimulated and occasionally scandalized audiences in his depictions of the manners and morals of early modern Parisian society. After his introduction in Glasgow to *Le Bourgeois gentilhomme*, Cairncross had moved on to *Les Femmes savantes* (*The Learned Ladies*), which appealed both for its satirical portrayal of 'precious' behaviour among aspirational middle-class women and for an implicit feminist questioning of the assumptions behind the manners and affectations of the society. Molière's empathy for the position of women was more evident in some of his other works – for example, *The School for Wives* – and they became an important aspect of Cairncross's interest in his ideas. He admired the combination of humour and humanism in Molière, while his freethinking spirit was in accordance with his own growing outlook on life. In *Dom Juan*, the excesses of the 'libertine' were heresies in the world of conventional morality and religious orthodoxy – and after its early withdrawal, brought allegations of atheism and blasphemy directed at Molière himself. Through the character of Dom Juan Molière was able to question hypocrisy and the constraints of orthodox thinking. For Cairncross, Dom Juan illustrated 'just how dubious are the orthodox certitudes and canons of this world'.[14]

> Hypocrisy is a fashionable vice and all vices that are fashionable turn into virtues. These days the role of a man of principle is the pick of the parts you can play, for to profess hypocrisy is to acquire remarkable advantages. It is an art, and practising it invariably commands respect. People might see through it, but they dare not speak out. All mankind's vices are subject to criticism and anyone is free to attack them openly. But hypocrisy is a privileged vice. With a gesture of its hand, it can stop the mouths of everyone and is left in peace to enjoy unlimited immunity. With its cant and humbug it binds all those who practise it in close fellowship, and whoever clashes with one of them brings down the rest of the pack on himself. … How many men do you think I know who use such clever tactics to cover up the disorderly conduct of their youth, shielding themselves by donning the cloak of religion, and then, robed in the cloth of its respectability, have everyone's permission to be as wicked as they like?[15]

If Molière's search for freedom was evident so too was his use of humour and satire in scrutinizing the ways of the powerful. His status as a freethinker, sceptical of orthodoxy, precocity and prudery resonated with Cairncross's early principles. However, it was not of the stuff to drive him into organized politics, join demonstrations or write a campaign leaflet. In any case, he had little time for politics during his first year at the Sorbonne. *Action Française*, a right-wing monarchist movement, was the main political grouping among the students and held little appeal for him. This was the period before the Popular Front brought left-wing governments (composed of communists, socialists and others) to both France and Spain in 1936. The French Communist Party (PCF) was a small, isolated sectarian group in the university with seemingly little to interest the nonconformist Cairncross. He found the films of that period more enticing than any political movement. These included *Topaze*, Louis Gasnier's 1933 film version of Marcel Pagnol's 1928 play, which deals with the predicament of a teacher who abandons the honest principles he taught his pupils when confronted with the realities of corrupt business practices. His studies came first, however – he admitted later living much of his first year at the Sorbonne 'wrapped in a kind of academic cocoon'.[16] His year at the Sorbonne had been a success, and after excelling in his certificates (for French literature and philology) he sought and won approval to transfer his studies from Glasgow to Paris for a second year. His Paris education had expanded his horizons and had been the perfect place to develop his interests in French literature.

Following his end-of-year exams, he returned to Scotland for the summer vacation. At home, he was 'Johnny' again, and he was once more reacquainted with his family, to whom he recounted his various European adventures. That summer he enjoyed a walking holiday in the highlands with his brother Alec and, one of Alec's friends, Walter Salant. Recapturing his 'roving spirit', he managed to become separated from his two elder companions, only to be rediscovered the following morning breakfasting over a campfire with a group of boy scouts.[17]

Cairncross arrived for his second year knowing that most of his studies would now focus on German language and literature, which required the 'exacting task'[18] of translating from German to French, which took his understanding of both German and French culture to a new level. Hitler's accession to power in 1933 meant a change in the atmosphere at the Sorbonne. During his second year he encountered many more German Jewish refugees among his fellow students, intent on finishing their studies but uncertain when they could return home.

He later assisted one Jewish family he met during this period to relocate to England in 1938. He found that many of the German students were reluctant to discuss politics but from his conversations with them, and with François Bondy, a German-born Sorbonne contemporary who would later become a distinguished Swiss political writer and translator, he got to know more about the escalating crisis in Germany. Cairncross's political curiosity did not amount to joining any organization, and the only meeting he later recalled attending during that year was for an appeal for the release of the German communist leader Ernst Thalmann, who had been arrested by the Gestapo.[19]

However, he was committed to helping those on the receiving end of fascism, and the experience of his long cycling tour (reaffirmed by shorter holiday visits to Germany and Austria outside term), combined with what he was told by German students in Paris, convinced him of the need for a well-organized movement in support of them. Paris, at this time, was a refuge and meeting place for many exiles from Italian fascism and German Nazism as well as Comintern representatives from Moscow and agents of all kinds. Contrary to some later claims by espionage writers, it was meetings with exiled Italian anti-fascists rather than Soviet communists that would be of lasting significance for Cairncross.

> I had had talks with members of the Giustizia e Libertà group (a liberal movement of which the Rosselli family were prominent members) and their friends in Paris and they had given me illustrations of the severe losses suffered by the movement initially because of their lack of experience in ... agitation.[20]

In the period after the murder of socialist parliamentarian Giacomo Matteotti in 1924 and the subsequent clampdown on the opposition, many Italian intellectuals and anti-fascist activists had been forced out of Italy. One of the most prominent and influential was Carlo Rosselli, a young Jewish intellectual whose oppositional activities included setting up a clandestine journal Non Mollare (Don't Give Up) and helping to free the veteran socialist Filippo Turati, for which he was sent for a two-year confinement to the Aeolian Island of Lipari, off Sicily. There, he wrote most of his classic work, Liberal Socialism, a critique of orthodox Marxism, which drew on an eclectic mix of ideas ranging from the liberal philosopher Benedetto Croce to the reformist traditions of the British Labour Party. He and others escaped from Lipari in 1929 and made their way to Paris to join other exiled Italian anti-fascists. In Paris, Rosselli and his allies founded *Giustizia e Libertà*, which would become one of the leading anti-fascist resistance movements of the liberal left. Among exiled Italian intellectuals in Paris was Gaetano Salvemini, Rosselli's mentor, who would later move to the United States to take up a professorship in history. The wider group of exiled liberal socialists and republicans produced a plethora of publications and organizations, including the Mazzini Society, and would later constitute the core of the non-communist partisan groupings which helped to defeat fascism.[21] Later in Rome, Cairncross through his wife's relations and other friends would get to know many of those who participated in these movements, including Raimondo Craveri and Enzo Tagliacozzo. In Paris, in quite different circumstances, he learnt from the Italian dissidents – and not from Comintern agents like Willi Münzenberg – the importance of effective clandestine organization in the work of anti-fascist resistance. It was in Paris that he was drawn to the ideas of European anti-fascism which was a logical outcome of his experiences travelling on the continent since 1932. This was the big political change which would shape his decisions and choices in the coming years.

At the end of his second year in Paris he returned to Germany for the summer vacation to take up an au pair role in Berlin at the home of a Jewish family, which he combined with teaching English to their son. While there he was introduced to some of their musical friends and accompanied them to the theatre and opera to see (among other things) a performance of *Così fan tutte* portrayed in military costume. On one 'chilling occasion' he witnessed Hitler, now in power, standing erect in his car to receive the adoration of the crowds.[22] This experience cemented his growing anti-fascist principles and alerted him to Nazism at first hand. His time in Germany immediately before and after Hitler came to power was a fleeting affair in comparison to that of Christopher Isherwood whose immersion into the world of the cabaret artists and seedy bars at the moment of rising political tension inspired some of his best novels. But for a young Scottish student, it was a formative experience.

After graduation from Glasgow University, Alec had started a PhD in political economy at Cambridge in 1932, at the moment when Keynesian influence was at its peak. He would go on to produce only the second doctorate to be awarded in that subject at Cambridge. His younger brother had been impressed by Alec's reports of university life there and, on his brother's encouragement, applied through the Open Scholarship system to complete his undergraduate degree in modern languages. Fortunately, one of the examination questions was on Molière and not for the first time Cairncross was able to impress his examiners with his outstanding composition. With his *Licence-ès-lettres* from the Sorbonne he was able to miss the first year and go straight into the second year of a Cambridge degree. By now he had completed four years of study, had travelled extensively in Europe and was ready to take on anything England's prestigious university had to offer (Figures 1–5).

Figure 1 The Cairncross family. Baby John with parents and siblings. Reproduced by kind permission of the Syndics of Cambridge University Library.

Figure 2 Alec and John in Lesmahagow, 1921. Reproduced by kind permission of the Syndics of Cambridge University Library.

Figure 3 'Johnny' (far right) with (left to right) brothers Alec, Andrew and unknown friend (in a kilt), rambling in the Scottish Highlands. Reproduced by kind permission of the Syndics of Cambridge University Library.

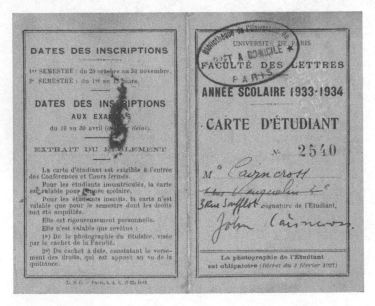

Figure 4 Student at the Sorbonne, Paris. Reproduced by kind permission of the Syndics of Cambridge University Library.

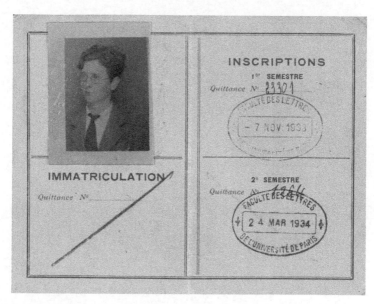

Figure 5 Student at the Sorbonne, Paris. Reproduced by kind permission of the Syndics of Cambridge University Library.

Chapter 4
Cambridge

At the time John Cairncross arrived at Cambridge in October 1934, Britain was in serious economic and political crisis. It was at the peak of the Great Depression, and the sight of the Hunger Marchers passing through the town a few months earlier had brought the plight of the unemployed to the attention of privileged Cambridge students. Politically, Britain was stumbling along, its system and structures lacking in authority and conviction. 'Betrayal' was also in the air: the Labour government elected in 1929 and headed by Ramsay MacDonald, an 'illegitimate' son of a farm labourer and domestic servant, had been unable to deal with the onset of economic crisis and by 1931 had metamorphosed into a national government, to the indignation of its left wing. The Communist Party (CPGB), the Independent Labour Party (which George Orwell among others would briefly join) and Oswald Mosley's 'New Party' all reacted with hostility – the latter shifting rapidly from an opportunist populist faction of the left to the British Union of Fascists (BUF), which was formed in 1932 as an authoritarian movement of the far right. In the year since Hitler had come to power, Mosley's BUF made a significant impact and had even won the sympathy of some influential figures (Lord Rothermere's *Daily Mail* included) and held several large rallies: one of which, at Olympia in June 1934, had produced violent clashes with anti-fascist opponents.

At Cambridge, the combination of anti-fascism and left opposition to the crisis in the Labour Party had resulted in the creation of a large socialist society (CUSS), in which the communists at Trinity College (where Cairncross studied) were the leading proponents. The two leaders were John Cornford and James Klugmann; both were intensely political and brilliant organizers who thrived on leading debates and recruitment drives late into the night. The previous autumn, in the midst of what was becoming an escalating international crisis in the aftermath of Hitler's rise to power, they had organized two peace demonstrations to coincide with the armistice commemoration. The demonstrations, which brought clashes with right-wing opponents, caught the imagination of their cohort, with the prospect of another war now a serious concern. Klugmann, Cornford and their comrades had forged good links with the Cambridge Anti-War Council, which received broad support from local church groups and pacifists, while in the university the CUSS continued to thrive as the main vehicle of left-wing politics. The following year the Comintern would instruct communists to officially endorse a 'Popular Front' strategy of uniting all those opposed to war and fascism, which was followed shortly after by Popular Front governments in France and Spain. In Cambridge by 1934, Klugmann and Cornford had already succeeded in ensuring their communism appealed to liberal-minded students and other believers in social justice and peace who had lost faith in a crisis-ridden political system and for whom the Labour Party was no longer an alternative. This made for some unusual recruitment and communist 'cells' composed of people who had only the vaguest acquaintance with the British proletariat.

In the two years since starting his PhD in political economy at Trinity College, Alec Cairncross had observed with interest the politicization of the undergraduates and reflected on the differences between them and the undergraduates he had known at Glasgow.

I was amused to find how radical these young aristocrats were, how ready to toy with communism, how confident that they knew the mind of the average worker; whereas the predominantly lower-middle class students of Glasgow were intensely conservative, or at least liberal and certainly did not idealise a working class that they knew at first hand: it was also revealing to see how much political sympathies rested on temperament and taste rather than on reasoned arguments, still less on any programme of action (except for the seizure of power) or analysis of the measures that might improve the functioning of the system as a whole.[1]

Like his brother, John Cairncross had no need of Marxist education classes to discover the British proletariat: he had grown up with them and studied with them at school. After four years of university education, including two in Paris, he had wider life experiences than many of his new contemporaries. No respecter of hierarchy or pretension, he would not have been slow to bring this fact to their attention. As his *Licence-ès-lettres* from the Sorbonne enabled him to enter directly into the second year of his Cambridge Tripos, he therefore missed some of the more innocent and immature antics of the freshers. His experience of studying in Europe was significant and to a degree set him apart from his undergraduate contemporaries. It was some way from the cosmopolitan background of Eric Hobsbawm, who arrived at Cambridge the year Cairncross left, but his early days adjusting to university life in England might well have left a similar impression.

'Britain was a terrible let-down', Hobsbawm reflected.

Imagine yourself as a newspaper correspondent based in Manhattan and transferred by your editor to cover Omaha, Nebraska. That is how I felt when I came to England, after two years in the unbelievably exciting, sophisticated, intellectually and politically explosive Berlin of the dying Weimar Republic. … For my first years in Britain I felt I was just marking time, waiting till there was a chance to carry on the conversation where it had broken off in Berlin.[2]

Cairncross must have been struck by the rituals and pomp of the university in which he matriculated in October 1934. According to Victor Kiernan, one of his Trinity College neighbours, it was a place of 'contrast and incongruities'. On the one hand there was a 'highly paternalistic' 'gentility'; the university was 'a haunt of the *jeunesse dorée*, who were there to amuse themselves in a playground of snobbery and upper-class lotus-eating'.[3] On the other, 'There was a galaxy of talent, even genius – more than at any time in its history.'[4] Their own college, Trinity, was both the wealthiest and arguably home to the most gifted students.

It would have been a departure from anything John Cairncross had previously encountered. One of the attractions of being at the Sorbonne was its facility for informal living arrangements and easy access to the culture of a great European city. Now he was among the ancient quads of Trinity, where it was still expected to arrive back in your rooms by

11.00 pm and to wear gowns about town. Alec Cairncross had found
the 'well-to-do-English' an entirely different species from anyone he had
previously encountered: 'Normans' in their 'upper-class accents' ('even
in its slang'); 'their physique, complexion, their looks were quite unlike
what one found in typical Glasgow students'. He was even moved to
compose a sonnet in their honour:

> Gods in whose image I have not been fashioned
> Full-chested gods, handsome and debonair,
> With voices measured, cool and unimpassioned
> Sophisticated gods oozing with savoir-faire.[5]

His younger brother would have been reassured, then, to start his
student life at Cambridge by sharing rooms in C4 of Nevile's Court with
his older sibling. For the duration of his time at Cambridge John would
be part of a loose cohort of Scottish students who shared their suspicion
of the 'English P.S.' (public school) crowd. 'I am getting over the first
feeling of revulsion of having come into contact with the English P.S.
boys, but I still feel more at home with your brother than I do with them',
one of Alec's friends reported back to him on arriving in Cambridge. 'I
find them too much like hothouse plants.'[6]

Cairncross would come to resent what he saw as typically English
'class-ridden conventions' at Cambridge, but he also bemoaned the
attitudes to women and lack of opportunities for the sexes to meet.[7] He
saw this as indicative of an unnatural repressive atmosphere towards
sex and sexuality exemplified by the Friday night train to London (known
as 'The Flying Fornicator') when male undergraduates, apparently
starved of female company in the colleges, trooped off to Soho for their
weekend entertainment. 'It was at Cambridge', he reflected later, 'that
I began to understand how it was that in the books of Wodehouse a
bedroom scene was one in which getting drunk was manly [and] having
sex was thoroughly immoral'.[8]

His whole Cambridge experience, as he reflected later, left him with
mixed feelings. At times he found it 'oppressive' and 'mentally alien'; yet
in other respects it was clearly 'enriching'.[9] Whatever difficulties he had in
assimilating at Cambridge, he eagerly embraced its intellectual offerings.
For the next two years his academic interests would take precedence over
anything else. Among the academic staff who helped him settle in at the

college was Trinity's Senior Tutor, J. R. M. Butler, a progressive-minded former Lib-Lab MP for the Cambridge University seat who was the son of the former master of Trinity (Henry Montagu Butler) and who would later become Regius Professor of history. His academic mentor for the duration of his time at Cambridge, however, was undoubtedly his French tutor, Professor Henry (Harry) Ashton. Ashton was a grammar-school-educated son of a Lancashire schoolteacher who had recently held a post at the University of British Columbia in Canada, arriving at Gonville and Caius College, Cambridge, in 1933. He had developed a strong interest in Molière's life and thought and was committed to bringing the originality of his ideas to the attention of his students. His *A Preface to Molière*, published in 1927, explored the impact of Mollère's social background and intellectual influences on his plays. For Ashton, it was 'impossible to separate literature and history. They are so inextricably mingled that one cannot be understood without the other. This is particularly true of Molière's works because they portray the social life of his day and show a critical attitude towards certain aspects of it.'[10]

Although Cairncross was by now well acquainted with Molière, Ashton's emphasis on the historical context of his work was a major influence. It was for Ashton that he wrote his first essays on Molière's *Tartuffe*, and it was under Ashton that Cairncross embarked on the substantial detective work which would later result in *New Light on Molière*, where he argued that *Tartuffe* was originally produced in three rather than five acts. Cairncross also shared Ashton's appreciation of the humanity of Molière, notably (as Ashton put it in his book) 'of the rightness of human instincts', and 'avers[ion] to hypocrisy', as well as his freethinking disposition. He was 'independent of character, with no disposition to toady to the great'.[11]

For two years Cairncross shared his tutorials ('supervisions') in Ashton's rooms at Caius with Douglas Parmée, an exceptional modern languages student who had entered Trinity the year before on a teacher-training scheme. Parmée would go on to be a distinguished fellow at Queens College and a notable and prolific translator of the works of Zola, Maupassant, Flaubert and Laclos. He and Cairncross became firm friends. They had much in common, with their love of French literature and aptitude for translations and writing. After Cambridge they met again at Bletchley Park, and Cairncross was best man at Parmée's wartime wedding. Their studies in Cambridge would bear fruit with their respective works of translation, albeit produced in very different circumstances. Years later, Parmée was 'greatly amused' to read in the 'Fifth Man' revelations that Cairncross had been taught by Anthony Blunt. This was 'journalistic fantasy', Parmée wrote to his old friend. 'For one thing, he [Blunt] had no competence in any literary sphere, as far as I am aware. In fact, I suspect you, and indeed I, could have given him teaching in French literature!'[12]

In 1934 Anthony Blunt was midway through a four-year research fellowship on 'artistic theory in France and Italy during the Renaissance and the 17th century'.[13] He was not a formal member of the teaching staff, though he was an active member of the Modern Languages Club and could have offered informal teaching on art history. However, he was a popular and influential figure at Cambridge. He had been part of the Bloomsbury set around Dadie Rylands and Julian Bell (with whom he had an affair) while an undergraduate and was held in high esteem by some in the Cambridge generations below him for whom recognition in prominent social circles was as important as academic achievement.

Blunt had recently returned from Germany where the horror of the Hitler regime was brought home to him by the persecution of his friend, the art scholar, Walter Friedlander, who was forced to leave his academic post and move to Britain. Indeed, the year 1934 had been one of a political awakening for Blunt. When he had arrived back in Cambridge at the beginning of that year from a sabbatical in Rome, he had been shocked by the 'Marxist' turn among the students, in the aftermath of the autumn peace protests and the spring hunger march.[14] Until this point Blunt had shown little interest in politics; on his own admission he was more of a 'Bloomsbury' aesthete, who had been a regular guest at Charleston, the Sussex farmhouse rented by Duncan Grant and Vanessa Bell and frequented by their Bloomsbury friends. Now he took more interest, partly through the influence of his close friend Guy Burgess, who, unable to complete his examinations, had graduated from Cambridge in 1933 on the back of an aegrotat, and had initially begun a PhD studentship (which he later abandoned). Burgess had been politicized by the events of 1933 and had been persuaded by James Klugmann, the 'political theorist' of the Cambridge communists (in Blunt's words), to join the communist group at Trinity. Klugmann had graduated with a double first in 1934 and was also a significant influence on Blunt during the discussions they shared on European history and culture in the latter's rooms. In comparison with Klugmann and Burgess (let alone communist dons such as the economist Maurice Dobb or Roy Pascal of the German department), Blunt had even less knowledge of Marxism than he had of French literature at this point. In fact, Pascal had earlier referred to his lack of historical context in a review of one of Blunt's earliest works. Nevertheless, as he extended his artistic and literary circles over subsequent terms his status in the university grew, notably among younger undergraduates. According to his friend Stuart Hampshire, Blunt was 'a marvellous figure of great glamour' and was the centre of attention at parties.[15] In contrast, Cairncross, according to Hampshire, was 'an absurd and rather untidy scholar, very bright and academic. He was socially from the lower rather than the higher, very talkative, sort of chaotic.'[16]

Blunt was also a member of the Apostles (the Cambridge Conversazione Society) and had been instrumental in recruiting Guy Burgess to its meetings, along with other Marxist recruits. One consequence of his access to wider literary circles was that he had been taken on as the *Spectator*'s art critic, where he filled his pages with reviews of exhibitions he had visited and with critical commentary on other art historians. His Marxism displayed all the fervour and dogma of the recent convert, where complex questions were quickly transformed into neat historical categories of class struggle and the imminent certainty of political change. In his contribution to *The Mind in Chains*, an instantly forgettable collection of essays edited by Cecil Day Lewis in his brief communist phase, it was Blunt's role to set out the predicament facing the artist in capitalist society.

> Now that the class struggle has grown more acute and has become the dominating factor in the world situation, any artist who cuts himself off from his class is automatically excluded from the possibility of taking part in the most important movement of his time and is therefore forced to take to some sort of escape, to find some consolation in his art for the reality with which he has lost touch in life.[17]

John Cairncross knew Blunt as a member of the French staff and as a Nevile's Court neighbour and visited his impressive, if sparsely furnished, suite in which Poussin's *Rebecca at the Well* had prime position, for meetings of the Modern Languages Club. Blunt's 'clear exposition' and lecturing ability, from which countless Courtauld students would subsequently benefit, was evident to Cairncross, though he was less taken with his orthodox Marxist assumptions. At this time, Cairncross recalled, Blunt appeared as a 'natural disciple of Marx. For he drew on the master's theories to underpin his own views.'[18] Cairncross was even less impressed with what he perceived as Blunt's limited knowledge of French literature; hardly surprising, perhaps, as Calrncross by comparison had spent several years reading and researching the seventeenth-century classics in their original language. As far as Cairncross's primary academic interests were concerned, Blunt did not compare favourably with either Harry Ashton or his Sorbonne professors.

> He struck me as a typically English case of someone having gained a certain reputation because of his good knowledge of the French language acquired when his father was chaplain at the embassy in Paris, and which supposedly guaranteed his understanding of French literature.[19]

Nor was Cairncross, the Scottish sceptic and international student, likely to be much impressed with Blunt's rising social status among his undergraduate contemporaries. He knew 'the importance attached by most English friends to convention and rank which went well with a general hostility to, and ignorance of, continental ideas. There was only one point of view, and all the other approaches were automatically rejected. I found the rigidity of this insular attitude a kind of ideological corset.'[20]

Much was made later by espionage writers and historians of Blunt's ability to cultivate impressionable and vulnerable students who were in awe of his standing in literary circles, but Cairncross was unlikely to have been swayed by his social milieu. Quite the contrary. Indeed, Molière's questioning of the manners and postures of 'precious' social climbers resonated with Cairncross's own irreverence towards his English social superiors. No doubt he would have concurred with the observation of one of his brother's friends who, after arriving at Cambridge the following year, wrote to Alec, '[After] what I have seen of Cambridge so far, I feel capable of writing another' of Molière's 'Les Précieuses.'[21] *Les Précieuses ridicules* ('Affected Ladies') was Molière's caricature of the attempts of persons of rank to convince an obsequious audience of their latest philosophical sophistication; it might, in Cairncross's own observations, have made a seamless transition from seventeenth-century Paris to 1930s Cambridge.

> It is the custom here, you know, [Mascarille said to Madelon], for authors to read their latest efforts to persons of rank like ourselves, to secure our approbation and gain a reputation for their work, and as you may well surmise, when we give one verdict, the parterre does not dare give another ... .

> 'I quite understand', [Madelon responds]. 'What a wonderful place is Paris! A thousand things happen every day which one never hears of in the provinces, however avant-garde one may be.'[22]

Cairncross was not alone in his aversion to some of the social climbers who mounted Trinity's staircases. Louis MacNeice, Blunt's close friend from Marlborough, who was now lecturing at Birmingham University, also had misgivings about his friend's new stardom. He thought the 'charades', 'private gossip and tittering' embarrassingly reminiscent of their time at school.[23] According to Blunt's biographer, 'MacNeice was depressed by his circle and their incessant parlour games.'[24] MacNeice had even put Blunt in his first novel, as Cyril Hogley, an 'intellectual snob', 'predator' and lover of dirty jokes who had become totally absorbed by Oxbridge's insular world. It was not a flattering portrait.

Cairncross found Professor Frederick Green much more amenable. An Aberdeen-born, St Andrews-educated First World War veteran, Green had recently arrived in Cambridge as the Drapers Professor of French, having held previous appointments in Durham, Paris and Cologne. After seeing action as a young commissioned officer attached to the Royal Scots he became an intelligence officer in the VIII Corps, where his knowledge of French and German was utilized in the interrogation of French and German prisoners of war. In 1918, he was awarded the Military Cross for his bravery in helping check German advances at Amiens. On Armistice Day he was present and officiated (as a senior German speaker) in the surrender negotiations, helping to prevent the lynching of German officers by angry crowds. After the war, instead of returning to St Andrews where he was expected to take up a lectureship, he went to Cologne where he experienced life in Germany after its military defeat. He later wrote an unpublished short story based on his wartime experiences, entitled 'There's No Such Thing'. It was a satire on the vanity and snobbery he had encountered among his senior officers at VIII Corps HQ. Sir Derek Funkaby, Sir Elmer Buffles-Froyd and Thwaites-Brown were (according to Green's daughter) 'thinly disguised' characters based on the 'incompetent amateurs' he had served under.[25]

It is not difficult to see that Cairncross would have taken to this Scot, who in life experience and outlook was far removed from the classic Cambridge don. Their shared Scottish background meant a familiarity with the different education system north of the border. Green's university thesis had been on the poet Robert Fergusson, who had led a brief bohemian life in Edinburgh at the time of the Scottish Enlightenment. Some of his poetry had been written in Lowland Scots, and Cairncross, like Green, was an admirer of his life and work. Clearly Green's critique of his vain superior officers would have resonated with Cairncross, as Cambridge's hierarchies, pretentiousness and rituals became an everyday reality for him. No doubt they shared their experiences of post-war Germany, and although Green (according to his family) was reluctant to expand on the details of his military experiences, the wider impact of the war on Germany would have been a topic of mutual interest. As an expert on Stendhal, Maupassant, Proust and Rousseau, among others, Green's academic specialisms were of interest to Cairncross and Parmée. The respect Cairncross held for Green and the encouragement he received from the professor would be reciprocated later in the Second World War. In 1943 Green, a captain in military intelligence, helped Cairncross get his transfer from the GC&CS at Bletchley Park to Section V of MI6, which dealt with counter-espionage.

In the German department Cairncross was taught by Arthur Knight and Roy Pascal. He held a dim view of Knight, who in his 'rather brusque manner would rattle through his carefully-prepared lectures so that no one could absorb them'.[26] Pascal, on the other hand, was one part of the small circle of communist dons who met at the Chesterton Lane home of economist Maurice Dobb, the long-serving and stalwart communist, who also chaired the Cambridge Anti-War Council. Cairncross was on friendly terms with Pascal, whose book

The Nazi Dictatorship, published in 1934, was one of the first attempts to explain the origins of the Hitler regime. Pascal had wide interests in German literature, expressionism and romanticism, and his expertise extended to the works of Thomas Mann and Johan Wolfgang von Goethe. Under him, Cairncross could add more context to some of the events and experiences he had witnessed in Germany and Austria. The two remained in touch after he left Cambridge.

His studies came first but given his strong anti-fascist principles combined with a critical outlook on life, it was inevitable that he would attend political discussions on the international situation. In his time at Cambridge they included communist student meetings calling for actions against war and fascism, and pacifist discussions making the case for sanctions. According to a Scottish friend and contemporary, Cairncross 'brought refreshing level-headedness' to an otherwise 'pretentious' discussion of the prospects of the growing peace movement.[27] He was not by nature or disposition someone who joined political parties or movements and did not have the ideological commitment or discipline or indeed the loyalty required to uphold party lines. Cairncross was, however, a natural and outspoken contrarian. He and his friend Douglas Parmée remained critical of the limitations of the university curriculum, scornful of some of the pretentiousness of undergraduates and despaired at the inadequacies of the National Government as it lurched unconvincingly between Ramsay MacDonald and Stanley Baldwin, but this did not amount to the adoption of a particular world view. Cairncross was nevertheless impressed by the work the Trinity College communists had done in building up an anti-fascist consensus among the wider student body. His decision to join the communist group as a student – distinct from joining the full Communist Party of Great Britain – was not a remarkable development; for him, though, it would turn out to be much more of a fateful one than the many others who passed through the student communist group. Students at Cambridge and elsewhere during the Popular Front period of the mid-1930s were broadly divided into three groups. These were the committed ideological communists like James Klugmann and John Cornford who were in touch with Communist Party HQ in King Street and who saw their role in delivering the party line and building its visibility among students and in the town. Their commitment as open, public communists was not in doubt and they were prepared to make significant sacrifices for the cause. Secondly, there were those who held communist beliefs but were less open and active in political meetings as they were destined for top jobs in government, FO or the civil service. Cairncross has erroneously often been classified in that camp, as a dedicated party loyalist prepared to work underground as a mole to serve its interests. In fact, he was a classic example of the third group, a looser cohort of students drawn to the communists because of their opposition to fascism and their organizational strengths as effective leaders of the left. As a fellow Trinity student who joined around the same time put it,

> We were interested in ideas; we wanted to believe. But most of us joined the movement because it was the best-led, most active movement in the university, advancing the short-term objectives we felt were right … we took no party assignments with us when we left Cambridge at the end of each term.[28]

It was on this basis that Cairncross attended some of the meetings in Trinity in 1935. He was a communist student member who attended its meetings on a casual basis; he was not an 'activist' in the sense of attending demonstrations or selling the *Daily Worker* at factory gates nor, as far as we know, did he hold any office within the group. His contribution was less than that of some of the later well-known public figures who also passed through student communism in the same period. Denis Healey was the Oxford Communist students' 'cultural secretary' who organized a discussion of Picasso's powerful painting *Guernica*, after that town was bombed by German Nazis and Italian fascists during the Spanish Civil War in 1937. Philip Toynbee became the first communist president of the Oxford Union in 1936, while Richard Crossman, though not a communist, was one of several Labour students working with (and in awe of) Abe Lazarus, the brilliant interwar organizer and orator of the Oxford party. Even Charles Rycroft, recruited after hours of careful persuasion by James Klugmann, managed to fit in an anti-fascist demonstration before and after lunch at the Reform Club.

It was James Klugmann who won over Cairncross. From a wealthy North London Jewish family, and another brilliant modern languages student, Klugmann by October 1934 was a postgraduate studying under Ashton. His research covered a later period than Cairncross's specialisms, focussing on the social origins of French romanticism and intellectuals at the time of the French Revolution, but they shared common interests in French history and politics. Klugmann would divide his time between Cambridge and Paris, where he briefly benefited from the supervision of Daniel Mornet at the Sorbonne. However, Klugmann, as one of the leaders of the communist student group at Cambridge, had so impressed his party elders at its Covent Garden HQ that he was already earmarked for future leadership. In between studying at the Bibliothèque Nationale, he worked as secretary of the Rassemblement Mondial des Étudiants, a Comintern-backed student organization, founded by Willie Münzenberg, whose role it was to organize world student congresses and back campaigns, notably for the republican side in Spain after 1936 and for China in its battle with Japan over Manchuria. Where other student communist activists and leaders went to Spain to fight, Klugmann would play his revolutionary role in galvanizing left-wing student activists across the globe. In 1938 he would lead a much feted student delegation to India and China where they met Jawaharlal Nehru and Mao Zedong.

In Cambridge Klugmann had earned his promotion through his success as joint organizer of the Cambridge communists, first with David Haden Guest and (after the latter's graduation) with John Cornford. Both Guest and Cornford were later killed fighting in the Spanish Civil War. The leadership combination of Cornford and Klugmann was ideal for the times. Cornford, the younger by four years, and from an academic Cambridge family, was, in addition to being a brilliant student and a promising poet, a highly committed activist. In contrast to Klugmann, whose natural political habitat was small discussion circles, Cornford did much of his organizing among workers outside the university. Cornford openly rejected the university's rituals, 'dressed down', agitated outside bus garages and lived with a young working-class woman with whom he had a child at the age of seventeen. Klugmann, while equally committed, was a gentle persuader who could talk for hours about European history, culture and politics. He and Cairncross, who had no interest in joining workers' campaigns in town, had much to discuss.[29]

Cairncross found their discussions stimulating and was attracted by the quietly spoken, convivial and erudite Klugmann, who, like himself, was a voracious reader and bibliophile, and whose main hobby outside politics was book collecting. Klugmann's depth and range of argument surpassed Blunt's reductionist Marxism, and he had convinced scores of Cambridge undergraduates of the intellectual appeal of Marxism, not as a crude doctrine, but as an explanatory framework not only for understanding what was wrong with the narrowness of the university curriculum but also for grasping the historical context of the causes of the international crisis. Marxism, he argued, 'made everything rich'. It provided an understanding of European history, a framework for understanding culture and, not least, a guide to political action. Klugmann's optimism in the explanatory power of Marxism seemed to be vindicated for a time, as increasing numbers of middle-class students, writers and teachers (way beyond the 'aristocrats' Alec Cairncross had referred to) were attracted to the Popular Front. It is inaccurate to see the Cambridge communist generation as somehow divorced from the wider climate of the mid-1930s, which saw a generation of poets and writers turn to communism, brought large numbers of subscribers to the Left Book Club (when it was founded in 1936) and stimulated broad support for the republican side in Spain. Two factors were crucial in Cairncross's decision to join the communist group in Cambridge 1935, which after Klugmann's move to Paris was led for a while by Gavin Ewart, a young Anglo-Scottish poet whose loose association with communism had been stimulated through his friendship with Esmond Romilly at Wellington School.

First, the communists took the strongest anti-fascist line among the political groups at Cambridge, which remained for Cairncross the one political cause which required his full commitment. That might have been the reason why he was described as the 'fiery cross' in the May 1935 edition of *Trinity Magazine* and not, as subsequently claimed by espionage writers, on account of his supposedly hard-line communism. The following year, in its 1936 edition, he had evidently mellowed, according to even this tenuous criterion, as one 'who learns a new language every fortnight'.[30] His anti-fascism was not something on which he was prepared to compromise, and he was by now very well-informed about the most effective and broadest alliances that needed to be made.

Secondly, the communists attracted some of the strongest students, and by 1935, Cairncross believed he was one of the brightest of his cohort. 'Every communist student a good student' was a slogan not only adopted by the Cambridge communists but also evidenced by a series of high achievers among the communist group, notably Klugmann, Kiernan and others who had recently graduated with firsts. Cairncross may have been opposed to social elitism, but he was (and always remained) an intellectual elitist; his self-confidence in his own capacities explained some of his controversial actions and decisions and was often the cause of disputes with publishers, editors and rival academics.

However, his own thinking had not followed Klugmann's down the path of an all-embracing philosophy for living. It would not be his creed or faith. He did not idolize the working class, or feel impelled to defer to its cultural norms and habits (as Cornford and others had), nor had he much interest in the trade union movement. The Soviet Union was not an alternative paradise and he had no particular desire to join some of his comrades in visiting it. Joining the communist group at university – a 'bed and breakfast party' as Denis Healey had described the Oxford version – was not the same as the full Communist Party of Great Britain, with its rigorous commitments to branch meetings, weekly activities and ideological rigidity. Moreover, even when capitalism was shaking at a time of international political and economic instability, he did not share Klugmann's contention that the revolution was near. He had studied political economy and had learnt from his brother's Keynesian circle that there were other solutions to capitalist crisis. He had been impressed, among others, by the work of Vilfredo Pareto, the Italian social theorist whose work on elites he found useful in understanding fascism and Nazism. He also counted a Trotskyist, Etienne Tamboury, among his friends while he regularly found himself in disagreement with other hard-line communists, like Paddy Costello, over Soviet policy. There is therefore little to suggest that the 'Party' asserted any hold over him.

Indeed there were significant differences in character, outlook and the levels of political commitment between him and Klugmann. Despite the more tolerant attitude of the CPGB leadership towards students and intellectuals, Cairncross was not prepared to submit himself to the disciplines accepted by rising communist intellectuals like Klugmann. In fact, he would have reflected the 'bourgeois' tendencies condemned by Rajani Palme Dutt, the CPGB's leading theoretician, only two years earlier in the pages of *Communist Review*, when he warned would-be intellectuals: 'First and foremost he should forget that he is an intellectual (except in moments of necessary self-criticism) and remember only that he is a communist.'[31]

He would have had no problem in seeing himself as an intellectual first, driven as he was by endless curiosity, scholastic gifts and a fiery independence. The priority of defeating Nazism and the lack of faith in the British government's capacity to resist its rise was the main political ideal he shared with Klugmann and others; communists, he felt, had made the running and were winning the arguments among students.

As he reached his final year, his academic prowess and wide interests suggested that he was set for a university career, and he duly gained a first in modern languages. However, some had seen traces of arrogance in the way he set out his views. Though popular with Ashton and other tutors, he was not close enough to college or university authorities (nor prepared to ingratiate himself in the way that was often thought necessary), to try for a fellowship. By the time he graduated in 1936, Alec had taken up a post at Glasgow University. Certainly his life would have taken a different course had he followed his brother in that direction.

Chapter 5
The Foreign Office

In his posthumously published autobiography John Cairncross admitted that he had always held the ambition to pursue an academic career. Certainly he was capable of it. He had excelled in his studies, and by the time of his graduation in the summer of 1936 he had spent six years studying at three universities (Glasgow, Paris and Cambridge); it would be difficult to imagine a more richly varied undergraduate portfolio. Moreover, he had acquired that taste for independent research which was the calling of the serious-minded academic; his work on Molière had impressed Professor Ashton and others. He had already decided that he had something original to say about the French playwright and believed that with more time for research he could reveal the underlying mystery of the intellectual origins of *Tartuffe*. However, his prospects for gaining a research fellowship had not been helped by his reluctance to cultivate the Cambridge Fellows. He did not frequent the circles useful at the time for a Cambridge career, and in any case he was put off by what he saw as pretension and sycophancy. Nor was he a member of the Apostles, an established route to academic prominence. Guy Burgess was a member and had all the conversational gifts and aptitude for gossip and flattery that eluded Cairncross, but apparently lacked the tenacity and purpose required of an academic researcher. Among Cairncross's tutors, Harry Ashton was not part of the social hierarchy at Cambridge, and Professor Green shared Cairncross's scepticism over the rituals and hierarchies of the place. Anthony Blunt, still a junior research fellow at the time of Cairncross's graduation, may well have kept an eye on him. Blunt was recruited to work for the Soviets by Guy

Burgess in early 1937 (i.e. some months after Cairncross left Cambridge) and, as a talent-spotter, he himself recruited two of Cairncross's near-contemporaries: Michael Straight, the wealthy American socialite, and Leo Long, a postgraduate student from a working-class family. Contrary to some later claims, however, there was no preordained plan hatched at Cambridge for Cairncross to infiltrate the FO under Blunt's, or anyone else's, direction.

Cairncross's decision not to follow an academic career, one that would have severe consequences for him later, was not merely because of his unwillingness to conform or kowtow to his professors nor solely because of their failure to encourage him, though no doubt that was a factor. He also wanted to avoid becoming a financial burden on his parents who had helped support him over the previous four years. The FO held a special appeal for him. His travels had opened his mind to new experiences, most recently in a short Easter break to Spain earlier in 1936. After a 'horrendously long journey' by train from Paris to Barcelona, he arrived in time to see troops marching through the city on a national holiday to cries of 'Viva La Republica'. He enjoyed Spanish hospitality after finding himself (not for the first or last time) short of money and having to be helped out by the generosity of the hotel owner.[1] This visit, just a couple of months before the outbreak of the Spanish Civil War, added to his already well-formed views about the international crisis, while his informed judgements and linguistic abilities encouraged a belief that he could reach a senior diplomatic post. He had also grown tired of Cambridge and its cloistered existence and petty rules.

Though he knew little of London, the capital city offered the lifestyle he had aspired to in Paris. A few years earlier, Ian Smith, his former Glasgow flatmate and friend of his brother, had visited the capital to take his civil service examinations and, though he was ultimately unsuccessful in that venture, had raved to Alec about London's attractions. In contrast to what he saw as Glasgow's provincialism, Smith marvelled at the modern life of the Metropolis, with 'women with more lipstick and painted eyebrows', and every kind of fashion. Even his lodgings at the Central YMCA in Great Russell Street was 'a great place with automatic lifts, swimming pool and charming waitresses. If this is what being a civil servant implies, then a Bohemian life for me.'[2]

Such a life would have appealed to John Cairncross too. He would be more at the centre of things in London, with art and culture at his fingertips. His stays in Paris and travels in Europe had broadened his mind, but he was still naïve about life in some ways. In the future his family would admire his success with women, as he introduced them to one or other of his girlfriends, but his experience with the opposite sex up to this point was limited, and while he had enjoyed the company of women students at his three universities, he had always put his studies first. He lived frugally and was still unused to parties, big social gatherings or travelling by taxi. However, any aspirations for higher living had to be put on hold as he took temporary accommodation in a Paddington bedsit to prepare for his exams. Money was tight and, unlike other applicants, he was not able to enjoy the facilities of a 'crammer' to get him through his FO and civil service exams.

In 1936 civil service examinations followed a very traditional format, with a general question paper on literature, political economy and international affairs. Cairncross, like many others before him, was able to give studious attention to past papers. The examination format suited him, although its practical value for a diplomatic career and its narrow range of topics had become the subject of criticism. Academic experts, including William Beveridge, complained at the absence of sociological topics, while the previous year's disquiet over the lack of questions on 'everyday science' had even been heard in the House of Commons. Others claimed, with justification, that the exams favoured Oxbridge syllabi while other universities were rarely consulted on the content of the papers. The exam system would be partially revised the following year, but Cairncross was glad to be able to answer questions on French literature and political economy. For the latter he received coaching from Hans Singer, the German economist who after fleeing his country in 1933 was offered a Cambridge University post on Keynes's recommendation. Through Alec, Cairncross had got to know Singer at Cambridge and had so impressed him with his German that on one occasion Singer had passed him off as Johann Kernkreutz at a social function attended by anti-Nazi German exiles.[3]

Cairncross was in Berlin, staying with the family whose son he had tutored two years previously, when he received a telegram from his proud family in Lesmahagow informing him that he had come top in both FO and civil service exams. It was a remarkable achievement for the son of an ironmonger, and The Glasgow Herald proudly reported Cairncross's success to its readers. Among those of his contemporaries graded below him was Con O'Neil, Etonian and recently elected Fellow of All

Souls, who would go on to be British ambassador in China and lead the negotiations on British entry to the European Economic Community. Alec Cairncross would later say that coming top in both exams was for his brother 'the high point in his career'.[4] However, considering the trajectory of his life thereafter it was an achievement that would bring him mixed blessings.

On his return to London, Cairncross had to sit his viva, which proved to be a more uncomfortable encounter. Naturally outspoken and intellectually curious, he could not help setting forth his views on the current international situation and the dangers of German expansionism. Another question concerned the poetry of the late A. E. Housman, who had been a reclusive near-neighbour of his at Trinity College. Cairncross thought he had 'blundered' by pointing out the 'somewhat affected' or 'over-pretty' aspects of the acclaimed English poet, who 'had a special appeal to English ears and sensibilities'.[5] Nevertheless, he remained top of the candidates list and in October 1936 took up a position as third secretary in the American department at the FO.

His salary precluded the bohemian lifestyle that Ian Smith had wondered at, and he had to be content with a room in Gunterstone Road, Barons Court, then a secluded London district, sharing the house with another civil servant. Here he lived frugally on an annual starting salary of £275, and it was some time before he was in a position to enjoy the benefits of the metropolis. His appointment to the FO did, however, transport him to a new world of power and rank, and he was struck by 'its whole aura of tradition and influence' the first time he entered its majestic buildings.[6] It took him a while to get used to the daily routines of Whitehall (he was never entirely comfortable within its environs) but at the same time was impressed by its prestige and grandeur.

Autumn 1936 was a critical time to be entering the FO, with Japan's occupation of Manchuria, the outbreak of the Spanish Civil War and Mussolini's invasion of Abyssinia. The previous year Hitler had decided to rearm Germany in breach of the Treaty of Versailles, which confirmed Cairncross's worst fears picked up from his travels in Germany. The FO itself had contained divergent views among its leading officials on how to deal with these events. When Cairncross joined the FO, Robert Vansittart was its permanent undersecretary, the highest position held in the FO by a non-politician. Vansittart was a staunch opponent of the Hitler regime and opposed Anglo-

German rapprochement; he would later be an outspoken critic of appeasement. As early as 1933, during the Austrian crisis, Vansittart had warned that 'it would be dangerous in the extreme for His Majesty's government to be caught unprepared. ... Hitler may vary his methods but he will not abandon – save under compulsion – his firm intention of destroying Austrian independence.' He even saw Russia as a potential ally in stopping German advances in Europe and Japan's ambitions in the Far East.[7] Earlier in 1936, Vansittart had sent a memo to the cabinet calling for tougher action against Germany. At that time, Vansittart's position gave him a leading role in foreign affairs policy, one that put him at odds with politicians, though this would change significantly when Neville Chamberlain became the prime minister in 1937. Chamberlain 'moved to control foreign and defence policy' and introduced a new diplomatic strategy from above, one which sought bilateral agreements with Germany and other aggressors and which critics later attributed to a weakening of Britain's security and status.[8] At the same time Vansittart's role was diminished, and in 1938 he would be removed from his post.

It was against this background that Cairncross took up his position in the American department. For many, this would be a stepping stone to a distinguished career in the FO and diplomatic service. His role involved reading dispatches and passing them on with his annotated comments to senior officials, to filter documents, to select, monitor and prioritize their importance. Cairncross had the intellect and acumen, excellent linguistic skills as well as a good knowledge of the international situation to prepare him for a career in the FO. Yet, as his career progressed, reports suggested that he lacked some of the administrative skills, the diplomatic manners, tact and the necessary conformity to procedure. His first days brought some uncertainty, on his part, over whether he would entirely fit in, as he perceived a certain aloofness and even difficulty in understanding his Scottish accent, though this may have been as much to do with his aversion to what he considered English conventions and rituals.

It was the inability to contain his political views, as the cataclysmic events unfolded, that would widen the distance between him and some of his colleagues. At a time of political and international crisis he found it impossible to hide his dismay at the direction of British foreign policy, or his contempt for those he considered pro-fascist sympathizers within the ranks of politics, the military or aristocracy. Added to that, he was not deemed 'clubbable' in a way that was expected among the wider FO community. In his reliance on intellect and general academic knowledge, he had something of the 'cult of the amateur' that had dominated the civil service since the Northcote-Trevelyan Report had defined its role over eighty years earlier. (It would later be subject to critical scrutiny in the Fulton Committee investigation into the civil service published in 1968.) He had not received specialist training; the management processes were unclear and civil servants worked in a cloud of secrecy for much of the time. Added to that, Cairncross's own character and personality was often at odds with the outlook of his superiors. His background was different, and on joining the FO he had to learn an etiquette that was 'foreign' not only to his relatively humble background but also to his newly discovered European outlook. He was outspoken and opinionated, and as the international crisis deepened, he found it increasingly difficult to fit in. Among those taken aback by his views on Germany was Sir Robert Craigie, one of the FO's senior diplomats, to whom he made an untactful chance remark at a colleague's wedding.

This helps explain why his FO career never took off in the way he envisaged; in fact, his work was regarded as unsatisfactory for much of the time, and throughout his FO employment he would find himself moved to other sections in the hope that this would improve. In November 1936, just weeks after his appointment, he was reprimanded (on Vansittart's recommendation) for leaving a cupboard door open.[9]

His first move to the Western department in early 1937 seems not to have been a result of any particular failing on his part, however; it was more an indication of priorities as the conflict in Spain (which came under its domain) escalated. He therefore found himself, a European anti-fascist, in the Spanish section in the FO during the critical time in the Spanish Civil War. Nationalist opponents of the republican government, led by General Franco, were making severe inroads into regions loyal to the government, which in November 1936 had to move its HQ from Madrid to Valencia. FO attitudes to Franco, whose insurgents in the early years of the war surpassed the brutality of even early Nazi atrocities, were divided; some took the view that, like Mussolini and Hitler, it was a useful bulwark against communism. The British government, a national government which was led by Stanley Baldwin (until he was succeeded by Neville Chamberlain at the end of May) had adopted a policy of 'non-intervention', which was the official position of the British Labour Party in opposition, and therefore one that Cairncross was obliged to follow in his day-to-day work. For communists and others in the Independent Labour Party, as well as international socialists and democrats, the Spanish Civil War was the cause célèbre of the mid-1930s. The Labour Party, too, under its new leader Clement Attlee, would move to more open support for the republican side once it was clear that Franco was backed by Hitler and Mussolini.

Cairncross had already reached the conclusion that the expansion of fascist influence was the biggest threat facing democracies, but this put him in a difficult position in his new role. As he later reflected,

The atmosphere in the Spanish department was fairly balanced, but I witnessed at first-hand the effect of the sham non-intervention for Spain. There was little inclination to favour either side, with just a few with the Republicans and the majority non-committal.[10]

One of the first people he met when he arrived in the Western department was Donald Maclean, with whom he shared an office. It was the first time they had met. Maclean, who had graduated in modern languages from Trinity Hall in 1934 prior to Cairncross's arrival in Cambridge, had originally intended to take up a teaching post in Russia, but after being recruited later that year to NKVD, the Soviet intelligence service, on the recommendation of Kim Philby, he had been persuaded to join the FO, a decision which pleased his family. He spent the year before taking up his FO post in October 1935 cramming for the exams, liaising with his Soviet contact, disavowing his communism and attending debutante balls.[11] In his FO examination Maclean had performed particularly well in the interview part, with the panel, consisting of politicians and diplomats known to his late father (who had been a member of Ramsay MacDonald's government in 1931), accepting his explanation for his early attraction to communism. Maclean clearly felt at home in FO circles, and his connections, together with more experience in the role, gave him a head start over his new colleague situated at the other side of his desk. Two other junior FO staff also shared the office, which was next to the offices of the head of department and his secretary.

In the Spanish section, Cairncross worked under the eccentric and easy-going William Montagu-Pollock, an earlier graduate of Trinity

College who would later have a distinguished FO career, serving as charge d'affaires in Sweden during the Second World War: higher up the ladder were Walter St Clair Howland Roberts, the head of department, and the undersecretary George Mounsey, who in Cairncross's estimation was 'mildly pro-Franco'. Under the supervision of Roberts ('middle of the road') and Frederick Hoyer-Millar, the son of a timber merchant and owner of Blair Castle in Perthshire, Cairncross's job was to liaise with agents in Spain to secure the release of British subjects held in Franco's prisons in exchange for prisoners held by republican authorities. As a civil servant required to uphold the government's position of neutrality, he was obliged to couch his comments in the moderate tones of one who hoped that 'Britain's policy of non-intervention is gradually being appreciated', and that General Franco would demonstrate appropriate restraint. He found this approach increasingly difficult to sustain, and his annotated comments on reports of the movements of Franco's 'insurgents' occasionally got him into trouble with his superiors. It sharply illustrated his unease with official positions on Spain. One source of conflict was the pro-Franco reports he was required to comment upon. Major Francis Yeats-Brown, a senior British military officer who had received a 'friendly welcome' during a visit to Franco forces, was keen to drop in at the FO and share his 'impressions' of his meeting with the general. Yeats-Brown had been accompanied on his trip by Douglas Jerrold, newspaper editor and vocal supporter of both Mussolini and Franco, who in 1936 had helped fly Franco from his isolation on the Canary Islands to Morocco, from where he began to launch his coup, thus heralding the start of the Spanish war. Yeats-Brown's undisguised admiration for General Franco clearly bridled with Cairncross. 'It may be mentioned', Cairncross noted in his comments, 'that Major Yeats-Brown is a fascist'.[12]

Shortly after, Cairncross received a report from Major General Sir W. Maxwell Scott, the great-great-grandson of Sir Walter Scott and another military officer, who was keen to inform the FO of 'the facts' on the 'Situation in General Franco's territory' in March 1937: namely that republican prisoners had been 'liberated', the Spanish people in his areas were prospering and the fault lay with the republicans and their supporters. Cairncross commented,

It is impossible to discuss Sir W. Maxwell Scott's report in detail without writing a minute of approximately the same length. Sufficient to say that he has swallowed the insurgents' point of view en bloc and that his report is consequently biased, inaccurate and occasionally rather naïve (it is if his belief that 90% of the people of Eastern Spain urge Franco's victory).

As such, the document is useful rather as an example of political propaganda than as an objective analysis of the situation in Spain.[13]

As Cairncross received further reports of Franco insurgencies, he noted the 'ghastly set of pictures' of mutilated bodies made available a year after Franco's attack on Madrid and commented on the successful resistance to Franco advances on Guadalajara in mid-March. As his superiors looked for reasons to explain the failed mission to Guadalajara, he pointed out that the 'low morale of the Italian troops' was a possible contributory factor, but had been omitted from the telegram dispatches. 'It's not their war!' Hoyer-Millar retorted in his scribbled response to Cairncross's observation, seemingly regarding his junior's comment as misplaced idealism and naivety.[14] Yet, the reluctance of senior FO officials to accept that other fascist governments were supporting Franco could be said to be naivety on their part.

The collusion of fascist governments in supporting Franco was first confirmed in reports made by the writer Arthur Koestler, the most notable of the exchange prisoners dealt with by Cairncross. Officially, Koestler had been in Spain as a foreign correspondent for the *News Chronicle*. Yet, unknown to the FO, Koestler was in fact working for the Comintern and had been sent to Spain shortly after the Franco insurrection had begun in the summer of 1936. Initially, he had wanted to join the republican army, but he was persuaded by Willi Münzenberg and Otto Katz, his Comintern bosses, that for propaganda reasons he would better serve the cause by working undercover in insurgent areas as a reporter investigating foreign aid given to the nationalists. As Koestler explained later, 'The purpose of my visit to enemy headquarters was to collect evidence proving German and Italian intervention on Franco's side.'[15] Katz, who was well connected in left-wing journalistic circles in London, provided him with his accreditation as a 'Special Correspondent' for the *News Chronicle* and further eased his passage by providing £200 in expenses and a new suit with which to impress Franco's circle. He set off from Southampton for Lisbon, from where he would enter Seville, the nationalist base. Soon after reaching Lisbon, the sight of German airmen wearing Spanish air force uniforms marked with a swastika was immediate evidence of Hitler's support for Franco, confirmed to Koestler by a leading nationalist general. In Seville he met more German officers (including one who recognized him from previous encounters), which meant he had to escape to Gibraltar at short notice. On his return he discussed publishing a new 'Committee of Inquiry into Alleged Breaches of the Non-Intervention Agreement in Spain' with Katz and Münzenberg; they had previously initiated a similar investigation into the causes of the Reichstag Fire of 1933. As with the Reichstag Fire inquiry, the 'new committee of inquiry' found broad support in London among such figures as the Duchess of Atholl, Phillip Noel-Baker and Eleanor Rathbone. In any case, communists were now (as Koestler put it later after he had abandoned communism) being converted into 'anti-fascists', 'with geranium-boxes on the windows, and a gate wide open to all men with goodwill'.[16] His claim to be the first foreign journalist to expose fascist support for Franco was real, however, and was given wider confirmation following the German and Italian bombardment of Guernica and other detailed atrocities.

On the recommendation of the Spanish foreign ministry, Koestler returned to Spain to search for documents left in Madrid that would provide further evidence of Nazi support for Franco. He managed to complete this task before the nationalists reached the city. The Spanish government had set up an international news agency, with Katz heading its Paris office; it was on their recommendation that Koestler was sent to Malaga, via Valencia (where the government now had its base) on another *News Chronicle* assignment. After Franco's troops finally reached Malaga at the beginning of February 1937, Koestler was arrested at the home of his friend, the British zoologist Peter Chalmers-Mitchell, situated on the edge of the city. His arrest had been aided by Italian soldiers (some of whom were singing *Giovinezza*, the anthem of the Italian fascists), and despite the negotiations Chalmers-Mitchell made on his behalf, Koestler was taken to the cells, expecting to be hanged. Here he witnessed several beatings carried out in front of him. Kept in isolation from other prisoners, and regularly told by the guards that he would soon be executed, Koestler's main contact with those around him was the occasional singing of the *Internationale* from nearby cells or the 'oily' voice announcing names of prisoners to be collected. Conditions improved when he was transferred to the nationalist base of Seville, where he could choose books from a well-stocked library and was able to establish better relations with the guards, though he still expected to be killed. A visiting representative of the Hearst Press told him he was suspected of being a spy and, asking if he was 'aware of the consequences of his actions', raised the question of whether a deal with Franco was possible. Otherwise, 'it means death', she told him. She also told him that 'Mr Hearst' and the News Chronicle had both made representations to Franco and that he 'might possibly grant a commutation'. In fact, William Randolph Hearst had dramatically changed sides from a left of centre democrat to a sympathizer of the far-right regimes of Europe, and members of his press group were working in Franco's press and propaganda HQ.[17] Koestler gave a brief written statement in which he said he would be grateful to Franco for the commutation of his sentence on political grounds, while restating his socialist convictions. For days afterwards, he remained tormented by the suggestion that Franco might grant him a reprieve. 'I was incapable of collecting my thoughts. Death sentence, life-long imprisonment, the correspondent of the Hearst Press, the Propaganda Department, the Phalangist uniform and the perfume were altogether too much for my poor head.'[18]

Five weeks after his arrest there was still no indication that he would be released, and despite some improvements such as a letter from his wife, time spent mingling with other prisoners on the patio and better food provisions, he was reminded of the prospect of death on a daily basis. Several of his patio companions were not seen again, and it was only after faking heart problems that he was able to make any contact with the British consul. His prison diary of Monday, 10 May recorded:

The consul came. ... It had still been impossible to obtain from Franco an assurance that he would not have me shot. He said, it is true, that he did not think my death was of such importance to Franco that he would risk offending the foreign office but this was somewhat vague comfort. I asked if there were a possibility of my being exchanged with a prisoner of the Valencia Government, but he said that at the present stage he did not think it likely.

Koestler added, 'I must have made an odd impression on him, and it seemed to me that he looked at me several times in astonishment and some irritation.'[19]

Nevertheless, two days later he was told to pack his bags. He had spent 102 days in prison. After signing a declaration that he would not be 'meddling in the internal affairs of Spain', he was met by what turned out to be one of Franco's leading war pilots, and the husband of a woman whose release had been arranged in exchange for his own. They were driven to a field on the outskirts of the city where his pilot flew him to the border with Gibraltar – the two of them, crammed into a tiny Baby Douglas monoplane, debating the merits of the two sides in the Spanish conflict. He arrived in Britain on 14 May, where he was made aware of the strong support he had received from the British public, including not only writers but also MPs of both main political parties.

Though Cairncross's official involvement in Koestler's release was a minor one (his junior position in the Spanish section did not allow him significant responsibility other than a supporting role), he subsequently revealed that he had 'pressed for action' on Koestler.[20] The operation seems to have been handled by the FO's man in Madrid, Milanes. However, there is almost certainly more to this story of Cairncross's involvement in Koestler's release. Cairncross's friendship with James Klugmann had continued after Cambridge, and it is possible that Klugmann, the former co-leader of the Cambridge communist group who was now the secretary of the World Student Association (RME), the Comintern organization set up by Münzenberg and Katz, would have known of their work and been aware of Koestler's role. Initially in Paris to carry out research under Harry Ashton and Daniel Mornet, Klugmann had by this time become a full-time political organizer, galvanizing international left-wing students under the guidance of his Comintern bosses. A major part of the RME's work was to raise 'aid for Spain' and, in alliance with the burgeoning number of pro-republican groups, to try to exert pressure on governments and public opinion. It is inconceivable that Spain was not the main topic of conversation between Klugmann and Cairncross and for that reason the latter would have known more about Koestler than his FO colleagues. It is also revealing that Cairncross's move to the Spanish section in February 1937, unlike later transfers on competency grounds, was one that he himself might have helped secure. It also coincided almost exactly with Koestler's capture.

Another significant explanation for Cairncross's likely contribution to Koestler's release can be found in his recent acquaintance with

Harold Nicolson, the diarist, National Labour MP and, after a brief dalliance with Oswald Mosley's 'New Party' (predecessor of his Blackshirts), a strong opponent of Franco and appeasement. Cairncross had got to know Nicolson slightly through Guy Burgess, whom he had met for the first time at a party in early 1937. Unknown to Cairncross, Burgess and his close friend Anthony Blunt had both been recently recruited by the NKVD, and they had targeted Cairncross for similar recruitment once they knew he was set for the FO. Donald Maclean and James Klugmann were also aware of the attempts to recruit Cairncross at this time; Burgess had begun to seriously cultivate Cairncross after a Sunday gathering involving Blunt, and his friend Louis MacNeice in Cambridge and in London used his wide social circles to introduce him to more interesting people, including Nicolson and others. Cairncross, though sceptical of the pretentiousness of his upper-middle-class contemporaries, was nevertheless 'flattered' to begin mixing in such social circles. Nicolson, who had been a diplomat and formerly an attaché in Madrid, was one of the influential figures behind the campaign to release Koestler from Franco's prison and enjoyed excellent contacts at the FO. Cairncross confirmed as much in his later interview with M15 interrogator William ('Jim') Skardon in 1952,

> Round about September 1937 he [Burgess] asked me to a party at his flat in Chester Square at which a number of celebrities, including Harold Nicolson were present. Nicolson, who had been told I worked in the FO Department dealing with Spain, asked me about KOESTLER who was then imprisoned by the Franco authorities. He asked me if I could do anything to help and when I said I doubted it, he asked for the name of the Head of Department and the Under-Secretary which I gave him.[21]

Nicolson, who was extremely well connected and would later serve in the Ministry of Information, no doubt lobbied undersecretary Mounsey. However, Cairncross's meeting with Nicolson could not have been in September 1937 because Koestler had already been released four months earlier. As we shall see, May 1937 was the month that Cairncross, with the help of James Klugmann, was recruited to Soviet intelligence. Could this have been his first assignment as a Soviet agent?

Koestler's own MI5 file confirms that the security services had no knowledge that he was employed by the Comintern prior to going to Spain, merely that 'his leanings are definitely towards the left'.[22] In *Spanish Testament*, his own account of his imprisonment published within months of his release, Koestler unsurprisingly omits any mention of his involvement with the Comintern or Münzenberg and Katz. He writes, 'As a journalist of liberal convictions and author of fragments of pacifist novels … I was bound to be tempted by the idea of getting into rebel territory.'[23] The Duchess of Atholl, who wrote the foreword to the book and was also none the wiser about Koestler's Comintern links, noted that it was 'only a fortunate chance had enabled him to enter General Franco's territory, for journalists of the "Right" alone were being admitted'.[24]

The Comintern was not officially part of Soviet intelligence, even if it did inhabit a world of propaganda, intrigue and covert operations. After its adoption of the Popular Front strategy in 1935, which committed it to work with all those opposed to fascism, the Comintern's activities became bound up increasingly with broader campaigns. Klugmann, as the secretary of the RME, was a paid Comintern leader, adept at explaining the anti-fascist politics of the Popular Front, which for an 'internationalist' like John Cairncross, would have appealed, notably in light of the British government's reluctance to take sides. As the Spanish Civil War intensified, the Spanish section's position would have seemed anathema to Cairncross. John Cornford had been killed fighting in Spain a few months before, and others of his Cambridge generation would die fighting for the republican side. He knew of Klugmann's work for the Comintern and like many others approved of its Popular Front activities. The friendly, engaging and lucid Klugmann had been a good friend to Cairncross and was one of the few people he respected as an intellectual equal. Klugmann had also been a mentor to Donald Maclean since their time at school. Soon Cairncross and Maclean would have a lot more in common, even if only one of them would be aware of the implications of their acquaintance.

Chapter 6
Agent Molière

Born into an Austrian Jewish family in 1904, Arnold Deutsch had been a brilliant student of philosophy, physics and chemistry at Vienna University in the early 1920s. Attracted to left-wing politics as a teenager, by 1924 he had moved from Austrian youth organizations into the Austrian Communist Party, on a path that would lead to a permanent breach with his social democratic and religiously observant father. Sent to Moscow by the Austrian Communist Party in 1928, Deutsch's technical skills and aptitude for propaganda work, combined with his ability to operate on his own initiative, brought him to the attention of the Comintern, which employed him as a courier in OMS (its international liaison department), in Vienna from 1928 to 1931. From there he was sent to Greece and the Middle East and on to Paris in 1932, by which time he had been recruited by the OGPU, a section of the Soviet Secret Police which in 1934 became part of the NKVD, the Soviet intelligence network, officially titled 'The People's Commissariat for Internal Affairs'. In the Austrian revolt in 1933–4, the Austrian parliament was suspended (rendering the social democratic opposition weak and ineffective), which culminated in the brief civil war between the army and the left during 12–16 February, in which both of Deutsch's younger brothers participated. Now sought after by the police, Deutsch left for an OGPU assignment in London. By this time he had already made his first recruit: the communist activist and photographer Edith Suschitzky. Like Deutsch, she was a communist from a social democratic family and, as with many other Austrian communists who had been forced underground after the suppression of opposition and the imposition of fascist rule, now sought exile. Among Suschitzky's friends and comrades was Litzi Friedmann, who shortly followed her to London with her new boyfriend, a Cambridge graduate named Kim Philby, whom she had befriended, influenced and fought alongside in the street battles in Vienna. Suschitzky's escape to London had been helped by her marriage to Alex Tudor-Hart, a left-wing English doctor.

Deutsch arrived in London as an 'illegal', that is to say, a Soviet intelligence officer who did not operate under the protection or formality of the Soviet Embassy or held diplomatic privilege. For his cover, he entered Britain on a student visa, enrolling in a psychology course at London University, and apparently taking his studies seriously until the last examinations. He had a particular interest in the ideas of his countryman Willhelm Reich, whose attempt to marry Marxism with Freudian psychoanalysis in explaining the links between sexual and economic oppression was seen as heretical within communist orthodoxy, and dangerously controversial outside it. Deutsch's status in Britain, always precarious, was supported by his cousin Oscar Deutsch, who owned Odeon Cinemas. Deutsch worked for him for a while, in the company's advertising department.

Arnold Deutsch, codenamed 'OTTO' or 'STEPHAN', was a thirty-year-old independent minded (as far as Comintern constraints allowed) and intellectually curious cosmopolitan, who spoke fluent English and German, with passable skills in French, Italian and Dutch. Short and stocky, he was a likeable companion, capable of great empathy, notably for those younger or of similar age. He also had a plan.

Through her friend Litzi Friedmann, Edith Tudor-Hart – by now under NKVD codenames 'EDITH' or 'STRELA' – had become acquainted with Philby and recommended him to Deutsch. Deutsch saw the potential of recruiting young graduates with communist sympathies like Philby (whose father had been in the British secret service) with the potential to rise within the higher echelons of the British state. For most of his time at Cambridge, Philby had been a social democrat, but through the influence of the communist-dominated CUSS (for whom he acted as treasurer) and under the tutelage of Maurice Dobb, the long-standing communist economics don, he had been won to more radical ideas at a time when capitalism appeared doomed and the Soviet Union was winning admiration for its economic plans. Dobb had put him in touch with members of the Comintern's 'Red Aid' group in Paris and through that network

Philby reached Austria. His experience in Vienna during its revolutionary upheavals was the defining moment for Philby, where, under the influence of his landlord's daughter Litzi (with whom he fell in love) he saw action on the streets, as communists led the opposition to the fascists.

In 1934 Edith Suschitzky introduced Philby to 'Otto' in Regent's Park, through a typically circuitous route used by agents, involving several taxis and buses. They got on well, and Otto's initial appeal to Philby, one he repeated to all his recruits, was that he was needed by the Comintern in the international struggle against fascism; only the Soviet Union was capable of resisting the march of Nazism, he told Philby. Philby would be of more use to the Comintern, Otto added, by 'penetrating' spheres of influence, rather than through the activities of an ordinary communist. This was a point that Philby might have viewed with some irony, given his recent attempts to join the Communist Party of Great Britain had been thwarted by its bureaucratic procedures. Otto also asked him to supply a list of names of others of similar background who were sympathetic to the cause and had outstanding career prospects ahead of them.

Philby quickly produced a list of seven of his Cambridge contemporaries, with Donald Maclean at the top and Guy Burgess at the bottom. Maclean was next to be recruited later in 1934 by which time he had abandoned plans to teach English in Russia or study for a PhD on Calvinism and Marxism in favour of a diplomatic career at the FO. Guy Burgess, through his friendship with Maclean, and despite a growing reputation for indiscretion and unreliability, was recruited by Otto at the end of 1934. Anthony Blunt was recruited later in early 1937, while still on his research fellowship at Cambridge. All four were known to each other and in some cases (Burgess and Maclean and Burgess and Blunt) enjoyed close friendships.

By the time of Anthony Blunt's recruitment, Deutsch was in the final year of his stay in London. It had been a difficult time, occasionally having to justify his resident status and moving house several times. For a year from November 1935 he lived in the art deco Isokon building in Lawn Road, Hampstead, built the previous year by the architects, Wells Coates and Jack and Molly Pritchard. It may have been recommended to him by Edith Tudor-Hart, who as a photographer was fascinated by its architecture and the 'minimalist' living quarters. In the Isokon he was part of a larger milieu of refugees – approximately a third of the residents – from Nazi rule, which included, at different times, at least three other spies. A short distance from Edith's flat on Haverstock Hill, it was a bohemian, freethinking artistic community which reflected a range of dissident opinions.[1] Deutsch was later joined by his wife Josefine (herself an NKVD wireless operator) and their young son. His status in Britain during 1937, however, was increasingly under scrutiny, while his relations with Moscow deteriorated. The British police had refused him a work permit (he had after all entered the country on a student visa), while another spy network at the Woolwich Arsenal base set up by Deutsch's NKVD boss Theodore Maly was in the process of being exposed by the MI5 agent Olga Gray, who was working undercover within the CPGB hierarchy. In the same period Edith Tudor-Hart lost a diary with valuable information and contacts which caused Deutsch to be recalled briefly to Moscow. Nevertheless, against this background of uncertainty and insecurity, Deutsch continued to receive young talented recruits. The most notable in 1937 was John Cairncross.

Cairncross, at this time, was little known to other members of what would later be dubbed by Moscow as 'the Magnificent Five', after the Western film *The Magnificent Seven*. Indeed, he was never knowingly part of a 'ring'. The others had all graduated before he arrived at Cambridge, and Anthony Blunt was the only one he knew during his time there as a student, though of course he had maintained his good friendship with James Klugmann. Like Cairncross, Klugmann was ideally suited to academic life but by the 1930s he had become so caught up in the tumultuous struggles of the time – depression and hunger marches at home, the Spanish Civil War and the Popular Front government in France – that he abandoned his research to take up a role as a student leader, organizing congresses and campaigns. He later described the period as one defined by 'commitment' and he was content to sacrifice an academic future for what he saw as bigger causes. His loyalty was rewarded later when he was appointed to several leading roles in the CPGB.

As an open communist, Klugmann had chosen a different path to his contemporaries, Philby, Burgess and Maclean. He had known Donald Maclean since they were close friends together at Gresham's School in Holt, then under a liberal regime and accommodating the sons of notable public figures, including Roger and Brian Simon and Peter and Bernard Floud, who would all go on to be communists. Klugmann was more politically mature than Maclean, more steeped in Marxist understanding and a good organizer and served as an early mentor as the latter moved towards the left. Although Maclean was at Trinity Hall, they both took the same degree and campaigned together as leading activists in the communist group and the CUSS. That changed after Maclean's recruitment to the NKVD in 1934, when he distanced himself from his former comrades and cut his British communist links. While in Paris working for RME, Klugmann would have known of Maclean's recruitment to the NKVD, and indeed it is quite likely that on one of his regular visits to London Maclean consulted him about it, but it was not a world he sought for himself. As an open communist he believed with others in his party that 'two sorts of work' – open public campaigning and secretive manoeuvres – would conflict, and while communists of his generation knew that clandestine espionage took place they were aware that such actions derail important gains made through open political work.

By then Klugmann had already been earmarked by the CPGB as a future leader. As an intellectual, he quickly absorbed the necessary humbleness and deference to members and leaders of what was a predominantly proletarian party, one which attempted to reflect the cultural ethos of the skilled working class. This was something beyond Philby, Burgess and Maclean, even if they had been so minded. Cairncross did not share the depth of Klugmann's convictions, but their common interest in French and German literature formed the basis of a continuing friendship after Cairncross joined the FO and Klugmann was one of the few people with whom Cairncross kept in touch.

The friendship between Klugmann and Cairncross, however, would have fateful consequences. After he had been recruited to the NKVD on the prompting of his close friend Guy Burgess, Anthony Blunt had assumed the role of talent-spotter, for which, with his pastoral care for younger undergraduates, he had some facility. He paid particular attention to those promising graduates with left-wing sympathies who were likely to take important roles in government, foreign affairs or international finance. His recruits included the wealthy American Michael Straight, whom he had exploited in the aftermath of the death of Straight's close friend John Cornford in Spain in December 1936: Blunt manipulated Straight's vulnerability at this low point, taking advantage of his grief at Cornford's death to remind him that his friend had given up his life for the cause and that he could make his own contribution to the international struggle by taking an influential banking job on Wall Street, where he could disclose confidential details of economic strategy. 'Our friends ("the international communist movement") have given a great deal of thought to it', Blunt told his friend. 'They have instructed me to tell you that this is what you must do', he added, to dramatic effect.[2] Straight had sufficient private wealth to make his own choices and was expecting to be offered the chance to stand as a Labour MP. Blunt's persuasive tactics, however, sent him back to the United States.

Blunt knew Cairncross had just started a career in the FO and thus fitted Deutsch's criteria of potential agent. Once Burgess made contact with Cairncross in London in early 1937, Blunt invited him to Cambridge on the last Sunday in February for a convivial gathering which included Blunt's school friend, the poet Louis MacNeice. Cairncross held a keen appreciation of poetry and sought the company of writers: he was flattered to be invited. He had no knowledge then that he was being targeted to work for the Russians. Many years later he concluded that, on the train journey home from Cambridge that day, Burgess had made his pitch to recruit him. Reporting back to Moscow on Monday, 1 March, the day after the meeting in Blunt's rooms, Burgess confirmed the details of his approach as well as another meeting he held with Cairncross the previous evening. He was cautiously optimistic about the possibility of him being recruited, despite his assertion that Cairncross was not a committed communist but rather a 'typical petit bourgeois who always thinks that he can achieve a great deal in bourgeois society'.

> Cairncross: I befriended him and we returned to London together. I asked him to give me a ring and to come and see me. He came yesterday evening and spent the whole evening with me. It seems to me that I managed to interest him in my person. That is already clear from our conversation. He promised to come again. ... I had long talks with him on French and English ideas, on French history etc. From discussing these questions, we moved to politics. ... He was led by purely cultural considerations, in contrast to social and radical ones. ... In his view Marxism, from a cultural point of view can contribute to the solution of theoretical problems and he discussed these questions with us from that angle. He was never a member of the party in the real sense of the word, but I think that we should

work with him and involve him, though I am inclined to think that it would not be entirely without danger to approach him directly, at least until such a time that Tony [Blunt] or another party member has taken him to hand.[3]

Burgess's belief that Cairncross could be a 'risk' was amplified by the 'dangers' posed by Cairncross's social background and personality, indicative of Burgess's disdainful snobbery. Cairncross, he noted, 'comes from a lower middle-class family and is of humbler origin than I. He speaks with a strong Scottish accent and one cannot call him a gentleman.'[4] Burgess offered further observations on Cairncross's limitations.

His personal and social maturity conceals a danger. He has never had the time or the money to enjoy life, he has always suppressed himself and denied himself everything for the sake of the future. Now he is close to his goal. Though I think we may count on his goodwill, nevertheless his personality is fraught with many dangers and all this is not without a certain risk.[5]

From Burgess's comments it is not clear whether his scepticism over Cairncross's potential value as a spy is derived from his political unreliability – 'never a member of the party in the real sense of the word' – or his social inadequacies.

Burgess did pick up, however, on Cairncross's career ambitions as well as his growing grievance towards the FO's hierarchies and his reservations about government policy on Germany. Burgess followed up the Cambridge meeting with further invitations to social gatherings (which included the meeting with Harold Nicolson, when the latter asked him about Koestler), as well as a botched attempt to meet up with him in Paris around Easter 1937 – when Cairncross failed to appear at a rendezvous Burgess had arranged at a homosexual café.

Burgess suggested that it would be better if the actual recruitment involved a party member Cairncross could trust, as there was too great a risk for himself and Blunt, now active NKVD agents. Such an approach would not be likely to cause initial suspicion on Cairncross's part as he and other student communists would have been aware that the CPGB maintained its own clandestine links with Moscow; in fact,

shortly after joining the FO, he had been informally approached by
Gavin Ewart (who succeeded Klugmann and Cornford as leader of the
communist cell at Trinity) for useful information, and had also ignored a
suggestion over lunch by Roy Pascal, his former German tutor, that he
meet up with one of his contacts to discuss 'political developments'.[6]
These approaches, however, did not have the backing of Moscow or
the offer of an espionage role.

As Cairncross's closest friend in the CPGB, Klugmann was himself
recruited to the NKVD by Deutsch, with the cooperation of the CPGB
leadership, for the one-off assignment of recruiting Cairncross.
Klugmann himself regarded such matters with distaste and insisted on
it being authorized by the communist leaders. In May 1937, at the time
when Cairncross was working in the Spanish section to help secure
the release of Koestler and others, Klugmann arranged to meet him in
the early evening at the entrance to Regent's Park. They walked to a
secluded area of the park where Cairncross was introduced to Arnold
Deutsch; Klugmann, Cairncross recounted later, then disappeared into
the bushes, and they were not to meet again for thirty years. Though he
was unaware at the time of what he was being drawn into – 'Otto', as
usual, initially framed his offer in the language of the Comintern's fight
against fascism – he would come to regard Klugmann's role in setting
him up for NKVD recruitment as that of a 'catspaw', and a betrayal
of their friendship. Klugmann, for his part, regarded it as a necessary
duty on behalf of the Comintern and the cause to which he had already
committed his life. As he would later confess to a senior CPGB official,
in an interview at the party's HQ in King Street Covent Garden that was
recorded by MI5 microphones hidden in its rooms, 'If I'm asked to do
it then I will.'

In their early meetings, Otto and Cairncross got on well: the elder
Austrian's cosmopolitan background and interests appealed to
Cairncross, who had spent a memorable time in Vienna, Deutsch's
home city. They spoke in German and no doubt Cairncross shared
with the older man the memory of cycling holidays, conversations with
Austrians and Germans, and how five years before he had been made
aware of the threat Nazism posed for the world. Cairncross's interest
in Marxism, for what it brought to an understanding of history and
culture, was one he shared with Deutsch, who was far from a dogmatic
ideologue. Deutsch's attraction to bohemian living among the Lawn

Road fraternity would also have been agreeable to Cairncross, whose growing criticism of the prudery of bourgeois morality, bolstered by his readings of Molière and others, had yet to extend to any significant change in his own lifestyle. Deutsch's interest in Willhelm Reich's recently published *Sex-Pol* essays has probably been exaggerated in subsequent attempts to explain his appeal to the 'sexually promiscuous' members of the Cambridge spies. Certainly, radical ideas on the liberalization of marriage, divorce and abortion laws, 'free love', and the general hypocrisies of 'bourgeois morality' – controversial views at the time even by the norms of the German Communist Party – would have interested Cairncross, who would later write a short history of polygamy. However, Cairncross stated later that he never discussed Reich's work with Deutsch, which would not, in any case, have been a revelation to him. Deutsch's view of Cairncross was favourable and, in a typically insightful report on his new recruit – whom he recommended Moscow Centre give the codename MOLIÉRE – he praised his intellectual strengths, while noting his modesty, humble origins and what he attributed as the influence of early religious upbringing on his 'pedantic, industrious, zealous and thrifty' attitudes.

'He is modest and simple. When I met him the first time and took a taxi this was an event for him – it was the first time in his life he had ridden in a taxi.'[7]

On Cairncross's part, his luxurious journey home had given him much to think about.

> [After] I made my way home in a taxi I immediately took a strong drink and the good and the bad aspects of the meeting flashed through my mind. For my reaction was not just one of shock. I was still eager to work in any way I could but not as a Soviet agent, (but) for the alliance between our two countries. But in addition I recalled how my Italian refugee friend in Paris had talked of the organisation of an anti-fascist movement in his country. And how he had always insisted on the need for expert guidance in building up a resistance movement. If there was no support, the price to be paid in life and freedom was immense. And so I thought … how this expert knowledge could perhaps be exploited, since I had so little faith in the British resistance material should Britain ever be invaded or capitulate, to help organise an underground movement – on the

assumption that one must always prepare for the worst even if one does not expect it. And so finally I fell deeply asleep.[8]

Deutsch was struck by the growing tensions between Cairncross and his FO superiors, which became a frequent part of their discussions at their later monthly meetings, normally held in a park or other public space. Like Burgess, he saw that Cairncross was unhappy in his work, felt politically isolated and was consistently at odds with the prevailing attitude to Franco, Mussolini and Hitler. It was also clear to Deutsch that the FO had reservations about Cairncross's office work. Maclean, Cairncross's FO colleague, had reported on the unfavourable impression Cairncross had created in the office; according to Maclean, Cairncross was 'careless' in his work while his attitude to his superiors and those around him had not won him many friends.[9] Cairncross's problems at the FO presented both a danger and an opportunity for his Soviet controllers, while he was hardening his own opposition to British policy on fascism.

Cairncross later recalled that once he had started meeting Deutsch the choices of action available to him were limited. Deutsch had reassured him at their first meetings that he was free to withdraw from their arrangement, citing the example of Goronwy Rees (without naming him), who had been recruited by Burgess but had later had second thoughts. Rees, a close friend of Burgess, would be troubled by his own recruitment for years afterwards. His concern prompted a botched attempt to warn MI5 at the time of Burgess and Maclean's disappearance in 1951 and produced a series of tabloid articles on his former friend for *The People* in 1956, which cost him his position as the principal of University College of Wales, Aberystwyth. Once he had begun seeing Deutsch, Cairncross knew it would not be easy to report to his FO superiors details of his meetings, which would hardly put him, a troublesome colleague without strong social connections, in a positive light. In any case, politically isolated and with a growing desire to do something about what he saw as a disastrous foreign policy in a rapidly deteriorating situation, he felt a moral obligation to act.

It seems clear that the NKVD exploited his wider naivety, feelings of job insecurity, political idealism and desire to widen his social circles. Deutsch, who had a warm affection for his young recruit, advised him to move from Barons Court to Warwick Square, Pimlico, which was enabled through expenses provided by the NKVD.[10] Here in an impressive white-stucco Italianate building he enjoyed larger accommodation with three rooms and furniture provided by Mrs Ashton. He was closer to the restaurants and cultural venues of the West End, with the possibility of a lifestyle more suited to both his own individual aspirations and Deutsch's belief that more social circles would enhance his cover.

For the first four months of his recruitment, from May to September 1937, during what became an unofficial induction period, he was given tips on carrying material, avoiding suspicion and travelling to meeting points; he did not at this point pass on any serious documentation. He was being prepared to replace Maclean who was expected to move to Paris: a move, in fact, delayed until 1938. However, these plans were put on hold and in some jeopardy following Deutsch's recall to Moscow. In the summer of 1937 Deutsch finished studying at London University and intended to work for his cousin Oscar at the Odeon Cinema Company. However, his application for a work visa was refused and he received a visit from the British police which precipitated a prompt departure to Paris. In Paris, he met Theodore Maly, effectively his boss since 1936, and Kim Philby who Soviet intelligence were sending to Franco-occupied zones, officially as the Spain correspondent for *The Times*.[11]

After the departure of Philby and Maly, who had been recalled to Moscow, Deutsch invited Cairncross to join him at the Paris International Exhibition, where, among the vast exhibition rooms, the Nazi and Soviet regimes presented contrasting artistic visions of the future. Totalitarian art dominated the exhibition, while the portrait of Neville Chamberlain in fishing attire, hanging in the British pavilion, may have raised a smile. In the evening, Deutsch offered his companion some lighter amusement by introducing him to a belly-dancing club.[12]

There were bigger questions for Deutsch to worry about than the renewal of his British visa, as the Moscow 'show trials' and purges got underway. Maly's recall to Moscow was part of the purge, and he was subsequently charged and found guilty by the Military Collegium of the Supreme Court of the USSR of 'harming the interests of the USSR (malicious violation of the security rules, disclosure of state secrets, refusal to carry out orders in combat conditions).'[13] Along with many other victims of Stalin's purges, Maly confessed to being a German spy and was executed. Maly had been running the Woolwich Arsenal ring until it was broken with the help of Olga Gray, MI5's agent in the CPGB hierarchy, who worked closely with the ringleader of Woolwich Arsenal, Percy Glading. He had come under suspicion by Moscow because of his links with another agent Walter Krivitsky, who had recently defected. Krivitsky's defection also had implications for Arnold Deutsch as Krivitsky had been aware of his work and, under instructions from Moscow, Deutsch 'put the network on ice' between November 1937 and February 1938. Deutsch, although under suspicion, was transferred to other duties on the recommendation of Laventy Beria, who was carrying out the purges under Stalin's orders and would shortly become head of NKVD. Deutsch died in 1942, sunk by a U-boat, on his way to the United States where, as an illegal, he was to be reacquainted with Michael Straight, another of his (and Blunt's) Cambridge recruits.

Although the precise details of what happened to 'Otto' were unknown to Cairncross, the general picture he was confronted with had left him in limbo. His predicament was complicated further by his troubles in the office. Walter Roberts, his head of department, had found his work 'slipshod', 'inaccurate' and 'untidy'. Following the first year of his probation, there was 'considerable doubt about Cairncross's suitability for the service. He showed little sign of sound judgment or ability to conform to office routine.'[14] His willingness to present his unsolicited opinions on Franco no doubt rankled his FO superiors. Overall, his work was said to be 'unsatisfactory', and at the end of 1937 he was transferred again – this time to the FO's central department, headed by William Strang, which dealt with Germany. Here, he could witness at close hand the rising tensions between the British government and Germany, with the burning question of appeasement in the air.

Chapter 7
Appeasement

How was it that John Cairncross, who in an outstanding achievement had topped the results of the FO and civil service examinations, was now deemed an 'unsatisfactory' probationer after his first year in the job? The examinations had provided a test of knowledge and reasoning on familiar topics, and he had always flourished in academic settings. The job itself required more than intellectual rigour and agility, however, and his diplomatic skills and approach to office work had clearly fallen short of what was expected. Nevertheless, there was more to it than this. He could not relent in his conviction that government policy on international affairs was mistaken. As far as he was concerned, it was not just a political failure that had led to an underestimation of the threat of fascism in Europe: it was an intellectual failure. It was based on a misconceived strategy which was now helping to accelerate rather than hold back Europe's degeneration into war. The fallacy of this position had been brought home to him in the Spanish section where it had become clear that the government's 'non-intervention' policy was flawed; yet, even that was being undermined, in his view, by influential pro-Franco elements. He feared there were forces in politics, the FO and among privileged social hierarchies, who continued to see fascist regimes as a useful bulwark against communism: concerns he took with him into the German section. All this had left him restless, impotent and angry. No doubt his concern that the failure of British government policy and FO strategy to address the fascist threat provided some self-justification for working for the Soviets. Another reason for his lack of faith in the

FO was what he regarded as its privileged culture and atmosphere, typical, as he saw it, of a closed English elite. His resentment was picked up by colleagues, while there was probably a failing on his part to engage (within the limits of the FO) with potential allies who had sympathy for the republican cause.

During 1938 Cairncross witnessed at close quarters the prelude to what he and others saw as the 'betrayal of Czechoslovakia' at Munich in September. He was increasingly at odds with Chamberlain's position that Hitler could be appeased through negotiation. The removal of Robert Vansittart, an awkward critic and leaker of FO material to sympathetic journalists, and his replacement as permanent undersecretary by Alexander Cadogan strengthened Chamberlain's hand; 'It was first blood to the appeasers.'[1] The British government's line enjoyed some support from among the wider public for whom there was no great enthusiasm for another war. Nor was appeasement entirely a left–right issue. Left-wing groups such as the pacifists in the Peace Pledge Union, and the former Labour leader George Lansbury, as well as other socialists were reluctant to press the case for action against Hitler while some of Chamberlain's strongest support came from influential socialites around the Cliveden Set, as well as *The Times* whose owner, Lord Astor and editor, Geoffrey Dawson, remained loyal to Chamberlain throughout the crisis.

There was sympathy for Hitler from many who saw him as a defence against communism, while some in the high ranks of British society supported the cause of National Socialism itself. In the course of his work in the Spanish section of the Western department, Cairncross had experienced at first hand the enthusiasm for Franco and had been made aware of the collusion between the different fascist powers. Support for Hitler was evident in a range of organizations, whose members included people in prominent positions of influence. Aside from those for whom peace with Germany was important in resisting communism, others openly endorsed the regime's antisemitism. Cairncross knew well the fascist threat posed by Oswald Mosley, whose 'Blackshirts' (the BUF) had held violent marches and meetings from the early 1930s. He also suspected there were some strong supporters of Hitler among businessmen, parliamentarians and aristocrats, but it was only when he took up his FO post that he became aware of its seriousness.

One example was the Nordic League, founded in 1935 by the Conservative MP Archibald 'Jock' Ramsay. This was an overtly antisemitic organization which sought a 'race-conscious' Britain, adopted 'Perish Judah' or 'PJ' as its chanting slogan, distributed Nazi literature and concluded its meetings with a rendition of the Nazi anthem 'The Horst Wessel' song.[2] An organization with roots in Germany, it attempted to bring its politics to the British scene. Its speakers incited more agitations against Jews and reiterated the obsession that fascism was the only real counter to the 'Red Menace'.

The Anglo-German Fellowship, also established in 1935, was apparently inspired by a speech from the then Prince of Wales (who, as Edward VIII, abdicated the following year). It was less overt in its prejudices, but broader in its influence and reach. Financed by companies like ICI, Price Waterhouse, Thomas Cook and Unilever, it ostensibly promoted peaceful relations with Germany. It co-hosted regular meetings at the German Embassy and enjoyed a warm relationship with Joachim von Ribbentrop, who took up his position in London as the German ambassador in 1936 and would be Hitler's foreign secretary from 1938. Its members included influential parliamentarians and public figures, including Lords Londonderry, Redesdale, Rennell, Galloway, Brocket and the Duke of Wellington; also on its list were Duncan Sandys, son-in-law of Winston Churchill, former FO official and MP, and Geoffrey Dawson. One of the pro-German MPs John 'Jackie' Mcnamara, Conservative member for Chelmsford, who allegedly had links with Hitler Youth, employed Guy Burgess from 1935 as a 'mix of secretary, travelling companion and personal assistant'.[3] Burgess saw his link to Mcnamara as an ideal cover in disguising his work for the Soviets and used it to reassure those who asked if he had severed his links with communism. He recruited Kim Philby into the Anglo-German Fellowship, who (on his own admission) 'did much of the legwork involved in an abortive attempt to start, with Nazi funds, a trade journal designed to foster good relations between Britain and Germany'.[4] While attempting to establish the journal, Philby attended talks in Berlin with the German Propaganda Ministry. For a while he also edited the fellowship's monthly magazine, the *Anglo-German Review*, which carried 'glowing accounts of Germany written by travellers ranging from expert professionals to holiday tourists'.[5] In its January 1937 issue

Archibald Crawford KC, after visiting a criminal trial in Munich, informed readers that he had 'never witnessed justice being more patiently or more impartially administered'.[6]

As well as hosting cocktail parties for Nazi leaders at Claridge's and other notable venues (with swastikas adorning its walls and tables) members of the fellowship were regular attenders at the Nuremberg rallies. The 1937 rally, according to Julia Boyd, attracted a galaxy of notables, including Colonel Sir Thomas Cuninghame DSO and Lady Cuninghame, Lieutenant Colonel John Blakiston-Houston, Robert Grant-Ferris MP, Sir Nevile Henderson, British ambassador, several members of the House of Lords, Captain George Pitt-Rivers, Sir Assheton Pownall MP and Professor A. P. Laurie, and Sir Barry Domvile, who recorded the occasion in his diary. The British visitors, regarded as prominent VIPs by the Nazi organizers, were given a tea-party reception at which Hitler formally welcomed them. As Hitler was introduced to his British guests, 'He remained stiff and expressionless until introduced to Francis Yeats-Brown, when he burst into smiles.' Yeats-Brown, whose pro-Franco views Cairncross had objected to in his FO notes just a few months earlier, was known to Hitler, who had admired the film version of his book, *The Bengal Lancer.* Hitler 'thought the film such a valuable demonstration of how Aryans should deal with an inferior race that he had made it compulsory viewing for the SS'.[7]

Burgess and Philby, in their willingness to adopt a new political fashion as cover for their espionage, displayed the ruthlessness of the professional undercover agent alongside their natural arrogance and, on the surface, a revealing malleability of political principle. In contrast, John Cairncross was incapable of keeping his views on fascism quiet even from his office colleagues. His one cause, European anti-fascism, was now driving his actions and choices to an almost obsessive degree. If he can be characterized as having any ideological position, it was in this deep-rooted opposition to appeasement which he saw as a rapidly growing menace. That he ended up secretly working for the Russians and continued to do so confirmed that he had little faith in the strategy of British government or opposition in doing its duty in *resisting* the tide of Nazism. If this was also a sign of arrogance on his part, the appeasement crisis strengthened his conviction that he had made the right choice in the short term. His experience in travelling through Germany and Austria and studying in France, where he had befriended members of Carlo Rosselli's *Giustizia e Liberta* movement, had alerted him to the need for organized resistance, with Russian support. As he reflected later,

> I felt that the British communists were not capable of forming ... a resistance movement. Indeed, the English character does not move along these lines as does, say, the Irish. Russia, on the contrary, had both the strategic base outside the country and the experience in clandestine activities to develop an underground movement. All my continental friends with knowledge in this field were unanimous as to the need for experience and skill. ... They had impressed me with the need for careful and professional preparation: otherwise the result would always be high losses, both in effort and success as well as lives. Looking back, this attitude seems a generous and speculative illusion, but my experiences on the continent had convinced me of the strength of German willpower and drive and I was eager to seize upon what may sound a desperate project in defence against a future of complete isolation. As in the First World War, Russia was needed to be able to force a fight on two fronts if it came to hostilities. Already weakened by the strain of the First World War, Britain under Chamberlain's leadership might, I feared, arrive at an understanding with Germany.[8]

It was at this critical moment, in the months before the Munich crisis, that John Cairncross took up his new post in the German section in the FO's central department. Initially, his new section promised to be a more congenial and welcoming environment. William Strang, the head of the central department of the FO when John Cairncross joined it, was of similar Scottish origins to his younger and junior colleague. From a family of tenant farmers in southeast Renfrewshire and northwest Lanarkshire who was born and brought up in Essex, he shared some of the linguistic inheritances as Cairncross (his parents spoke a bilingual mixture of 'Lallans' and English) while his own relatively humble origins did not make the diplomatic service an obvious career choice.

> To be born into a Scottish Household in a rural English environment is to be faced with a need for adaptation and adjustment, conscious or unconscious, going beyond what is normally called for in the formation of personality.[9]

He had to confront the difficulty of being an outsider in an English world at an earlier stage than Cairncross; his willingness to adjust, however, no doubt eased his later transition into the culture of the FO.

> As a child I was conscious that my parents and I were different from the people around, to go into an English house was to meet something alien and, at first, a little intimidating. ... One had to be alert and sensitive and by trial and error to select what seemed the best model to follow.[10]

Like Cairncross's early years in Lesmahagow, Strang was 'bookish', eagerly supplementing his studies at the village school (and later Upminister Grammar School), with extensive reading of Thackeray, George Eliot, Dickens and Shakespeare. He found French more difficult, and though, on the back of an Essex County scholarship, he would go on to read it at University College London, he 'could make little of Molière'.[11] On graduation in 1912, he studied at the Bibliothèque Nationale in Paris, where 'I learned to think in French and to distinguish the tone of French life and the texture of French thought'.[12] He served in the First World War after 1915 and, after seeing an advertisement in *The Times*, joined the diplomatic service in 1919 as a third secretary (as Cairncross was to do, in 1936).

Unlike Cairncross, however, Strang was prepared to make the compromises and adjustments necessary for a career in the FO; he was a 'diplomat' in his internal office relationships as well as with his dealings with foreign officials.

> Entry into the Foreign Office and Diplomatic Service gave me a measure of confidence in myself which I had not hitherto possessed ... was it true that in this formerly aristocratic service there was a career open to those without family influence or private means? And was I adaptive enough to learn its ways and absorb its traditions without doing violence to a personality formed in another environment and on other traditions?[13]

Strang developed a strong enough aptitude for administrative work that it enabled him to oversee the support of a ministerial office, and he became an expert in the traditions and procedures necessary for effective diplomacy. His rise through its ranks placed him at the centre of crucial and controversial moments at the FO in the interwar period. In 1922 he was transferred to the FO's northern department as a second secretary, which dealt with the fledgling Soviet Union. In this role two years later, he had to respond to the publication of the notorious 'Zinoviev Letter' – an instruction purportedly from Moscow inciting British communists to take up revolutionary measures. In the most detailed study of this affair, the letter was later found not to be 'genuine' and the work of a former Tsarist officer Ivan Pokrovsky, 'with the knowledge if not active assistance of British intelligence officials in Riga'. However, at the time it was accepted as genuine by the FO and willingly disseminated by 'security, intelligence or military communities [who] were willing to make the letter available to right-wing interests opposed to the Labour government and its Russian policies'.[14] The publicity over the letter caused sufficient damage to prevent the re-election of Ramsay MacDonald's first Labour government and would be a constant reminder of the vulnerability of the Labour Party and the British left to accusations of collusion with Moscow. Sections of the Labour Party (and the British left) would thereafter remain suspicious of the security services and MI6, notably at times of elections and on taking office. The affair did long-term damage to the reputation of British intelligence in creating the impression that it was amenable to cover-ups and conspiracy.

After being posted to Moscow, Strang was required in 1933 to negotiate on behalf of three engineers at the Metropolitan Vickers Electrical Company who had been arrested on spying charges. His dealings with the Soviet authorities, which had extracted forced confessions from the engineers (though they were later released), alerted him to the nature of Soviet justice even if the full details of the repressive nature of the state were not yet evident. He visited the engineers in prison and had to provide daily accounts of their trial, which gave him first-hand experience of the way the state operated.

In the autumn of 1933 he was made the head of the League of Nations section of the FO. This was the kind of role he had coveted, but he was also aware of the limitations of the League: that 'mutual obligations' without arms to support them when necessary were futile. He believed that this lesson was not learnt during the 1930s, as he witnessed the advance of Mussolini in Abyssinia (Ethiopia). In Strang's view, had Britain and France taken the initiative on behalf of the League of Nations, not only might Mussolini have been stopped but they also 'would have sent warning to Hitler that he could have been halted'.[15]

This meant that when Strang succeeded Ralph Wigram as the head of the central department in 1937, he was well aware of the dangers of Nazism and the difficulties facing anyone intending to negotiate with Hitler. He would be at the centre of the appeasement policy and accompanied Chamberlain to the crucial meetings with Hitler and his advisers at Bad Godesberg, Berlin and Munich in September 1938, and advised him on the negotiations.

He was therefore an important source for Cairncross. Despite the differences in age and rank, a friendship of sorts developed between them, perhaps strengthened by their common Scottish origins and interests in France and French literature. It was Strang who formally recommended Cairncross for membership of the Travellers Club, the venue for many of Cairncross's lunches at which he extracted from FO colleagues some key details on government policy towards Germany.[16] Membership of the Travellers Club improved his access to the key figures; it was a regular rendezvous for informal social gatherings of diplomats and the FO hierarchy. Strang was sufficiently convinced of Cairncross's suitability for the club to provide an in-depth account of his qualities at its Election Committee. In support of Strang's proposal, Cairncross's case was seconded by David Scott, the head of the Consular Office, before a detailed discussion of the candidate by the committee, with his election concluded by the passing round of the ballot box in which members were asked to place the traditional wooden balls in a 'yes' or 'no' tunnel. Membership of the Travellers Club was routine among diplomats though the selection process was not a formality. Membership marked a point of distinction for Cairncross who now found himself in relatively exclusive company – an outcome that would have matched his own sense of esteem as well as meeting with the approval of his Soviet controllers, who had urged him to make such connections from their earliest meetings.[17] Indeed, Cairncross's Travellers Club membership was paid for by Moscow for 'representational purposes'.[18] Deutsch had encouraged membership as he knew the Travellers was frequented by leading FO heads and diplomats, and Donald Maclean was already a member. As Cairncross passed on the summaries of some of his lunch meetings, Strang had therefore unwittingly aided a process whereby his own close dealings with Chamberlain would be relayed to the Soviets.

Cairncross's successful application for membership was not merely a cynical ploy on his part nor was it a particular surprise. Many of his FO peers were members, and he was already lunching there as a guest before his membership was confirmed. He valued his friendship with Strang while lunch meetings ensured that he was up to date with developments at a crucial time. Cairncross was only a junior member of the central department, but he had access to important documents as the Munich crisis unfolded, and his friendship with Strang, though not close, was also of much interest to the Soviets, given that Strang was head of the central department, the office responsible for dealing with negotiations with Hitler, and had accompanied the British Prime Minister Neville Chamberlain at all the vital meetings. Strang confirmed later that once the negotiations began his view on the prospects for peace hardened.

> It became clear that the Nazis would stop at nothing; that sooner or later they would have to be resisted by armed force ... that was thus more than a probability and that consequently – and this was vital – we should all make speed to rearm ourselves in order to be ready for the emergency when it came.[19]

Strang was in a difficult position. On the one hand, he was not impressed by 'glib' talk of opposing Hitler by people who remained against rearming; on the other hand, he 'was not very comfortable' defending Chamberlain's position, a feeling that clearly worsened as events unfolded. Chamberlain remained determined to continue with his policy, one that he himself had devised and took responsibility for (while supported by Lord Halifax, Horace Wilson and Lord Simon). According to Strang, Chamberlain's

> mind was dominated by two thoughts ... a hatred of war so deep that he would think that heavy sacrifices would be justified in order to avoid it

and he also

> believed that Hitler and Mussolini were men whose word could be relied on; that it was possible to come to agreements with them

which could transform the international situation for the better and give peace to Europe; and that by his personal influence with them he could hope to bring such agreements about.[20]

For Strang, Chamberlain's first consideration was 'laudable' but 'hazardous', while his second was a 'misjudgement, all the more serious in that it continued to be entertained even in the face of strong evidence to the contrary'.[21] Strang, working to the orders of Lord Halifax, had to keep the central department on board as the Czechoslovakian crisis developed over the issue of autonomy for Germans in Sudetenland, with Hitler waiting to invade the country if the demands of the German Sudetens were not met. As events escalated during 1938 and hastily arranged meetings between French, British and Czech officials could not reach agreement, the prospect of war increased. The French were reluctant to provoke Germany into a war they could not win, the Soviets had their own internal conflicts which precluded the prospect of entering a war and Chamberlain remained convinced that Britain was not prepared for war; in any case, he believed that there was a real chance for a negotiated settlement with Hitler.

At three meetings over two weeks in September 1938 Strang flew with Chamberlain and Sir Horace Wilson to Germany to meet Hitler and his entourage. The first of these on 15 September took place at Hitler's mountain home at Obersalzberg, Berchtesgaden, in Bavaria. The flight over was Chamberlain's first time in an aeroplane, and Strang described him as his normal self: 'aloof, reserved, imperturbable, unshakably self-reliant'.[22] On arrival Strang found 'a somewhat macabre tea-party at a round table in the room with the great window looking out towards Austria'.[23] Over lunch, Hitler told Chamberlain that 300 Sudeten Germans had been killed and he would be prepared to go to war for the land if necessary. After lunch with Ribbentrop, Chamberlain, Strang and Wilson flew back. Over the next few days Britain and France reached an agreement that the Sudeten areas should be handed over to the Reich – a decision which inevitably brought opposition from the Czechs who continued to press for arbitration. Further meetings were arranged for 23–24 September, and Strang flew out to Bad Godesberg with Chamberlain and Wilson who were accompanied at the meetings by Nevile Henderson, British ambassador to Germany. Strang recalled that 'the meetings took place in an atmosphere of extreme tension and the outcome was in the highest degree unsatisfactory'.[24]

Hitler demanded Sudetenland be evacuated for German occupation between 26 and 28 September (i.e. in three days' time). Strang, during long 'tedious hours', remained waiting in the hallway with Hitler's entourage: finding leading Nazi officials, senior army officers and foreign affairs staff in a jovial mood. Strang observed Chamberlain's reactions to the Führer's demands: 'For all his efforts, Mr Chamberlain could not, apart from getting the dates changed to October 1, move Hitler from his main position.' The Führer 'gave affirmation' – his 'last word' and Neville Chamberlain agreed to 'communicate it'.[25] According to Strang, Chamberlain had been given 'rough treatment' by Hitler.[26]

Back in London, further meetings between Chamberlain and Daladier – according to Strang, 'among the most painful which it has ever been my misfortune to attend' – achieved little (with Chamberlain, according to Strang, ignoring Daladier's concerns), and agreement was reached with Hitler for another conference in Munich. The House of Commons supported the position of the prime minister (its few opponents included the communist MP Willie Gallagher), and once again Strang flew out with Chamberlain to meet Hitler. Benito Mussolini produced a draft paper for the conference which obliged the Czechs to leave Sudetenland and allow German occupation between 1 and 10 October. It was clear to Strang that the proceedings of the Munich conference went way beyond the conventions of professional diplomacy and the spirit of international negotiations. He described the gathering as a 'hugger-mugger affair', 'chaotic', lacking in order and continuing well into the night until, at 2.00 am on Friday, 30 September, an agreement was signed, and fifteen minutes later, after it was made clear to the Czech Prime Minister Jan Syrový that he would receive no military support from France and Britain, the latter reluctantly agreed. Strang saw this as primarily a 'German-Italian occasion'; Goering, 'haughty and punctilious' in white uniform, SS officers circling and, while the British and French returned to their hotels, Hitler and Mussolini had dinner together.[27]

At their hotel, however, Strang found Chamberlain in a contented mood. As far as the prime minister was concerned he had completed what he had set out to do. He had helped 'save' the peace and, in his view, had played a significant role in strengthening Anglo-German relations. Chamberlain asked Strang to draft a statement on Britain's future relationship with Germany – one that would appeal to the Führer. Over breakfast, Strang put together three paragraphs before handing it to Chamberlain, and promptly replaced the second paragraph with his own version. The statement began by declaring:

> We, the German Führer and Chancellor and the British Prime Minister have had a further meeting today and are agreed in recognising that the question of Anglo-German relations is of the first importance for the two countries and for Europe.
>
> We regard the agreement signed last night and the Anglo-German Naval Agreement as symbolic of the desire of our two peoples never to go to war with one another again.
>
> We are resolved that the method of consultation shall be the method adopted to deal with any other questions that may concern our two countries, and we are determined to continue our efforts to remove possible sources of difference and thus to contribute to assure the peace of Europe.

The disputed second paragraph concerned the reference to the 'Anglo-German Naval agreement', which Strang had not included in his draft. He pointed out to Chamberlain that it 'was not a thing to be proud of'. Chamberlain told him that it was precisely the 'type of agreement' he should be seeking. Strang also failed in his attempt to persuade Chamberlain to let Daladier know of the naval agreement in advance. Daladier would later express 'shame' at the Munich Agreement, but Strang saw nothing of that in Chamberlain's persona, as he greeted cheering crowds from his hotel balcony. 'As he sat down to lunch, the Prime Minister complacently patted his breast-pocket and said: "I've got it."'[28]

Arriving back in the rain at Heston, greeted by heaving crowds and union flags in the gardens of surrounding houses, a beaming and triumphant Chamberlain was given a hero's welcome. Lord Halifax presented him with a letter from the King before he told waiting reporters that 'the settlement of the Czech problem which has now been achieved is only a prelude to a wider settlement in which all Europe might found peace. Here is the paper that bears his name upon it as well as mine. ... The agreement was symbolic of the desire of our two peoples never to go to war again' (loud cheers). 'Three cheers for Neville.' 'For he's a jolly good fellow.'

The prolonged House of Commons debate on the Munich Agreement over the following days drew more support for the prime minister, although critics of his policy were more evident there than among the wider public. Duff Cooper, Secretary of State for War and the leading opponent of appeasement in the cabinet, announced his resignation, convinced that Chamberlain's chosen 'guarded language of diplomacy' and the 'conditional clauses of the Civil Service' would not stop with Hitler. He had long argued that a show of military strength was the only way to deal with the German dictator: 'That is the deep difference between the Prime Minister and myself throughout these days. The Prime Minister has believed in addressing Herr Hitler through the language of sweet reasonableness. I have believed that he was more open to the language of the mailed fist.'[29]

Chamberlain's belief that Hitler had been won over by 'reasonableness' and his diplomatic skills was, however, widely believed at the time and even shared by the former Labour leader George Lansbury. Lansbury, who the previous year held private meetings with both Hitler and Mussolini during a personal peace mission, reminded other members that news of the agreement had gone down well in the East End. He carried on: 'I hear all this denunciation of Herr Hitler and Signor Mussolini. I have met both of them and can only say that they are very much like any other politician or diplomat one meets. ... You may treat with Hitler and Mussolini how you may but in the end the only way that will win peace is to show reasonableness.'

There were dissenting voices too, not least from Labour leader Clement Attlee, who condemned the 'shameful betrayal' of the Czech people, a point taken up in interventions by other critics on the left, including the communist MP Willie Gallagher and Ellen Wilkinson, the left-wing Labour MP. In the House of Commons there were supporters of Chamberlain's position who sought to exploit the occasion in the furtherance of closer ties with Hitler. Cyril Culverwell, Conservative MP for Bristol West, who the following month would publicly praise Hitler, demanded of the House: 'What has Hitler done up to now of which they can reasonably complain?' Endorsing the German occupation of Austria and the quality of life for the German people under the Nazis, he went on to explain:

I suggest that the policy of the enemies of Germany has failed, and it is time that the friends of peace had a turn. ... It is not that they [Labour/Socialists] fear Germany but that they hate dictators. They do not like the form of government which the German people are today enjoying (Hon members: Enjoying?). At any rate it is not for Hon members opposite to discuss the domestic affairs of Germany (Hon members: why?).

Hitler, he argued, had 'lifted' the German people from 'impoverishment' and 'humiliation'. Culverwell was one of several politicians and public figures who wanted to strengthen ties with the Nazi regime because of its hostility to communism, a position that intensified once war with Germany was declared.

Attitudes to appeasement cut across left and right, but the most consistent critics of Chamberlain's policy came from those who had accepted that loyalties (as Eric Hobsbawm put it) 'ran across and not just between nations' and that the existing liberal institutions of nation states, together with the impotence of the League of Nations, could not halt the 'march to conquest and war of the combination of states – Germany, Italy and Japan, of which Hitler Germany became the central pillar'.[30] Cairncross's own opposition to appeasement was based on this more internationalist view and, at the time of the Popular Front (before the disastrous Nazi-Soviet pact), an anti-fascism which sought to resist the attack on the values of Western civilizations. George Orwell later questioned the use of the term 'anti-fascist' as used in communist propaganda, but in the shared platforms between liberals, socialists, communists, some Conservatives and representatives of religious groups, it signified broad opposition to appeasement. Denis Healey, then a student in Oxford, thought 'Chamberlain's policy was politically and strategically disastrous, as well as morally contemptible', a view that he maintained in later years.[31] He joined many others in the Oxford by-election at the end of October in supporting Sandy Lindsay, the master of Balliol College, who was standing on an anti-appeasement platform. Lindsay was narrowly defeated by Quintin Hogg, the pro-Chamberlain Conservative.

The realpolitik at that time, the cumulative effect of appeasers on left and right, influential groups such as the Cliveden Set and distinguished newspapers like The Times, and a public opinion that remained against war, presented dilemmas for those convinced that fascism must be stopped. John Cairncross would have to continue his opposition outside the FO, however. His bosses continued to believe he lacked the diplomatic and administrative qualities necessary for the work. He was regarded as truculent, prickly in character and difficult to work with and ultimately deemed 'unsuitable for representation' in the view of his FO superiors.[32] He was moved from the FO to a more mundane role in the Treasury and took up his new position in the week of the Commons debates. On his own admission he had 'made no impact in the Central Department' and was isolated and frustrated at his inability to challenge what he regarded as the disastrous policy of appeasement.[33]

Chapter 8
A political career begins

John Cairncross would later describe his espionage role during the period of appeasement and throughout the Second World War as his 'political work'. Such 'work' included meeting former FO colleagues for lunch at the Travellers and later recording details of their conversations. From the appeasement crisis in 1938, he kept a diary (destroyed in 1941) which summarized the reactions of FO colleagues to the unfolding events. He had been close enough to William Strang and others in the German section to know something of the background, the personalities involved and the events leading up to the Munich Agreement. This was information which Moscow would be interested in obtaining to enable a clearer understanding of the British government's attitude to Germany and on that basis he passed relevant documents to his Soviet controller. The Munich Agreement itself became symbolized by the scrap of paper Prime Minister Chamberlain waved to the crowds who braved the rain at Heston Aerodrome on 30 September 1938, and his later promise, on the steps of 10 Downing Street, to deliver 'peace for our time'. This only confirmed Cairncross's worst fears and gave him the drive and determination to act.

He was not alone in regarding secret work of this sort as 'political'. His friend James Klugmann, for example, in his rapid rise through the officer ranks of the Special Operations Executive after 1941, later referred to his doctoring of official documents and favourable reporting of Tito's partisans over Draža Mihailović's nationalists in Yugoslavia, as 'concerted political work', of a kind necessary to persuade the Allies to shift their support to the former. Cairncross, by nature and outlook an 'aginner', in the words of an American friend, could not, on intellectual and emotional grounds, subscribe to any orthodoxy – communist or any other.[1] However, he was dedicated to pursuing his one political cause, which he had initially adopted as a curious and inquisitive teenager cycling through Europe in the years of Hitler's march to power, and not as the result of imbibing a communist line. Moreover, he preferred to think of his political actions as resting on *strategic* rather than *ideological* grounds; in other words, he believed that he worked for the Russians because it was necessary to join the international fight against fascism, especially when his own government was appeasing it.[2] He was further convinced that a political consensus which regarded communism as more of a danger than fascism had now settled in government. This was unacceptable to him. Among other things, it was evident in the British government's reluctance – endorsed of course by many of Cairncross's FO colleagues – to enter into agreements with the Soviet Union in resisting Hitler. Appointed to the FO at a time of international crisis and finding himself first in the Spanish section at a crucial time in the Spanish Civil War and secondly in the German section at the time of the Munich Agreement, Cairncross decided he could not sit by and watch events unfold without comment. Chamberlain kept increasingly tight control over his policy, and the warnings made by critics in the FO and cabinet went unheeded.

Cairncross could not contain his frustration at government policy towards Germany. He was aware that his own views were not shared by most in his FO section while his perceived grumpiness and cynicism did not endear him to them, despite his friendly relations with Strang and the occasional lunch companion. They seemed to regard their irascible colleague, an expert on Molière, as something of a misanthrope. His inability to fit in had been compounded by his disdain for some of the required administrative tasks, while it was clear to his superiors that he lacked the tact and negotiating skills necessary for his work. Any ambitions he held on entering the FO or expectations that he was at the cusp of a working life of travel and international diplomacy had rapidly diminished as the crisis took hold. In these circumstances he could not be a neutral observer or a disinterested civil servant.

Throughout his life Cairncross maintained sufficient confidence in his own intellectual powers to pursue his line of argument irrespective of received opinion. This was a trait that had been sharpened in his long experience as a university student and in the future would be a characteristic that produced academic papers, heretical challenges to existing scholarship and lengthy advice to BBC producers. In the environment of the FO in the mid-1930s, however, it made him appear arrogant and intransigent. One of his traits, according to his niece, was the absence of 'self-effacement', or 'the ability to see how he was perceived by others'.[3] That, combined with a social awkwardness in formal company, made him a difficult colleague. Another occasional feature of his personality was to come across as evasive through his reluctance to give a straight answer without first outlining a series of possible scenarios. Yet his self-confidence enabled him to hold to a position of principle – in this case, that his understanding of the implications of appeasement was correct and that there were serious flaws in the government's reading of the international situation.

From 1 October, the day after Chamberlain's return from Munich, his FO career ended officially, and he was effectively demoted as an 'unsatisfactory probationer' and relocated to the role of assistant principal in the Treasury. Here he did not have access to the kind of confidential material or information he enjoyed at the FO and spent much of his time looking after some of the administrative and resource requirements of the Post Office and the Stationery Office. However, he was eager to do something with the material he had obtained from his previous post working under Strang and share what knowledge he had obtained of the negotiations behind the scenes.[4]

With the new role in the Treasury insufficiently taxing, his thoughts remained focused on the escalating international crisis. Among those with whom he lunched at central London clubs and restaurants – important informal venues of power and influence in interwar Britain – were Jock Colville, his former Trinity College contemporary who was now Neville Chamberlain's assistant private secretary; Henry Hankey, who was in the Central European Office at the FO; William Strang himself and Sir David Scott. Colville, now free of his adolescent admiration for Hitler, spoke approvingly to Cairncross of the 'golden age of diplomacy' he thought was on the horizon under Neville Chamberlain, and agreed with Chamberlain's Home Secretary (and confidant) Samuel Hoare that war was still unlikely.[5] Cairncross found his colleague's viewpoint on Germany 'complacent' and would have done little to assuage his doubts.[6]

Cairncross's meetings and lunch conversations were an important part of his political work; he had never been an 'activist' in the conventional sense. Such occasions also enhanced his sense of importance and brought him closer to some influential circles, even if he always remained an outsider. As someone at this time with a growing number of acquaintances but no particularly close friends or serious relationship, he was also a loner to some degree – a condition which almost certainly assisted his work as an agent, and indeed he always considered that he was acting alone. Following the recall of Maly and Deutsch, he had no contact with his Soviet controller until seven months after the Munich crisis, and he was effectively left to work on his own initiative. Initial government jubilation at Chamberlain's Munich Agreement had been swiftly followed by the German occupation of Czechoslovakia in March 1939, and by the end of the month an agreement with France (but not with the Soviet Union) that they would come to Poland's aid if its independence was threatened. From then on, as the prospect of war with Germany increased, the case for involving the Soviet Union as an ally was a divisive issue in British government circles with Chamberlain opposed and always sceptical of the feasibility of such an alliance. Others believed an agreement was possible and necessary and continued to urge further negotiation.

By 1939 Guy Burgess had resigned from his post as a BBC Talks Producer and was working for Section D of SIS (MI6) which organized propaganda initiatives, including secret broadcasting to Germany. His other role as a Soviet agent was still unknown to Cairncross when they met again in July. Burgess knew of Cairncross's work in the German section and his links to Strang and others and was keen to see him again. Cairncross's contacts with the Soviets had lapsed to the extent Burgess feared that, as a 'novice' and a not altogether politically reliable agent, he might drop out altogether. After Donald Maclean, through his lover Kitty Harris (codenamed 'Ada': she was herself a Soviet agent), had alerted Moscow of Cairncross's move from the FO to the Treasury, Burgess re-established contact with him, aware that he 'has at his disposal the very best information available on Czechoslovakia'.[7]

Though they had met occasionally at social events, Burgess needed to have a good reason for approaching Cairncross with a specific request for information, and he chose the pretext that he was working for British intelligence with a particular responsibility for broadcasting anti-Nazi propaganda. This was true enough. Presenting himself as a like-minded opponent of appeasement, Burgess asked for information on Mussolini's discussions with Chamberlain, as well as the British government attitude towards Poland. For this he provided Cairncross with £20 worth of expenses. Cairncross shared with Burgess the official views he had heard and told him he would endeavour to seek out more during his lunches and meetings with his FO contacts. In this Cairncross satisfied himself that he was carrying out useful 'political work', unaware of course that Burgess was passing it on to the Russians. It seems surprising that Cairncross was not more wary of Burgess; he knew him as a well-connected socialite with a keen political brain but had also been warned about him by James Klugmann. Klugmann had recruited Burgess to the Communist Party in the aftermath of the Cambridge student protests back in autumn 1933 and of course knew of Burgess's involvement with Soviet intelligence, while he himself had played a pivotal role in directing Cairncross into the arms of the Russians. However, this did not detract from Klugmann's view that Burgess was an unreliable friend and ally. At this point in his life Cairncross remained flattered by Burgess's attention and acknowledged that he had opened doors for him. He was also eager to use the material he had gleaned from Strang.

Moreover, Cairncross's own relationship with Soviet intelligence became uncertain and strained during late 1938 and into 1939, predominantly of course as the result of the Moscow purges. Despite the recruitment of the Cambridge spies and the material they had passed on, Moscow no longer trusted the 'illegals' and in particular the relative freedom and autonomy of the kind Deutsch had enjoyed. Intelligence was more heavily monitored than before, and they now employed a different type of controller, whom they kept under tight watch. Indeed, Grigori Grafpen, who was initially put in charge of the London Rezidentura after Deutsch, was recalled in December 1938 and ended up in the Gulag. Anatoli Gorsky, codenamed 'HENRY', was the remaining 'legal' agent in London, and operated from the Russian Embassy, and it was he who finally renewed contact with Cairncross in April 1939, some seven months after his last meeting.

'Henry' was a very different character from 'Otto', who at least had been able to introduce them before his departure to Moscow. Cairncross remembered Gorsky as 'a Russian with distinctly Slavic features'. Unlike Deutsch, whom Cairncross regarded as a sophisticated 'continental intellectual' who shared similar cultural interests to his own and thrived in wide-ranging discussions, Cairncross found Gorsky a more orthodox, unyielding figure. He took over the running of the London agents only after attending a prolonged NKVD training session and on meeting Cairncross was unconvinced by his politics. They initially found it difficult to get on despite attempts by Gorsky to win him over by discussing his favourite composers and by thoughtfully presenting him with a recording of Pietro Mascagni's *Cavalleria Rusticana*. Cairncross's love of music prompted his new Soviet controller to assign him the new codename LISZT, after the Hungarian composer. Nevertheless, it would be a difficult relationship, made more complicated by the Nazi-Soviet pact.

Their first meetings occurred in the spring and summer of 1939, when Cairncross passed him documents on the situation in Germany, together with correspondence between Prime Minister Neville Chamberlain and one of his closest confidants, Samuel Hoare, the home secretary, as well as details of two former Moscow correspondents of *The Times*, Iverach McDonald and Peter Fleming (the brother of James Bond creator Ian Fleming), who had been working undercover for British intelligence. This last detail confirmed that Cairncross's political work extended into more uncomfortable areas beyond Russia's opposition to Hitler. It was a price he decided he had to pay. Far worse was to follow.

Cairncross and Gorsky did not meet again until January 1940, during which time the Second World War had begun and the Molotov-Ribbentrop agreement (the 'Nazi-Soviet pact') was under way. The Nazi-Soviet pact, a neutrality agreement between the Soviet Union and Nazi Germany, was disastrous for the broad anti-fascist movement and brought to an end the 'Popular Front' strategy which had aimed to build a broad consensus against Hitler. It was also catastrophic for Cairncross whose political work depended above all on the Russian opposition to Hitler. Some communists were aghast at the developments, while others were less surprised as they had experienced Stalinist tactics during the Spanish Civil War. Emerging evidence of the Soviet show trials was another factor in the disillusion with the Soviet Union, though the exodus from the British Communist Party over the 'Nazi-Soviet' pact was on a moderate scale compared to later events in the history of communism, such as the Khrushchev revelations about Stalin and the Soviet invasion of Hungary in 1956, or the invasion of Czechoslovakia in 1968. Many communists, unhappy, even incredulous, at the new position, went along with it out of loyalty to the party. However, Harry Pollitt, the long-standing general secretary of the Communist Party of Great Britain, was an initial casualty of the line and forced to stand down from his role while the Comintern pursued a new anti-war policy. The crudeness of the new position, namely in seeking opposition to what it called an 'imperialist war', was indigestible for many. Communists after all had spent the last four or five years equating fascism with war. For Cairncross, the new Soviet policy amounted to a rejection of his one political cause. It was

> disastrous for my plans, which now lay in ruins and made nonsense of my forecasts. I was convinced that the two new confederates would fall out and that Hitler would inevitably turn on the Russians after he had settled accounts with the West; but for the moment I had to soldier on in the highly uncomfortable position of being in touch with a friend of our enemy, with the danger of a German invasion of Britain far greater than before.[8]

In 1939 many regarded the pact as an outcome of the weaknesses of the British appeasement position, and the failure of the Anglo-French-Soviet talks to reach an agreement that would both safeguard Russia and help build an alliance against Hitler. Back in April 1939, the British government had suggested that the Soviets should make a 'unilateral public declaration on its own initiative' that if there was any aggression by Germany towards a European neighbour of the Soviet Union, the latter would come to the aid of that neighbour, if asked. This, according to Lord Halifax, the foreign secretary, 'would have a steadying effect on the international situation'.[9] Following this British proposal, the French government came up with an alternative plan which argued for 'bilateral' actions which the Soviets endorsed on 18 April within their own proposal that called for the Soviet Union, Britain and France to agree for a period of five to ten years a commitment to resist, through military support, aggression used against any one of the three; in addition, it would resist, with military support, any aggression towards the Eastern states between the Baltic and Black Seas on the Soviet border. Finally, it stated that the three countries would meet at the earliest date to set out the military aid to be deployed to this purpose.

Chamberlain and the British government delayed and procrastinated over the Soviet proposals, with the apparent 'desire to secure Russian help and at the same time to leave our hands free to enable Germany to expand eastward at Russian expense'.[10] On 3 May, that is, in the period between the submission of the Soviet proposals and the official rejection of them by the British government, Maxim Litvinov was replaced as the Soviet's Foreign Affairs Commissar by Vyacheslav Molotov, a disastrous turn of affairs. Litvinov was accused of disloyalty, and his Jewish background was now regarded as a 'problem' by Soviet leaders in any dealings that were to be done with Germany. Molotov, his successor, was an orthodox Stalinist ready to purge an older generation of intellectuals at the bequest of his leader. It left Ivan Maisky, the Soviet ambassador in London and a protégé of Litvinov, increasingly isolated as he attempted to negotiate with his British counterpart. The day before Litvinov's dismissal, Maisky was optimistic that an imminent change in the leadership of the British government would bring favourable grounds for agreement.

What is the current situation in England?

Summing up all the material at my disposal, I would describe it as follows. The attitudes of the broad masses of the population are sharply anti-German everywhere, except for a part of Scotland. ... The situation in government is somewhat different. ... Reconstruction of the Government. This is considered absolutely inevitable now and even the Beaverbrook press has started a campaign to this effect. But Chamberlain is stubbornly postponing the entry of such figures as Eden, Churchill and others into the Cabinet until the very last moment. ... Our proposals. There can be little doubt that the British Government will eventually accept them. Its situation is desperate. Yet Chamberlain stubbornly resists and has kept us waiting for the English answer for over two weeks now. Moreover, at first he even tried to hush up the Soviet proposals and conceal them from the public. However, thanks to the supporters of an Anglo-Soviet military alliance in government circles, our proposals were leaked bit by bit to the press and at the time of my arrival from Moscow their essence had become public knowledge. The opposition started exerting pressure in Parliament, and a lively debate got going in the press. ... I am inclined to take an optimistic view of the 'general line' in the development of Anglo-Soviet relations.[11]

However, the replacement of Litvinov with the intransigent Molotov and long delays in the protracted negotiations between the British and

Soviet officials from May to August dashed those hopes. The Soviets felt that the British side did not afford them the same respect they had shown Hitler and Mussolini by sending them FO officials rather than government ministers to conduct negotiations. In fact it was William Strang, Cairncross's old boss, who was initially sent to Moscow to agree to the deal and sign the pact. This irked the Russians, who wanted the foreign secretary or a senior member of the government, while Strang himself found the whole business 'humiliating'.

> Their distrust and suspicion of us have not diminished during the negotiations, nor, I think, has their respect for us increased. The fact that we have raised difficulty after difficulty on points which seem to them inessential has created an impression that we may not be seriously seeking an agreement; while the fact that we have yielded in the end would tend to remind them that we are still the same Powers who have (as they see it) capitulated in the past to Japan, Italy and Germany and that we are likely to do so again in the future.[12]

Chamberlain refused to countenance the possibility of Russia forging a pact with Germany, and this inevitably prolonged the negotiations while underestimating the risks involved with such slow progress. Russia was not given military assurances and did not secure agreement to intervene if the Germans attacked Poland or one of its Baltic neighbours – the Poles, pressured by Britain and France, unsurprisingly refused the Russians entry to their territory if under attack from Germany. Cairncross was clear where the blame lay.

> The ignorance and stupidity of the Chamberlain-dominated Allies had resulted in the most inept diplomatic negotiations since those between England and the American rebels 200 years earlier, making war inevitable in conditions which were little short of desperate. It was distressing to read later that Chamberlain accused the Russians of ending negotiations in bad faith, as if a country which had been quibbling for four months over petty issues was really only yielding to political pressure in negotiating at all.[13]

His understanding that the pact, which came into force in August 1939, was the consequence of Chamberlain's failed strategy did not alter the fact that this was a pact with the devil and made nonsense of the Comintern's previous strategy. He told Gorsky that he would not pass any more documents in such conditions. He viewed his predicament as a 'horrible situation', while accepting that the Soviet Union would need time to rearm in the face of the Nazi threat.[14] As Cairncross was not a member of the Communist Party he had no loyalties to a position nor, in the habit of Stalinists, could he undertake the ideological gymnastics required to adhere to a revised line which now effectively argued that former anti-fascist allies had become proponents of an imperialist war. Many communists did remain loyal, even if some thought the position absurd and untenable. Raymond Williams and Eric Hobsbawm, then Cambridge undergraduates (and later post-war anti-Stalinist intellectuals) co-authored a pamphlet, *War on the USSR?* which argued that the gains of the Russian Revolution were now under threat and needed to be defended against the forces (including Britain) that intended to attack the Soviet Union as a consequence of its war with Finland.[15] Drawing parallels with hostility towards the Soviet Union in the aftermath of the Russian Revolution, the authors observed what they called a 'dual policy of intervention – half aimed at helping the allies to win the war against Germany, but, as in 1918-1920, developing inexorably towards a full-dress war against socialism'. 'As in 1918', the future heavyweight intellectuals of the British Left argued, 'it is the rank and file, not the leaders, that matter. We must rally the students and the working people of Britain behind the slogan: No Volunteers for Finland! Hands off Russia!'[16] John Cairncross, who had no emotional attachment to Soviet socialism, was a long way from that position.

He was also aware of another threat. At the outbreak of war, the pro-German dissidents in Britain remained active propagandists before their internment. Indeed, MI5's Maxwell Knight – a former fascist himself – could not understand why the internal fascist challenge to Britain's security following the onset of war and the possibility of German invasion during 1939–40 was not taken more seriously. Though the Anglo-German Fellowship had declining influence and support, the Nordic League, originally established on Nazi money and sustained by its propaganda network, was still capable of attracting large audiences in Caxton Hall and other central London venues, its speeches fuelled with antisemitic hatred. The BUF, though not at its height, was still visible on Britain's streets, joining with others in attempts to 'Stop the War'.

As Britain reached the verge of war in August 1939, some of the more visible fascist protagonists were rounded up and interned under new defence regulations. One of those on the list was William Joyce, later the infamous Lord Haw-Haw whose radio broadcasts of Nazi propaganda would reach large British audiences. Joyce, an old friend and comrade of Knight's (and thought to have served briefly as one of his agents), was a former director of propaganda at the BUF, and though breaking with Mosley's organization had strengthened his contacts with Nazi agents with whom he exchanged material and information. However, shortly before he was due to be detained, he received a telephone call from his old friend warning of his likely fate. Shortly after, Joyce left for Germany to start his new career as a broadcaster for the Hitler regime.[17]

Other voices were driven by a combination of paranoia over the 'Red Menace' and antisemitic hatred, which continued to promote Nazi interests once war was underway. The Right Club, a secretive organization aimed at winning influential people within the apparatus of government, royalty and the military, expanded after war was declared. It was set up by Archibald Ramsay, the main instigator of the Nordic League, who was by now the most prominent pro-Nazi voice in parliament.

> The chief aim of the club is to coordinate the activities of all patriotic bodies which are striving to free the country from Jewish domination in the financial, political, philosophical and cultural spheres.[18]

In pursuing its aims, it maintained opposition to the war and, encouraged by Franco's recent victory in Spain, argued that Britain should join Germany in stopping communism. According to released MI5 documents, as the crisis deepened and the threat of invasion grew more likely it even positioned possible leaders who would help facilitate the takeover by German troops. There was concern that Ramsay, who as an MP was attending important House of Commons meetings, was a security threat. Yet he was not the only parliamentarian to hold membership of the Right Club. In all there were ten members of Parliament, who appeared on the list, including Sir Harold Mitchell, the vice chairman of the Conservative Party and Sir Ernest Bennett, a Labour MP, and six members of the House of Lords, including Baron Redesdale, father of the Mitford sisters and Lord Carnegie, husband of

Princess Maud. The Duke of Wellington and the Duke of Westminster were also on its membership list, with the latter contributing £1,000 to its kitty. It was even rumoured that the Duke of Windsor, the former king Edward VIII, was being considered as its future leader. Beyond politics, its members included Sir Alexander Walker, chairman of Johnnie Walker Whisky among industrialists, while the Right Club also targeted civil servants (Francis Hemming of the war cabinet secretariat was on its list) and senior members of the military. Unsurprisingly, the Right Club membership list also included Francis Yeats-Brown, Cairncross's old adversary.

The danger of Britain's 'Fifth Column' was only resolved in the spring of 1940, following the disastrous Norway campaign (in which Britain lost over 4,000 men) and when German invasion appeared 'almost inevitable' according to the Popular Front MP Vernon Bartlett. After keeping a long watch on an American Embassy official, Tyler Kent, a former Soviet agent who was close to Ramsay and other members of the Right Club, Maxwell Knight's MI5 operation entered his house in Bayswater on 20 May and found batches of Right Club files, including its secretive membership list. Among the documents in Kent's possession were files headed 'Chamberlain', 'Jews', 'Germany', 'Russia' and 'Americans and European Affairs'. The material was gathered with the opposite objective of Cairncross's own espionage – in other words, to help facilitate rather than oppose fascism. Maxwell Knight and Guy Liddell took their concerns to the Home Secretary Sir John Anderson, who reluctantly agreed to take action. Knight and Liddell feared the worst, and Knight submitted a six-page memo on the Right Club to the cabinet.

On 24 May Oswald Mosley was arrested at his Dolphin Square flat by Maxwell Knight who ran his MI5 operations from the same apartment complex, popular among civil servants for its proximity to Whitehall. During that crucial month, John Cairncross took a two-week vacation in the South of France. However, his holiday was interrupted by the advance of German troops along the Maginot line in the direction of the channel ports. Cutting short his stay, Cairncross returned to Paris, accompanying a 'beautiful French lady' who worked for the French government. Needing a ticket from the British Embassy to book his ferry ticket back to Britain he was reacquainted with Donald Maclean, who was in the process of breaking up with his lover and Soviet contact Kitty Harris in order to marry Melinda Marling, a young American woman he had met in the Café Flore in Paris's Left Bank a few months earlier. It was a particularly tense time for all the Cambridge spies as Moscow was uncertain about their reaction to the Nazi-Soviet pact, and one of Kitty Harris's last actions on behalf of her agent Maclean was to reassure Moscow that he and Philby still maintained 'confidence' in the Soviet Union.[19] It is extraordinary to think that as Cairncross helped Maclean destroy a mountain of British Embassy papers he was unaware that they were bound by a more secretive liaison. Cairncross finally boarded the ferry at Boulogne as German troops reached the outskirts of Calais, arriving back in London on 20 May, ten days after Churchill had been installed as prime minister. By this time, the crisis had escalated as the new prime minister had to respond to the failure of the French to hold the western front.[20] The accession of Churchill, an implacable opponent of appeasement, was welcome news for Cairncross. Less welcome was the message awaiting him that his brother Bill had been killed following wounds received at Dunkirk – tragic news he had to pass on to Alec before accompanying him back to Scotland for the funeral.

In marked contrast to Maclean's rapidly rising status in the FO, Cairncross's work at the Treasury was mundane, and he felt isolated from the foreign affairs discussions he had previously enjoyed. However, a new role became available in late 1940, at the time when Cairncross resumed contact with Gorsky, who had just returned from Moscow. This was the chance to work as a private secretary to Lord Hankey, the formidable and influential civil servant, who since October 1939 had been a minister without portfolio, serving in the war cabinet as a close adviser to Chamberlain. Cairncross had been friendly with Hankey's son Henry, whom he had known as a third secretary in the German section, and the prospect of working for Hankey senior fitted in with Cairncross's commitment to keeping an eye on the government's strategy, a role where he would have access to war cabinet minutes and FO telegrams. It was an opportunity that Gorsky urged him to take, as it was well known that Hankey was well connected to the highest offices.

It was under these conditions – a political 'no man's land' he later referred to it – that Cairncross briefly resumed his meetings with Gorsky in late 1940. By now Cairncross had moved from Warwick Square to nearby Dolphin Square, the same location, favoured by many civil servants and politicians, that had seen Oswald Mosley's arrest a few months earlier. He thought it would provide better protection from the Blitz, though shortly after moving in he narrowly escaped a bomb which fell in the adjoining room and had to move again, this time to lodge with Alec and his wife.

Cairncross and Gorsky continued to hold monthly meetings which would normally begin outside Lyons Corner House, Piccadilly Circus at 5.00 pm on Saturdays when Gorsky would ask Cairncross directions to the Strand Palace hotel, before embarking on a protracted circuitous journey to the outer suburbs and finally doubling back. Such caution was the prerogative of Soviet espionage, and Gorsky was a stickler for procedure, while generally more formal than his predecessor. He was a fashionable dresser in the style of an aspiring 'foreign gentleman' but in reality an orthodox Marxist who was less amenable than Deutsch had been to Cairncross's eccentricities, notably in arriving late or forgetting appointments, together with his technical incompetence and inclination to initiate a prolonged discourse on European culture. Gorsky told him to keep a lower profile and that in future they would avoid meeting in public bars or restaurants.

Prompted by Gorsky and through his acquaintance with Henry Hankey, Cairncross was able to set up a meeting with Hankey senior which was eventually accomplished over lunch at the Vega vegetarian restaurant near Leicester Square. This meeting ultimately resulted in Cairncross securing a position as Hankey's private secretary as he and Gorsky had hoped.[21] During the London Blitz in the last months of 1940 and the early part of 1941 Cairncross and Gorsky would meet to discuss the growing pressure on Churchill to make a deal with Hitler and the lead up to what would turn out to be the entry of the Soviet Union into the Second World War.

By late 1940, Lord Hankey was coming to the end of a remarkable career. He had been Britain's first cabinet secretary, had served in the war cabinet during the First World War and had enjoyed a long and distinguished career in the civil service. His knowledge of Whitehall procedure and approach to administration and government became a standard model for years afterwards. Well accustomed to acting as confidant to those in high office, the 'man of secrets' had remained close to Chamberlain as war got underway. Chamberlain had died by the time Cairncross moved to his offices in Whitehall at the end of 1940, and Hankey, disliked (though not unappreciated) by Churchill, had already left the war cabinet. Though formally outside the centre of power, he remained influential, however, directing committees and advising on preparations against invasion (for which he produced an eight-point memo) during the spring of 1940; and, from August 1940, recruiting radio engineers and technicians from the universities to gather material on German intelligence.

Hankey was Cairncross's key source in his political work. As his private secretary, Cairncross had access to his correspondence and was able to monitor and sometimes listen in on his telephone calls. He and Hankey built up a friendly relationship, and it is evident that Hankey, usually a stickler for security protocol, trusted his assistant. Since autumn 1940 Hankey had been chairing the Scientific Advisory Committee (SAC), composed of leading scientists and engineers whose role was to discuss and assess experimental work on the production of the atom bomb. Crucially, it advised TUBE ALLOYS, the cover name for the research programme that had been authorized to develop nuclear weapons during the war and which preceded the Manhattan Project that would be developed in the United States. The committee's earliest discussions, reflected in two papers, 'Use of Uranium for a Bomb' and 'Use of Uranium as a Source of Power', helped the United States in the early stages of their nuclear weapons programme.[22] Though these discussions had started before Cairncross joined Hankey and he did not have any official role within the committee, he decided they were of sufficient importance to pass the details on to Gorsky in September 1941. In October Cairncross forwarded another policy memorandum on the intended production of the atom bomb.

It is for these reasons, by alerting Moscow to the early progress of the Anglo-American atom bomb discussions, that Cairncross has been described as one of the first 'atom spies'. He had skilfully positioned himself close to a senior government adviser where he would get to see defence material, but the only information he could have passed on to the Russians at that time was the initial disclosure that British scientists intended to develop an Anglo-American atom bomb. Klaus Fuchs, a leading theoretical physicist and communist activist known to MI5 since the mid-1930s, was appointed to work on the TUBE ALLOYS project in May 1941 and his scientific expertise, together with knowledge gained from his close working relationship with Rudolf Peierls and Otto Frisch, provided Moscow with detailed technical insight on the production of the weapon.

Cairncross's status as an 'atom spy' pales by comparison to Fuchs and others. Moreover, Moscow began to distrust the voluminous material sent their way by Cairncross, partly because it did not seem feasible to them that Hankey, who was marginalized by Churchill, would have such a significant role.[23] In any case, they continued to give greater credence and importance to German intentions towards a possible peace deal with the British government and the latter's appraisal of the prospects for war between Germany and the Soviet Union. In spring 1941, these questions were at the top of Cairncross's political work as indeed they were for Lord Hankey (the 'BOSS' as he was referred to in Soviet intelligence).

From the beginning of 1941, as he recovered from a fall from a train and his impatience with Churchill's leadership increased, Hankey was pessimistic about the immediate future. His attempts to exert pressure on Churchill by calling on the remaining sceptics of the new approach, as well as some who continued to favour deals with Hitler, had failed. By spring of 1941 he was 'beset' by 'anxieties' and blamed Churchill for 'running the war as a dictator' – not helped by being surrounded in the war cabinet by a 'set of yes men'.

Nevertheless, his deliberations and discussions were of great interest to Cairncross and his Soviet controller as the crisis deepened in the aftermath of the Blitz, with German bombs threatening. The first documents Cairncross had passed to Gorsky just before Christmas included the war cabinet minutes, intelligence reports, FO telegrams and general material on the progress of the war as the British government saw it. The volume of documents increased during 1941 (and by the end of that year would total 3,449).[24] His role gave him access to the registry's documents, and he was able to provide a range of intelligence material, including counter-intelligence reports, details of secret SIS reports, War Office records, and the reports of the chiefs of staff.

The entry of the Soviet Union into the war in June 1941 strengthened Cairncross's commitment to his political work, and his meetings with Gorsky now became more regular, though he still had a habit of missing appointments. (On one occasion when Cairncross took a young woman friend to the opera, an irate Gorsky met him at the end of the performance.) Indeed Gorsky remained suspicious of Cairncross's politics and commitment to his work. Their discussions lacked the intellectually expansive topics Cairncross enjoyed with Deutsch, while Cairncross's attempts to probe broader political questions on the Soviet attitude to its new allies were thwarted by Gorsky's repetition of the official line. Nevertheless, for the remainder of 1941 Cairncross continued the routine of taking documents from the office and passing them to Gorsky. This largely consisted of cabinet minutes and FO telegrams, including the minutes of the SAC and British attitudes towards the Soviets as a new ally. These meetings were largely conducted in the outer suburbs of West London, occasionally through meetings in a public lavatory and always observed by the strict protocol of retracing steps or being driven through circuitous routes to avoid suspicion. Cairncross's lack of aptitude for technical matters would be a source of prolonged frustration to his handlers. Given a Minox camera by Gorsky to reduce the amount of paperwork he had to smuggle out of the office and to avoid his risk of getting caught, the ungainly Cairncross could not put it to any practical use. He would continue to work by carrying papers and documents around his person or in bags for the duration of his time as a spy.

His time working for Lord Hankey, however, was coming to an end. Hankey's despair at Churchill's leadership had increased during the critical months of 1941. After Hankey was moved to Paymaster-General, his loss of influence affected the quality of the material to which Cairncross had enjoyed access, but it also coincided with Cairncross's call-up in spring 1942.

Chapter 9
Bletchley Park

After the ending of the Nazi-Soviet pact, John Cairncross was reassured that the documents he had passed on – an enormous range, exceeded only by those provided by Donald Maclean – were contributing to the renewed anti-fascist campaign against Germany. The ending of the pact was marked by Operation Barbarossa in June 1941, when the Nazi invasion of the Soviet Union was intended to be the prelude to the conquering of substantial economic resources, including absorbing parts of the Soviet empire. The Soviet entry into the war with Germany and the realization that Britain at last had an ally in resisting Hitler brought widespread sympathy for the Soviets (and Stalin) among the British public, notwithstanding the threat to the regime's survival and the likelihood of massive losses as the Nazis entered Soviet territory. For John Cairncross, it meant he could return to his mission to help the Soviets defeat fascism with renewed vigour.

However, Moscow Centre was unconvinced of his true allegiances. Despite the impressive volume of documents he handed over, they consisted mainly of the attitudes of the British government towards the Nazi regime. Despite the replacement of Chamberlain in 1940 with Winston Churchill (who had long been in favour of collaboration with the Soviets), Stalin himself remained suspicious of Britain's true objectives and had continued to believe Britain might at some point still align with Germany. The attempts of Rudolf Hess to forge a peace deal through contact with the Duke of Hamilton after his solo flight to Scotland in May 1941 had only amplified this feeling and Cairncross's inability to provide any detail of this mission increased the suspicion that he and the other members of the Cambridge ring could be double agents on Britain's behalf. They could not understand how he was able to get access to such a large volume of material without arousing suspicion, while at the same time were unenthused by some of the quality of the information he was providing.

Despite the entry of the Soviet Union, it was evident to Cairncross that Britain remained reluctant to provide arms to the Soviets even after it had become an ally. More knowledge on this question was now a priority, and in the last months of 1941 Gorsky urged him to get more material. It was feared by Moscow Centre that Cairncross's imminent call-up – set for mid-January 1942 – would bring a halt to their source of information. However, on Hankey's intervention, the call-up was postponed and further delayed once Hankey had left the government in March 1942. By May, Cairncross and Gorsky had put into effect a plan to install him at the Government Code and Cypher School (GC&CS) (known to Moscow as KURORT) at Bletchley Park, Buckinghamshire. Cairncross accomplished the transfer after approaching Colonel Freddie Nicholls, the head of MI8, which was responsible for military communication interceptions. He had heard of Nicholls through his work for Hankey and arranged to meet him at the Travellers Club. Over lunch he explained to Nicholls that his expertise in the German language would be of more use to the war effort than as a soldier in the regular army. Nicholls was impressed and arranged for him to make a swift transfer to Bletchley Park within days of his call-up, at the beginning of August 1942.[1]

Cairncross arrived at Bletchley Park with the formal status of captain but effectively as a civilian member of a military section. He was placed in Hut 3, as a translator in the military intelligence section where his knowledge of German was regarded as an important asset. It was a crucial moment in Britain's war effort. In the preceding months Singapore had fallen to Japan, while the doubling in the number of German U-Boats resulted in Britain suffering heavy losses at sea. In response, Winston Churchill reshuffled his cabinet, introducing, among others, the left-wing Stafford Cripps after the latter's two-year stint as British ambassador in Moscow. Cripps's esteem among the British public had risen after Russia entered the war, and he remained a leading proponent in strengthening the Soviet Union's status as a wartime ally.

However, on being briefed on arrival at Bletchley Park, Cairncross was told by the receiving officer that the Soviets had not been made aware that the previous year the British had cracked the ENIGMA machine, the encryption device used by German military intelligence, because they were still regarded as untrustworthy allies. In reality, Churchill had already authorized the passing of information from Bletchley Park to the Russians in order to aid their resistance to the Nazi threat on the Eastern Front. Cairncross was unaware of this, and his own decision to provide them with ENIGMA decrypted details of German Luftwaffe military manoeuvres was partly made on his scepticism (and that of his Soviet controller) about the British perception of its new wartime ally. Among the early material he passed to Gorsky was a training manual on deciphering and a guide for understanding ENIGMA.[2]

After his frustrating career in the civil service, the role awaiting him at Bletchley appealed to Cairncross. After a brief training course in nearby Bedford – which did little to arouse his interest or enthusiasm – he found the work in Hut 3 stimulating. In his new role he was translating, editing and correcting and restoring lost words from the Luftwaffe decrypts provided by the cryptographers in Hut 6 next door. He was part of a group of mainly Oxbridge-educated academics, teachers and foreign language experts required to apply their skills as codebreakers for the war effort. He relished the challenge and found that codebreaking complemented his interest in translating literary texts: 'I found the editing of the German decrypts much like solving a crossword puzzle, or amending a corrupt text of a classical writer like Molière.'[3] He was also able to renew his friendship with Douglas Parmée, his old Trinity College chum, who was part of the Hut 3 group. Though he was part of an elite, it was an elite based on expertise rather than social background, and it renewed his sense of purpose to be involved with rigorous intellectual work. As one of his Hut 3 contemporaries described the role,

> It means reviewing known facts, sorting out significant from insignificant, assessing them severally and jointly, and arriving at a conclusion by the exercise of judgement: part induction, part deduction. Absolute intellectual honesty is essential. The process must not be muddled by emotion or prejudice, nor by a desire to please.[4]

However, the wider living conditions of Bletchley Park – or 'Station X' or 'BP' – did not appeal to him. Housed in an ugly Victorian mansion in an unprepossessing town 60 miles from London and roughly equal distance from Oxford and Cambridge, the working hours were antisocial and the work itself cloaked in strict secrecy; indeed it was not until the 1970s that the precise nature of the work was finally made public. Though set in pleasant enough surroundings with a lake full of ducks, a range of tree varieties and gardens expansive enough for summer games, 'It was not really a country-house at all, rather a monstrosity on the edge of Bletchley town, with suburban dwellings stretching up to the gates.' The building, according to Irene Young, who arrived at Bletchley Park shortly after Cairncross, was marked by its 'physical austerity ... something resembling public house Jacobean and lavatory-gothic'.[5]

Though he was thankful for meeting his old friend Parmée again, they had little opportunity to enjoy a convivial lunch together or late evening discussions on French literature. The secrecy and intensity of the work – arranged in three eight-hour 'watch' shifts from 8.00 am to 4.00 pm, 4.00 pm to midnight and midnight to 8.00 am – meant they worked in seclusion. He did not even know all the people who worked in Hut 3 let alone those in other Huts (which makes the claim in *The Imitation Game* that he worked alongside Alan Turing absurd). Working conditions in the prefabricated buildings were difficult: with poor air and ventilation they were kept warm in the winter months by oil stoves but with the windows shut because of the black-out the temperature oscillated between very hot and very cold across the seasons. He found it a 'semi-monastic' existence (and more of a cell-like atmosphere than anything he had experienced in the Trinity College communist student 'cell'), and after work he and others were promptly transported back to their lodgings in nearby towns. There were social activities, including rounders and tennis on the lawn and musical concerts on some evenings, but with the exception of a performance of a German Lieder concert and a Christmas pantomime, the only respite for Cairncross, who needed solid hours of sleep, was that at the end of a shift rota he could escape to his flat in London, only an hour by train from nearby Bletchley station. Most of his colleagues were accommodated locally, so his escape to the metropolis was perhaps another reason why he rarely mixed, and few Bletchley Park contemporaries remembered his short stay.

Prior to Cairncross's arrival, Hut 3 had endured some internal rivalries among talented individuals, a mixture of academics (which included the poet and author F. L. Lucas) and army officers used to dealing with different forms of intelligence, some of whom knew no German. Different opinions meant an absence of teamwork, and it was only after the appointment of Eric Jones, the former manager of a Manchester textile factory, that the personnel was reorganized, enabling an effective working routine and team spirit to be forged from its individual parts.

The work of Hut 3 comprised six translators or editors (including a team leader) whose role was to translate and elucidate decrypts that had been passed on from the cryptographers in Hut 6 (who were responsible for breaking the ENIGMA codes). The work of Hut 3 depended on the ability to provide swift interpretations, elucidations and summaries of the decrypts before submitting them to Whitehall. The layout of Hut 3 and the designation of roles within it testified to the intensity and precision of the work.

> Hut 3 was set up like a miniature factory. At its centre was the Watch Room – in the middle a circular or horseshoe shaped table, to one side a rectangular table. On the outer rim of the circular table sat the Watch, some half-dozen people. The man in charge, the head of the Watch or Number 1, sat in an obvious directing position at the top of the table.[6]

As the papers were received from Hut 6, they carried the original encoded text on one side and the decoded version arranged in five-letter groups on the other. The job of the Hut 3 Watchkeepers was to begin the process of translating, evaluating and commenting on the decrypts and drafting the final translation before passing on to the team leader for checking. An additional adviser would decide on the relative importance of the ULTRA intelligence (drawn from ENIGMA decrypts) and would arrange for its dispatch to the operational commands in London. A glossary of key terms and an index of decrypts were also important in consolidating the intelligence gathered. The busiest time was usually the evening shift when Hut 6 traffic reached its peak.

Cairncross was sceptical of the story he had been told on arrival that the Russians were not told anything of the ENIGMA secret. But he could not be certain, and the position was not clarified further even after he sought out the views of Jock Colville, by now working in Churchill's office. Nor did one of the Bletchley Park team leaders give much away after Cairncross sought his advice on British attitudes to Russia, over another lunch. 'As far as he knew, the Russians were not being given ULTRA. He did tell me, however, that the main reason for this decision was the fear that the Russian ciphers might be broken, and might thus in turn reveal that the German ENIGMA had been compromised.'[7] There was some fear within British intelligence that some German agents had penetrated the Red Army.

This presented him with a dilemma. In *The Enigma Spy*, Cairncross claimed that at the time he was posted to Bletchley he was 'determined' to relinquish his espionage role and 'sever my connection with the KGB (NKVD)', a decision he thought would be made easier now that Russia had entered the war as Britain's ally.[8] This uncertainty preyed on his mind during the first weeks of his appointment as it became immediately apparent to him that he had access to crucial intelligence at the moment when the Germans were advancing into Russian territory. He concluded, after some sleepless nights, that he could not justify ending his association with the Soviets. Given the precarious situation of the Russian forces in the face of Nazi aggression he had the opportunity to contribute to their defence – an option which, in any case, followed logically from his initial decision, on anti-fascist grounds, to pass documents to them in the first place.

He had passed thousands of documents over the previous two years, but for him ENIGMA was something of a qualitatively different nature, to be set apart from briefing documents and minutes of meetings on Anglo-German relations. This he considered to be serious intelligence that needed to be put at the disposal of the Russians. He accepted that what he was undertaking was espionage, and though his later attempt to define himself as 'an independent and voluntary agent, using the KGB as a channel to the Russians' sounds implausible given his connection with Soviet intelligence since 1937, he nevertheless set down conditions to his controller, as he sought to clarify how the material would be passed on and to what use it would be put.

If I can be defined as a spy, it is only in this solitary case, and it was my contribution of ULTRA for a period of a year which, I contend, gave meaning to and justified my maintenance of what had begun as a tenuous and unwilling link. Therefore when I met Henry I did not hand over any material before discussing with him the question of security. I explained where I was working, what I did and the dangers which the transmission of original ULTRA intercepts involved.[9]

Gorsky confirmed to Cairncross that ULTRA would be sent to Moscow by courier and would not be used by Russian signals. Reassured, Cairncross was now committed to providing regular ULTRA intelligence. Despite the intense secrecy surrounding Bletchley Park, security at the establishment was remarkably lenient. The German decrypts were discarded on the floor of the Watchroom after being processed and therefore easily available. He made his move early one morning in late August 1942 (within his first month at Bletchley Park), after he had spent a sleepless night on the floor of his room in Hut 3 weighing up his options at the end of the 4.00 pm–midnight shift. He had no problem smuggling the decrypts, concealed in his trousers, out through the main gates into Wilton Avenue and then the short distance to Bletchley railway station where he transferred them to a bag before catching the London train. It was his day off at the end of the shift cycle, and once he had spotted Gorsky at one of the suburban stations in West London, he followed him on a short tube journey before they alighted from the London underground separately, reconvening at a quiet location nearby to exchange the material. He passed Gorsky details of the German advances along the Eastern Front. According to the historian of GCHQ, 'The information provided by Cairncross proved to be important in launching an early attack upon the German tactical air force, much of which was destroyed on the ground.'[10]

The main ULTRA material provided by Cairncross covered two distinct areas of intelligence on the German military as it advanced on the Kursk salient in an operation known as CITADEL. First, he passed decrypts which provided information about the new German Tiger tank, which had been constructed in 1942 and was intended to defy Russian cannons by the toughness and durability of its armoured protection. Cairncross passed details of the new tank to the Soviets, which enabled them to produce shells capable of destroying it. According to the testimony of one of his later Soviet controllers, who had access to the KGB archives:

> The Soviet triumph in the great tank battle at Kurskaia Douga [Kurskaya duga] in July 1943, in which two thousand tanks fought each other to a bloody standstill for two days and nights, was thus partly attributable to John Cairncross.[11]

This material comprised the initial tranche of information in the early months following Cairncross's arrival at Bletchley. The second set of documents related to German military strengths and positions as the conflict on the Eastern Front intensified during late 1942 and into 1943, culminating in Operation Citadel and the Battle of Kursk in July and August 1943. At the end of April 1943 the British government made the Soviets aware of the immediate prospect of an attack on the Kursk salient and, based on their ENIGMA intercepts, also told them that the Germans had intelligence on the strategic location of all Soviet forces there. This was the 'sanitized' version of the decrypted material. Cairncross provided the 'unadulterated' form, which included the full texts of the intercepts – that is, not only the identification of the Soviet units but also their precise locations. Aided by the material he provided, the Soviets moved their regiments and were able to wrench the initiative back from the German forces. From his own basic analysis of ULTRA intercepts of Luftwaffe signals, he was able to pass accurate information on Luftwaffe squadrons, enabling a serious and selective bombing raid on enemy forces some weeks before the main move on Kursk. As Cairncross admitted later, he identified material which might help the Russian forces without holding any expert awareness of its specific use for military actions. He had little conception at the time of their relative importance to the battle then taking place. He certainly would have been unaware that (in the words of Yuri Modin) 'this preventive operation, which was followed by several others, was one of the major successes of the Soviet Air Force in the Second World War'.[12] It resulted in the destruction of some 500 German aircraft and enabled the Soviets to counter German aggression and repel their advance. The Battle of Kursk was the largest tank battle in history, during which the Germans suffered heavy losses of aircraft and weaponry on the ground. In early August it lost some of its key positions, and any threat to Moscow by this time had receded.

Cairncross was not the only source of ULTRA decrypts passed to the Russians. In addition to the official channels opened by the British government, Leo Long, a Cambridge contemporary and communist, recruited to Soviet intelligence by Anthony Blunt and by then working in MI14 (British Military Intelligence), also passed material to the Russians, mainly concerning land forces. Cairncross later rejected claims that his actions compromised British intelligence in providing 'unadulterated' versions of ULTRA (and therefore evidence that ENIGMA had been cracked), which could have reached the

Germans indirectly. Long could also have been another source. The British were leaking transcript material, though the Russians didn't believe it and remained suspicious of intelligence material given by the British. However, they were able to compare it with the material Cairncross sent; effectively Cairncross's material validated some of the intelligence the British were sending. In crediting Cairncross with playing the decisive role in the Battle of Kursk, the Russians arguably exaggerated his importance. It was only later that Cairncross received confirmation of the full implications of his actions. According to Yuri Modin, Cairncross was awarded the Order of the Red Banner and briefly shown the medal at a meeting in London, though Cairncross himself did not recall receiving the medal.[13] He later claimed that the full significance of his actions was only made clear when he was researching the battle for his book forty years later.

The stress of the shift system at Bletchley, combined no doubt with the anxiety of passing on secret documents – notwithstanding the absence of any obstacles put in his way to prevent it – meant that Cairncross was looking for a change in employment before he had completed a year at Bletchley. In fact, his initial curiosity in translating and editing German Luftwaffe decrypts had soon worn off. 'This is no place for me', he told Henry Dryden, a Trinity College contemporary, on passing him in the corridor of Hut 3 in December 1942, indicating to Dryden that life had been more agreeable under Hankey.[14] Over the next few months his eyesight worsened with the strain of reading decrypts, and his sleep patterns were now being seriously disrupted. Moreover, he was missing his life in London. The end of each shift rota provided a break sufficient enough for him to return to his London flat for a day, but this was not enough to satisfy his desire to return to the capital.

His appointment to GC&CS had interrupted a more enriching London social life. After being bombed out of Dolphin Square during the Blitz he had temporarily moved in with his brother Alec, before renting a new apartment in Lansdowne Court, Lansdowne Crescent, on the border of Notting Hill and Holland Park. Since moving he had made the acquaintance of some interesting academics and writers. A particularly useful contact was the Russian émigré Alexander Halpern, a former Menshevik radical, international lawyer and MI6 operative in the United States, and his wife Salomea, another Russian émigré and literary socialite. The Halperns were very well connected, and it was at their salon that he met Anna Kallin, who rented a room in their house. Kallin was then working for the BBC's European Services at Bush House and was an important contact for Cairncross who would make several programmes with her after the war. The Halperns' circle also included Moura Budberg, an émigré Russian aristocrat who had moved to Britain in 1935 and whose lovers Included Maxim Gorky, H. G. Wells and the British secret agent Robert Lockhart. Budberg, who unsurprisingly had come to the attention of MI5, was herself very well connected and acquainted with Duff Cooper, who had resigned from Chamberlain's cabinet after Munich and had recently been Minister for Information; Maisky, the Russian Ambassador; and a notable coterie of writers, editors and diplomats. 'It is said that she likes to consider herself the best informed woman in Europe', an MI5 memo recorded, and although her penchant for political gossip and intrigue led to suspicions that she was working secretly for the Soviets, there was no hard evidence to support it.[15] In fact, the nature of Budberg's departure from Russia made it more likely that she was anti-Bolshevik. She would have been an interesting acquaintance for Cairncross, who attended some of her cocktail parties. Though Cairncross had an aversion to pretentious social climbers, he was always keen to be in the company of writers and academics, and it was in this period that he met the philosophers Isaiah Berlin and Freddie Ayer. Mixing in such circles encouraged in him the feeling that his future would lie outside the civil service.

He left Bletchley at the beginning of June 1943, following an extended period of annual leave. Although he was there for less than a year, he was exhausted: 'The shift system was knocking the guts out of me.'[16] Though he remained committed to the war effort, he now believed he could make a better contribution in other ways. However, his determination to leave Bletchley had alarmed the Russians. Gorsky had been shocked by Cairncross's stated intention to leave and, after reporting back to Moscow, sought to persuade him to return; Gorsky even offered (according to Cairncross) an 'inducement' of £100 to do so. Cairncross was their only agent at Bletchley Park and losing that presence was a blow, while they were taken aback by his independent-mindedness, which was also against convention. However, it was his decision, and if it took his Soviet controllers by surprise then it only increased their suspicions of his real status. Gorsky had initially put in his mind the idea of a transfer from Bletchley Park to GC&CS's diplomatic section in London, but after Cairncross sought the advice of Pen Loxley, a FO colleague, he was told that his work at Bletchley was regarded as more important and that there would be little chance of a transfer.

It was through Cairncross's own initiative and contacts that he eventually found a way out of Bletchley Park. Fortunately for him, Professor Frederick Green, one of his old French tutors at Cambridge, had the wartime role of liaising between Bletchley and Section V of SIS (MI6), which was responsible for counter-espionage. On one of Green's visits to Bletchley, Cairncross told him of the effect the work was having on his health and confided that he would be better served in a London office where his German language and editing skills could be put to better use. Green had always thought highly of Cairncross, a fellow Scot perceived – like himself – as something of an outsider. Green impressed upon his colleagues in MI6 that Cairncross's background made him ideal for intelligence work. When Cairncross's bosses at Bletchley heard of his intentions, they insisted he leave GC&CS while his future employment could be resolved. Cairncross spent the first two weeks of June 1943 at home in his London flat, considering his future. He had much to think about. Gorsky's attempt to dissuade Cairncross from his move proved to be his last contact with him, and by the end of June he had been replaced by Konstantin Kukin (or Krechin, codenamed IGOR). Cairncross's mind was made up. He hoped that leaving Bletchley and Gorsky behind would be another escape route.

Chapter 10
Enter Graham Greene

The move to MI6 (Section V) in July 1943 was a welcome relief to Cairncross. He had removed himself from an exhausting shift regime and could return to live in his London flat. He also felt that the burden of his espionage had been partially lifted. He had delivered a significant cache of documents to his Soviet handlers, and even if he remained unaware of the true value of the material until later he was reassured that it was an important contribution to the ongoing battle on the Eastern Front. He hoped that the stress he incurred while extracting the decrypts, smuggling them out of Bletchley Park and handing them over to Gorsky in London, would now subside. Indeed over the next two years the volume of material he passed on was reduced significantly. This, combined with the renewal of his London life, enabled him to think more seriously about what he wanted to do in the future. He had kept up his Molière scholarship since Cambridge and was now tentatively planning an academic book on the playwright. The idea of an academic career or at least some more intellectually fulfilling vocation was on his mind. Moreover, these interests would soon be augmented by the most important friendship of his life, one that would provide him with a mentor, a lifestyle to envy, intellectual stimulation and, most crucial of all, a means to escape.

MI6 or SIS (Secret Intelligence Service) as it was mainly known to its officers, had been responsible for monitoring foreign intelligence since it was established along with MI5, its domestic counterpart, in 1909. It expanded during the First World War and in the aftermath of the Russian Revolution when trade deals brought more Soviet officials to Britain.

The work of MI6 included running foreign agents in different countries from 'stations' (often embassy buildings). It involved handling secret military documents and collecting, submitting and evaluating information obtained by both legal and sometimes illegal means. During wartime its work inevitably increased with the need for effective counter-intelligence.

Section V of MI6 which took responsibility for counter-espionage had seen its staff numbers rise prodigiously over the duration of the Second World War. Hugh Trevor-Roper, who joined Section V in 1941, found a 'very archaic' office, though a very busy one; on arrival he was immediately given a tough workload without adequate training or clarification of the expectations placed on his department. He felt that the initial settling-in period was more difficult than it need have been and amplified the disadvantages of taking up a position without the benefits of patronage, in the form of social or school connections. He was also surprised by the absence of a specific German department in Section V (only a regional one which it shared with Scandinavia), despite the fact that by 1941 Bletchley Park had broken the cipher of Abwehr, the German Military Intelligence Service.[1]

Cairncross owed his own move to Section V to a modest form of patronage in the case of one of his old French tutors (though his command of the German language was an obvious advantage). Throughout his time there he remained a relatively junior member and was only on the fringe of the impressive circles of future writers and academics. As such his name has been largely absent from the memoirs of some of the protagonists. When he started at Section V in June 1943, the offices were spread over three buildings in St. Albans, Hertfordshire, where they had been moved from MI6's HQ in Broadway Buildings, opposite St James's Park in central London. They would remain at St. Albans for only another month after his arrival, when, on the initiative of Kim Philby, they returned to Ryder Street, St James's. Kim Philby was then head of the Iberian department of Section V; among those working under him were his old school friend Tim Milne, Malcolm Muggeridge and Graham Greene.

Therefore, for the first few weeks until the office returned to central London in mid-July, Cairncross had to get up each morning at 6.00 am to catch the train from St. Pancras to St. Albans. He would then report to Glenalmond, the Edwardian building in which staff scrutinized the movements and operations of enemy agents, obtained through cipher intercepts and wireless messages. At least, it was a regular daily routine without the added burden of shift work, though his habit of poor timekeeping would continue to put more strain on his relations with his colleagues and superiors. Unlike Trevor-Roper, he was given a brief training in German counter-intelligence operations and was then set to work alongside William Steedman (one of several colleagues who had previously worked in Passport Control) editing and registering texts of the Abwehr's cipher. After the names of agents had been removed, these were then passed on for analysing, circulating and cataloguing. It was broadly similar work, if less intellectually challenging, to what he had been doing at Bletchley. Intermittently, he continued to share some of this material on German Intelligence with Gorsky and his successor Konstantine Kukin (IGOR) who replaced his codename LISZT with KAREL. Cairncross had hoped to escape these arrangements but with the increasing intensity of the battle on the Eastern Front his Soviet controller pressed for more material on German troop movements. It was still not clear to Cairncross how he might finally extricate himself from what had become a serious burden. Part of Cairncross's job was to destroy the intercepts, and this gave him the opportunity to provide plentiful quantities of material: 'When he started work there was a heap of old intercepts. He destroyed them (evidently registered their destruction), burnt some and passed about 1,500 on to us.'[2]

His MI6 assignment was to work as an editor on the intelligence traffic emanating from the German counter-espionage unit (which incorporated both the criminal police and the Gestapo, the Secret State Police). Once the Abwehr's cipher had been broken, Cairncross's job was to edit the text of the German originals which detailed the location of enemy agents. Section V's work in this area was important in identifying, arresting or 'turning' Nazi agents. In this way he was able to supply a resume of Abwehr movements along the Russian front, details of German intelligence's internal code and other material on Nazi agents. He was also able to provide details of Operation ULM, a clandestine operation involving German ski troops on the Eastern Front.[3]

From his own perspective, passing on such documents remained consistent with his commitment to aiding the Russians in their battle against Nazism. He had no problem smuggling material out of the building as it was commonplace for even senior MI6 officers, many of whom were overworked, to take work home with them. However, during his time at MI6, the Russians became less interested in his work, probably because they had Philby in the same section operating at a much higher level. They were also receiving similar material from Anthony Blunt who was then in MI5.

In the German section Cairncross worked under the direction of David Footman, a friend of Guy Burgess, who would himself later come under suspicion after the disappearance of his friend in 1951. Footman, 'always calm, balanced and equable',[4] had worked in the Consular Services in Egypt and in the Balkans until being recruited by MI6 in 1935. In that role he had secretly passed material given to him by Burgess to Lord Vansittart, a critic of Chamberlain, during the appeasement crisis, and his diplomacy skills and discretion at one point suggested to Burgess that he might make a good Soviet agent.[5] His friendship with Burgess had been cemented during the latter's time as a BBC Talks Producer, and Burgess had got him to do several talks on travel. In fact, by the mid-1930s Footman was an accomplished author having written travel memoirs, short stories and a novel entitled *Pig and Pepper*, a partly autobiographical account of a young naïve English vice consul working in the interwar Balkans who becomes immersed in a world of corruption, divided loyalties and danger. Footman remained part of Burgess's close social circles up until the latter's defection, and they would regularly dine together.

Cairncross's literary interests might have drawn him to Footman, had he read any of his work. However, Cairncross's reluctance to immerse himself in day-to-day office routines and continued scepticism of its hierarchies, occasional coldness towards colleagues, combined with his relatively low position in the office, ensured that their acquaintance rarely extended beyond workplace formalities. Footman was not impressed with Cairncross's attitude to his work and had to reprimand him for lateness. He thought him an 'odd person with a chip on his shoulder'.[6]

Though the more informal atmosphere was conducive to those of an academic disposition, Cairncross was never part of the social circles of Section V and did not join the likes of Malcolm Muggeridge, Footman, Pope-Hennessey, Stuart Hampshire and Trevor-Roper, in their after-work gatherings at The King Harry in St. Albans or the Kings Arms and Unicorn pubs after the relocation to St James. Nor did he have much to do with the bright hope of MI6, Kim Philby. Philby was in the midst of a rapid rise through the security services. Recommended by Hester Marsden-Smedley an MI6 officer working undercover as a *Daily Express* reporter, Philby was invited in 1940 to join Section D, MI6's sabotage and covert operations department, which would soon be incorporated into the work of the Special Operations Executive (SOE). This was the start of his career in British intelligence that would take him to its pinnacle. In 1941 he was appointed the head of the Iberian section of Section V of MI6, with responsibility for Spain and Portugal. Here he impressed his superiors and colleagues with his capacity for hard work, analytical rigour in interpreting intelligence, the ability to solve organizational difficulties with a minimum of fuss and loyalty towards colleagues. According to his old friend and MI6 colleague Tim Milne, he displayed a 'mastery of complicated procedures'.[7] On occasion, according to Milne, whose desk was opposite Philby's, he 'could also be uncompromising on anything he considered important. Somehow he usually got his way without antagonising the other party, often without letting him realise there had been a conflict.'[8]

For these attributes he was highly regarded, not only by his superiors, notably Major Vivian and 'C', Sir Stewart Menzies, but also by those who worked under him. Muggeridge, who worked for him as an officer in the Iberian department, noted his 'great energy and determination', while behind his charm saw 'a kind of boyishness, even naivete'.[9] Muggeridge had first met him when they were both journalists and rejected the view that Philby's appeal as a 'patrician charmer' was due to his background, upbringing and accent. If anything, according to Muggeridge, his 'appalling stutter', tastes, manners and dress were often less than conventional. His attributes had seemingly little to do with an 'old boy network'.[10] Philby's rivalry with Felix Cowgill, an unyielding anti-communist who was disliked by some of the Oxbridge 'intellectuals' in Section V, culminated in Philby being appointed head of the new counter-espionage division that Cowgill himself had initiated and one that Philby, backed by Moscow, had immediately coveted. Crucially, it put him in charge of the division responsible for dealing with communist agents.

Philby's status in MI6 meant that he had little to do with Cairncross, though the latter recalled a lunch together at the Travellers and another meal with Victor Rothschild, after Cairncross had appeared unexpectedly after confusing the date of the appointment.[11] Philby would presumably have known of Cairncross's espionage from Burgess, but there is no indication that Cairncross was aware at this time of Philby's role as a double agent. It was a rule of Soviet espionage that little information on fellow recruits was to be shared. However, despite the veil of ignorance that was suggested in some of the reports submitted by four members of the Cambridge spy circle, their own roles were well known to each other; and in some of the meetings, connections and handling of material, they often acted as a 'ring'. In this context Cairncross was out of the ring and remained unaware of the status of the other four until 1951. As far as the 'ring' was concerned, if Cairncross was its fifth member it was only on the basis of an unwelcome guest, someone who had been thought useful at the time but didn't fit in and – in light of his ignorance of the status of the others – more easily expendable.

In any case, Cairncross's own position in MI6 and role as a Soviet agent contrasted sharply with Philby's. Where Philby was a confident, impressive leader, the 'blue-eyed' boy of MI6 who had won over his colleagues and superiors, and was capable of disguising his true political allegiances, Cairncross remained more of a loner, habitually resentful towards authority, uncomfortable in his surroundings and, in his soft Scottish tones, politically outspoken and argumentative on occasions. MI6's environment was at least more congenial and less hierarchical than the civil service and more relaxed than MI5, with which it often clashed on procedural matters.

Unlike Philby, who was perceived as an exceptionally conscientious and capable leader on the way to the top of his profession – characteristics he was able to combine while revealing the identities of fellow British agents to Moscow – Cairncross's time at MI6 hardly epitomized the ruthless double agent. He was a marginal figure who retained a cynical outlook towards his superiors and held no career ambitions within the service. Philby normally avoided politics, according to Hugh Trevor-Roper, who even wondered if he had any significant intellectual interests; Cairncross, on the other hand, continued to make his views known and craved an intellectual release from the routines of the service. They had one thing in common. Philby, as several former colleagues reflected following his defection in 1963, was driven by a supreme arrogance sustained by an ideological certainty and loyalty to Moscow. On a different level Cairncross also exuded arrogance at times; in his case, his belief that he knew better was partly derived from his Presbyterian lack of self-doubt and the conviction that he was the intellectual match of those around him. That his colleagues did not recognize this only fuelled his resentment.

One person who did take him seriously as an intellectual was Graham Greene. Greene was working under Philby for the Iberian section of Section V, though Cairncross had only caught glimpses of him by the time of their chance meeting at St. Pancras, on the train to St. Albans. A tall, lanky figure he had vaguely recognized from the office joined his carriage and asked Cairncross about the book he was reading. This was *England Made Me*, Greene's 1935 novel set in the ruins of a failing economic system and its degenerate social and political values. Greene had researched his book in Scandinavia in 1933 and had modelled Erik Krogh, one of the main characters, on the self-made entrepreneur Ivar Kreuger, who had taken his own life after bankruptcy in the aftermath of the Wall Street crash. In the novel, Krogh's empire survives, though leaving in its wake a destructive trail of unscrupulous business dealings and failing private relationships. Anthony Farrant, another key character in the novel (apparently based on Greene's own brother Herbert), is an ex-public schoolboy who had charmed and cheated his way through life and exploited the generosity of friendships. It is easy to see how the book would have appealed to Cairncross, whose anger at the rotten English elite at the heart of the British class system still burned. Reflecting later on his motivations for writing the book, Greene remarked that the Great Depression and the rise of Hitler meant that 'it was impossible in those days not to be committed'.[12] Its decrepit traditions and rituals were indicative of a seedy and corrupt political system that helped prepare the ground for appeasers of fascism. Greene's novel encapsulates a picture of an international system where loyalties and borders were constantly shifting, and in which secrecy and betrayal were becoming accepted as part of its modus operandi.

Cairncross told his travelling companion that he was enjoying the book and that the same author had written an even better one, *The Power and the Glory*. This assertion met with the approval of his new acquaintance who praised it as 'a fine piece of work'. Intrigued by this reply, Cairncross asked him if he knew Graham Greene. 'I am Graham Greene' was the startling riposte, in what Cairncross later referred to as a 'veritable coup de théâtre'. It was the beginning of a long friendship which lasted nearly fifty years until Greene's death in 1991. For Cairncross it was the most important friendship of his life. In the following decades, Greene would variously take on the role of an academic referee for university applications; an intellectual mentor; a sounding-board for his literary ambitions; a publishing go-between; a housing adviser (when purchasing and selling his Capri property); a recipient of updated romantic sojourns; a character referee (when Cairncross was being pursued by the Italian courts) and, finally, as he was dying, an intermediary in providing legal advice and moral support at the time of Cairncross's public exposure as the 'Fifth Man'. In their many years of friendship, Greene is the one person to whom Cairncross afforded deference and unyielding admiration. There is an imbalance in the depth of the respective correspondence, with Cairncross's long, often rambling, updates eliciting shorter replies from Greene, whose wide circles put more demands on his time. But he retained a loyalty and affection for his friend whom he early on nicknamed 'Claymore', after the Scottish Highland broadsword.

Cairncross and Greene had little to do with each other in the MI6 office. Greene had joined SIS in 1941 with the help of his sister Elizabeth who was already in the service, and after being invited to a series of informal drinks parties for vetting purposes, he was trained as an agent at Oriel College, Oxford (then used by the secret service), before being dispatched to West Africa. When Cairncross met him, Greene had recently returned from working as an agent in Sierra Leone, where he had impressed his MI6 superiors as well as gaining valuable material for later novels, including *The Heart of the Matter*. Greene's travels with MI6 would be a fruitful resource for his writing, and the research for several of his novels was supported by MI6 expenses. On Greene's return from Freetown, Philby brought him into his Iberian section, where he took over as head of the Lisbon Desk in August 1943. *Our Man in Havana* drew extensively on his experiences in 1943–4, which included the meetings with 'C' and the description of two agents based in Lisbon. Paul Fidrmuc (known as Ostro) was a Czech businessman turned German citizen whose reports to the Abwehr detailed the dealings of imaginary agents, while Juan Pujol Garcia ('Garbo') was a Spaniard who simultaneously approached the Abwehr and MI6 before compiling fictional reports that despite claiming to be delivered from Britain were actually composed in Madrid with the aid of a travel guide to the UK and a glossary of Anglo-French military terms. Malcolm Muggeridge, based in Lourenco Marques in Mozambique and therefore under Greene's guidance as he set about spreading disinformation and attempting to run double agents, admired his controller. He was 'tremendously good at dealing with agents and working out cover plans and things like that and justifiably was highly thought of'.

Trevor Wilson was another in Greene's MI6 circle. Greene had met Wilson earlier in the war and they had much in common. Catholic like Greene and with a similar outlook on life, Wilson was a brilliant intelligence officer and fluent French speaker with a particular interest in the Far East; he would later become British consul in Hanoi. He and Greene became close friends, with Wilson an invaluable source of material for Greene's later works, notably *The Quiet American* that was set in Vietnam in the 1950s. In later years Cairncross would develop his own interest in the legacy of French colonialism in that region and spend many years working on the story of Constantine Phaulkon, the counsellor to the king of Siam who had been misrepresented by European writers and historians.

Philby was impressed with Greene's abilities in SIS, and once he had outmanoeuvred Cowgill to become head of the new anti-communist Section IX, hoped Greene would succeed him as head of the Iberian section. Yet Greene, over lunch with Philby and Milne at the Café Royal, politely refused the offer and instead in June 1944 resigned from MI6 to move to the Political Intelligence Department of the FO, expecting to witness the arrival of Allied troops in France (which in the end didn't materialize). A more plausible explanation for his resignation from MI6 is that with the war almost won he wanted to resume his writing and was tired of office routines. Philby was surprised at his decision and attributed it to Greene's aversion to responsibility. However, Greene's biographer, Norman Sherry, has suggested another possible reason. This was that Greene was aware that Philby was working for the Russians and did not want to compromise his friendship or be put in a position where he might have to turn his friend in. Whatever his speculations about Philby, he wouldn't have known the extent to which his friend was involved or that his determination to take on the head of the new anti-communist department was being urged as a top priority by his Soviet controllers.

In the late summer of 1944 John Cairncross transferred to Section I of MI6 which dealt with political intelligence reports emanating from

Germany. In this role he was able to pass on to Moscow details of Himmler's intentions to create a Nazi underground resistance network. In his last months in MI6 Section I, he continued to pass on material in the latter stages of the war, including details of a possible German offensive in Pomerania as well as British interceptions of Soviet radio and news of British agents in several countries across Europe and South America.[13] His Soviet controllers continued to be grateful for his work in passing on important documentation in the period after the Battle of Kursk. According to material uncovered in the Soviet Archives by Nigel West, at the end of October 1944 Cairncross was given a payment of £250 for his 'long and useful' work. He penned a note in reply, saying that he was

> delighted that our friends should have thought my services worthy of recognition and am proud to have contributed something to the victories which have almost cleared the Soviet soil of the invaders. …
> The premium presented to me is of the most generous nature, and I shall try to express my gratitude for it by redoubled efforts in the future.[14]

With the end of the Second World War imminent in June 1945 Cairncross left MI6 to return to the Treasury. Even if this was likely to be less propitious from Moscow's point of view, they approved the move as they had MI6 covered by Philby. Despite his offer of 'redoubling his efforts' for the Soviets, the happy outcome of the Second World War for Cairncross was that it marked the end of his role as 'an agent for the duration'. Or so he hoped.

For almost three years from the end of the Second World War, he would pass no documents to Moscow. The end of the war had brought some personal respite for Cairncross, against the bigger picture of a new beginning for Britain in the aftermath of the defeat of fascism and the election of a Labour government. The initial trigger for his release from espionage was the defection of Igor Gouzenko, a cipher clerk at the Soviet Embassy in Ottawa, Canada, within days of the cessation of hostilities. Moscow's concern at the possible implications of Gouzenko's defection for its agents put a hold on its activities in London. It was the most serious crisis facing its British agents and had occurred at the same time as the case of Konstantin

Volkov, which threatened to reveal the entire Cambridge spy ring. Volkov, the Soviet vice consul in Istanbul, who had previously worked on the British section in Moscow, was seeking asylum and offered the British consulate information on 'two agents inside the Foreign Office ... and seven inside the British Intelligence Service (including one fulfilling the function of head of a section of British counter-espionage in London)'.[15] That this crisis was averted (and Volkov dispensed with by Moscow) was due entirely to Philby's new position in MI6: as head of its counter-espionage section (and therefore one of those most at threat from Volkov) he was able to get access to the documents before any names were revealed, most notably those of himself and the two FO agents (Burgess and Maclean). Cairncross, as an agent in British intelligence, would also have been under threat of exposure.

The Gouzenko case also resulted in the prosecution of the first atom spy, Alan Nunn May, a near contemporary of Maclean at Trinity Hall, Cambridge, who leaked atomic energy secrets to Moscow while working at the Chalk River Laboratories in Ontario. The revelations concerning a former Cambridge communist threatened the status of Philby and the others. Due to the crisis emanating from the Gouzenko case, and the fear that the Cambridge spies were in danger of exposure, Cairncross's contact with his Soviet controller had been terminated and he did not meet the NKVD (now KGB) until 1948. In the view of Richard Davenport-Hines, the Cold War began from the moment Gouzenko extracted documents on Soviet espionage and defected from the Soviet Embassy in Canada – escaping a last-minute visit by thuggish KGB officers, thanks to the kindness of his neighbours.[16] The onset of the Cold War would change John Cairncross's life immeasurably. He was looking to leave the civil service for what he hoped would be an alternative career, preferably in academia (though his lack of publications was a hindrance in that regard) or even in business, which would take him far away from the world of espionage and where he could draw on his interests in political economy.

In *The Enigma Spy*, he stated that 'the moment for me actually to sever my KGB connection never came, but sometimes one is forced into a move which one should have had the energy or the initiative to make of one's own accord: in short, my problem was solved by events'.[17] Much debate has ensued over his failure to extricate himself from his KGB contacts in the period after 1945. If he had originally agreed to become a Soviet agent to serve the cause of anti-fascism before and during the war, why did he continue to work for the Russians once it had been replaced by the Cold War which turned Soviet 'allies' into communist 'enemies'? His autobiography does not provide a satisfactory explanation for these questions, and his reluctance to talk about it publicly fuelled suspicion.

The explanation probably has more to do with mundane practical circumstances, rather than ideological reasons. His failure to anticipate the moment for his departure was not without effort on his part, while it reveals a stubborn streak of self-preservation. In 1948 Labour prime minister Clement Attlee made clear his intention to remove communists and fascists from civil service departments where they would have access to sensitive material. In 1950, (Lord) Robert Vansittart, the former anti-appeasement permanent undersecretary for foreign affairs, turned his attention to the communists whom he believed remained active in influential positions in public life, including the BBC and education (where he estimated there were 2,000 active communist teachers).[18] Though nothing on the scale of McCarthyism, such measures saw resignations and dismissals of those with communist links, and even promising historians like Eric Hobsbawm, George Rudé and Christopher Hill found it difficult to obtain work in universities.

For the KGB itself, running agents in London was becoming more difficult in light of recent defections and the prosecution of Nunn May. More atom spies were to be prosecuted in the coming years. For all these reasons Cairncross was unsure of a clear escape route. To refuse to cooperate with the KGB could expose him to blackmail by them, with few likely sympathizers within the higher echelons of the civil service or FO if his espionage was leaked. On the other hand, he felt that reporting his own espionage to the security services now that the Cold War was well underway was also a non-starter. His mistake was not to act sooner, when he could have made the case that he was acting out of conscience in support of a wartime ally, but even then he could not be sure how he would be received.

Cairncross had his own reasons to seek release from his predicament. He saw his work for the Soviets as complete – a position that was reinforced in his estimation by the Soviet Union's expansionist activities in Eastern Europe, together with the unresolved territorial questions in Austria and Germany. His desire to end his espionage role set him apart, for example, from Burgess who felt isolated by the lack of communication in the more barren period immediately after Gouzenko's defection and Philby and Blunt who continued to be in touch with Moscow. In Washington, Donald Maclean, who maintained his double life as ideologue and diplomat (despite resorting to frequent drunken binges), was on the verge of what appeared to be a glittering career. As a first secretary at the American Embassy, his access to the key committees on Anglo-American atomic energy committees made him the most highly valued source for Moscow, and he continued to pass material for ideological reasons – his anti-Americanism was at its most virulent as the Cold War took shape.

Cairncross's wish to escape from the KGB was compounded by his disillusionment with his work in the civil service. Despite his appointment as a principal in the Treasury, by the end of the war he had himself concurred that he was ill-suited to the role of a civil servant. He was aware that there was a growing conflict in his life between how he was perceived in the narrow confines of the civil service and FO, where he had often appeared as socially awkward or aloof from colleagues, and his more propitious life beyond the office where he was now often in the company of writers, professors and poets.

Moreover, he now had a mentor. He and Graham Greene started to meet occasionally at the theatre or for drinks, and he was inspired by their meetings, as well as the new contacts he made through Greene. Cairncross had already got to know some editors, poets and BBC producers, but Greene was a step up from what he had been used to, and he hoped this would lead to fruitful collaborations. He maintained modest literary ambitions of his own, and penned some original poems and translations of verse for John Lehmann's *New Writing*, a 'book-magazine' which since the early 1940s had given space to an impressive milieu of young poets and writers. His first published pieces, translations of the Italian poet Umberto Saba and the exiled Spanish poet Luis Cernuda, would appear in Lehmann's publication.[19]

At the same time, he had continued with his work on Molière's original texts which he knew to be an original piece of scholarship, and began to seek out the possibility of an academic career, with his old tutor and friend, Harry Ashton, warmly supporting his applications. In addition to Molière he had also begun a collaboration with his elder brother Andrew, now an established Shakespeare scholar, for a book on Shakespeare's attitude to money and business. This book, intended for a French series, would allow John to do some detective work on the role of money during Shakespeare's life and deal with the translation. Despite some initial research, however, which continued to whet his appetite for academic life, the book did not come to fruition.

His determination to leave the civil service did not diminish and in 1948 he resigned his post at the Treasury to take up a position with the firm Courtaulds, which had recently been one of the first companies to establish an economic policy section. This was intended to utilize his interest in political economy and to offer a fresh start. However, for reasons that he does not – or cannot – explain in his autobiography, the personnel office at the Treasury put obstacles in his way, and he was later forced to withdraw his resignation. This intervention may have had something to do with his past communist involvement, given the greater attention to ex-communists in public service and business. While in MI6, Cairncross had got access to his own file and was aware that some loose left-wing connections had been assumed by British intelligence based on his receipt of a letter with a German provenance that had been signed off with 'fraternal greetings'. It may have alerted the personnel office at a time of escalating Cold War tension.

The idea of escape was in Cairncross's mind as the Cold War took shape. The Treasury transfer to Defence Personnel – a 'tedious assignment'[20] – where he was involved in officer grading in the transition to peacetime, at least enabled him to visit provincial towns and cities to meet officers at the various command posts. He travelled to Bath, York and elsewhere, adding cathedrals and other historic buildings to his itinerary while entertaining his hobby of collecting miniature whisky bottles which, after forwarding a few to his friend Graham Greene, would be replicated in the character of James Wormold, MI6's man in Havana in Greene's 1958 novel.

Travel was once more on his mind. His friendship with Greene helped spark a long love affair with Italy. In 1948 Greene had purchased a villa on the island of Capri with finance provided by Alexander Korda, who, with Carol Reed, had produced the film *The Third Man*, for which

Greene had written the screenplay. Greene would keep Villa Rosaio on Anacapri for forty years, using it as a place for writing and as a private retreat to meet his lovers – notably Catherine Walston and Yvonne Cloetta – as well as other writers on the island. When he was not there he often offered it to friends, and Cairncross took advantage of his hospitality and spent some vacations there prior to moving to Italy permanently. Capri, as an island of exile, must have appealed.

Chapter 11
Cold War and resignation

Yuri Modin was a twenty-five-year-old intelligence officer who moved to London with his young family in the bleak and freezing winter of 1947–8. The son of a soldier from Suzdal, an old provincial town north of Moscow, and a graduate of Leningrad Naval Academy, he had spent the previous three years in Moscow translating documents provided by the Cambridge spies. Proficient in English from an early age, he had immersed himself in their activities (working from the microfilms received from London), later claiming that he knew 'everything there was to know' about them.[1] However, he was inexperienced as an agent and on arrival in London – officially as a press attaché at the Soviet Embassy – admitted to some apprehension in taking over the control of the Five. John Cairncross, now codenamed Carelian (or Karel), was the first agent he was assigned after a set of trial meetings, before taking over the whole group. Korovin, Modin's KGB boss in London, when briefing him on the practicalities of dealing with Cairncross, pointed out his 'vagueness', and referred to his habit of being late and sometimes even missing appointments altogether. Modin wanted to build up a profile of the man he was dealing with. According to standard espionage procedure, he also designed a series of complicated routes, including doubling back to avoid detection, before resuming his journey to his first meeting with Cairncross at a pub in Bath Road, Chiswick, a short walk from Turnham Green underground station, in West London. Milovzorov, his predecessor – who had not got on with Cairncross in the brief time he had handled him – introduced him to Modin. In their meetings, Modin went by the codename 'PETER'. He was the fifth Soviet controller Cairncross had dealt with. He had graduated from the amicable and idealistic Otto, with whom he had held stimulating discussions on literature and philosophy, to the ultra-orthodox Henry, appointed as an outcome of the purges of the 'illegals', through to Igor and very briefly Milovzorov (whom Modin described as an 'ill-tempered lout').

'Peter' at least was agreeable, but Cairncross was still looking to sever his links with both the KGB and the civil service, where his relations with colleagues and seniors continued to be strained. In his three-year sabbatical from the Russians he made applications for university lectureships (with Graham Greene and Harry Ashton as referees), though his dearth of published articles or books put him at a disadvantage. His friendship with Anna Kallin had brought him opportunities at the BBC, and he had become a regular contributor to the Third Programme, where Kallin was a producer. The Third Programme had been founded in 1946 to broadcast classical music, aspects of art and culture and intellectual discussions. These were normally pre-recorded in the week preceding the evening broadcasts. Normally, he was one of a panel contributing views on aspects of literature or commentary on contemporary politics. In 1947 he took part in a discussion in English on the work of the Italian writer Alberto Moravia. Moravia was a cousin of the Rossellis but had wavered in his commitment to their anti-fascist cause, causing a rupture with the family after the murder of the brothers in 1937. Moravia's literature dealt with the more ambiguous situations of Italians under fascism and his recently published novel *The Woman of Rome*, which dealt with the themes of wavering commitment, betrayal and alienation, was the subject of Cairncross's discussion. Shortly after this broadcast he was due to give another talk for the Third Programme on 'The Aristocratic Society' but had to cancel it due to illness. He enjoyed working with Anna Kallin, who was born in Russia but educated in Germany and, according to Isaiah Berlin, was 'a typical Moscow intellectual, high-grade, highbrow … a brilliant and interesting woman'.[2] Cairncross shared Kallin with some interesting participants, among them a young Eric Hobsbawm, who in the same period Cairncross was discussing Moravia, contributed to several programmes, including a review of a French satirical weekly, a feature on Karl Kraus's play *The Last Days of Humankind*, and a talk on British pamphleteering since 1870.[3]

Cairncross's main radio commitment was on 'Point de Vue' for the French section of the World Service programme, conducted entirely in French. From the late 1940s until he left the UK in 1952, he made the regular journey to Bush House for early afternoon recordings, with transmission scheduled for later in the evening.[4] His producer for Point de Vue was John Weightman, who, like himself, was a French scholar and translator, and would later go on to be a professor of French at Westfield College, University of London and a regular writer and reviewer for the leading literary magazines. During the war Weightman, a grammar-school-educated son of a Northumberland miner, had included coded messages of hope in his French service broadcasts to occupied France. In addition to producing and convening the panel, Weightman also presented the programmes, which normally amounted to chairing a discussion between Cairncross and other guests (some of whom would join from a line in Paris). Weightman normally asked Cairncross and the other panel members to share with the French public their knowledge of British government policy or comment on aspects of British society. Among the topics Cairncross was asked to address were 'The English middle classes' (on which he no doubt offered some Scottish insight), 'The future of political parties in England', 'Nationalisation', 'Why the British are "isolationist"' and 'The Civil Service Today', on which of course he had some first hand, if jaundiced, reflections. Had they been aware of it, MI5 would no doubt have been interested in his 'Point de Vue' of 16 May 1950, when he was asked for his opinion on why so many scientists were attracted to communism, coming so soon after the prosecution of the atom spies, Alan Nunn May and Klaus Fuchs. Weightman became a good contact, and they would keep in touch in later years as Cairncross attempted to launch his academic career. In addition to Point de Vue, he participated in several other French service programmes, including 'Six d'un Auteur d'un micro'. He contributed to the odd edition of the Brains Trust for the Third Programme, and more regularly for the Canadian Broadcasting Corporation, where he was introduced under the pseudonym Philip Sandeman. For his broadcasts he was paid 10–12 guineas each time, depending on the length of the programme.

His BBC commitments and wider desire to escape from his KGB trappings made it more difficult for Modin to make contact, and Cairncross missed or postponed several meetings. He had not welcomed further contact with the Russians but neither did he take decisive action to break from them. He had not confided in anyone and had no confidence that his civil service superiors would empathize with his position. The Cold War only darkened his pessimism. By this time he also had other things on his mind. Through mutual friends he had made the acquaintance during the war of Gabriella Oppenheim, a well-connected young German Jewish woman who had first come to London with her family to escape Nazism and had been granted British citizenship in 1934. In London she had worked at the Jewish Refugee Committee to help others in the same position. Born in Frankfurt, from a family of commodity traders, she shared Cairncross's love of music and German literature. She too had a talent for languages, and since her exile had travelled extensively, as members of her large family were scattered around Europe and the United States. After the war she had moved to California to join relatives, but after Cairncross had made his feelings known she returned to England, where they married at Kensington Registry Office in March 1951. Though he had had previous girlfriends and enjoyed the company of women in visits to the theatre or concerts, it was his first serious relationship. They seemed ideally suited. His travels in pre-war Germany had alerted him to the predicaments she and others faced while he held a deep appreciation of Jewish culture and heritage. Marrying a 'continental girl' did not surprise his mother, who gently chided him: 'You always wanted something different.'[5]

His mother may not have been surprised at the news, but his Soviet controller Modin was taken aback. Gabi was the type of sophisticated bourgeois wife his Soviet controllers had warned him against. She had picked up the good business sense of her family and until recently had been selling leather goods in West Hampstead. Of liberal persuasion, she had had no flirtations with communism and was more interested in art and culture than politics. News of their impending marriage might have helped Modin understand the irregularity of their meetings, though he was authorized to provide expenses for their honeymoon, which they spent at Graham Greene's villa Il Rosaio, in Anacapri.

Of more concern to Modin was how to procure more official documents from his reluctant spy. As a principal in the Treasury department which dealt with War Office personnel, Cairncross had been able to pass on some details on armed forces requirements. The possibility of increasing the volume occurred since he had been appointed Deputy Treasury Representative to the Western Union Finance Committee in

1950. The Western Union was an alliance of the UK, France, Belgium, Holland and Luxembourg, established by the Brussels Treaty of 1948 with the aim of developing military, economic and cultural cooperation between member states, though it would shortly be subsumed in significance by the founding of NATO. Cairncross's assistant in this role was Robert Armstrong who would later, as Margaret Thatcher's cabinet secretary, be given the task of preparing her parliamentary answers to the questions surrounding his public exposure as a spy. Modin revealed in his later account that, he was able to induce Cairncross to supply plans for NATO bases in Germany, a matter of obvious interest to Moscow, though much of the 'large quantity of important documents' on military equipment and expenditure received from Cairncross at this time has not been specified.[6]

Meetings remained problematic for Modin, partly because he found Cairncross to be regularly late or rushing to arrive on time for their 8.00 pm monthly meetings. He had quickly abandoned his predecessor's preference for meeting in pubs and got into the routine of approaching his agent from behind or from a darkened side street off a main road, so that he could ensure he was not being followed. Many of these meetings took place in open spaces on the far western reaches of London Underground's District Line, in Ealing or Gunnersbury, for example. However, on renewing contact with Cairncross, Moscow Centre believed – contrary to Modin's view – that security would be strengthened by providing him with a car, a decision which almost ended disastrously for both agent and controller. Cairncross had already indicated his lack of technical competence by his inability to use a camera to photograph documents, thereby continuing with the onerous task of handling volumes of data. The use of a car was even more of a challenge. He had initially put off buying a car – with funds provided by Moscow – before admitting to Modin that he did not possess a licence. Nevertheless, after he finally succeeded in passing his test, he picked up Modin in his new Vauxhall in the West London suburbs. His lack of confidence in driving was evident to Modin, but he did not expect him to suddenly stall in the middle of a busy road. As he desperately struggled to restart the vehicle, his predicament was noted by a policeman who motioned him out of the car, checked his licence and took over the driving seat next to Modin, where he examined the car, pushed the choke in, restarted the vehicle and moved it to a safer spot on the side of the road. All this time Modin, in the passenger seat, feared he would have to say something in his Russian accent, more questions would be asked and the confidential Whitehall documents that they had in the car would be inspected.

> Although this took only a few seconds it felt like an eternity. I dreaded that he would turn and say something to me, but he didn't. He parked the car as the breathless Cairncross rushed towards it.

> 'Now sir', said the bobby, measuring his words, 'you really ought to know the choke should be pushed in once the car's started up. Otherwise she floods. Good day to you, sir'.[7]

This close shave could have been deeply serious for Cairncross if their joint identities, together with the documents they were carrying, had become known. More serious threats to his future were to come.

As the danger of continuing with his secret work increased during the Cold War, Cairncross's value as a spy diminished. Predictably, deterioration in his relations with his Treasury boss, E. G. Compton (which he attributed to the latter's 'despotic character and fault finding'[8]) meant that he was transferred, initially to the foreign currency control department, and later to the Ministry of Supply in May 1951. Here, he acted as assistant to Elizabeth (Betty) Ackroyd, a career civil servant and a formidable presence in a government service largely dominated by men, who would shortly be appointed the undersecretary and would later become the first director of the Consumer Council. In the Ministry of Supply he dealt with armaments questions and was able to pass over 1,000 documents related to the completion of Britain's armament programme. He reported that working with Ackroyd had become difficult but, by now, he and Modin faced a more serious threat.

VENONA, a team of codebreakers set up in 1946 by Meredith Gardner of the Army Security Agency (ASA), had been decrypting messages sent between Moscow Centre and the US security agencies and had accumulated a mass of material which suggested serious Soviet infiltration. Klaus Fuchs, who like Alan Nunn May, had been employed on the TUBE ALLOYS project and subsequently on the Manhattan Project where he worked on the Plutonium bomb at Los Alamos Laboratory, was initially identified by VENONA. After admitting his espionage under interrogation from Jim Skardon, Fuchs, like Nunn May, was given a heavy prison sentence. Moscow Centre knew of the existence of VENONA in 1947, but the extent of its findings was only made clear to Kim Philby on his return from an MI6 posting in Istanbul, prior to departing for Washington for a new post as its key representative responsible for liaising with the CIA. Before leaving, Philby was briefed by his MI6 bosses, 'C' (Sir Stewart Menzies) and Maurice Oldfield, of counter-espionage, who told him that they were looking not only for an atom spy but also for a British diplomat working for Soviet intelligence under the codename 'HOMER'.[9] HOMER was Donald Maclean's codename, and the realization that British intelligence was on the trail of his friend drove Philby into an emergency meeting with Burgess who in turn alerted Blunt. Between them they managed to pass on the VENONA details to Modin in early December. It had not been enough to save Fuchs, but this collaboration between the 'Cambridge Four' was followed by further intense conspiring as the net closed around them.

The fear of imminent exposure took its toll on the four and all sought partial refuge in drink. Fears for Philby were compounded when his own codename 'STANLEY' was identified as someone who had been working for the Soviets in 1945. Despite his constant drinking, Philby was able to retain sufficient composure to carry out his duties in Washington, which included weekly meetings with James Jesus Angleton, the CIA's head of special operations. Burgess's behaviour became increasingly worrying as he spiralled recklessly through a succession of jobs, which took him from a promising post-war position as a personal assistant to Hector McNeil, Minister of State at the Foreign Office, through its Far East Department and finally – following a drunken binge in Gibraltar – to a spectacular finale in Washington, as a second secretary at the British Embassy. Lodging with Philby (presumably so that the latter could keep an eye on him), his alcoholism and drug use provoked erratic behaviour, which included insulting the wife of William Harvey, the CIA's investigator responsible for Soviet espionage. Finally, he was ordered to return to Britain in early May 1951 after being charged with three speeding offences on the same day.

Maclean had tried to bring his work for Soviet intelligence to a halt soon after news of HOMER became known. However, his note to Moscow Centre to that effect was not picked up until months later, by which time he was in the middle of a breakdown in Cairo, where he had been posted as a Counsellor and Head of Chancery. Here, drunken binges with his friend Philip Toynbee, including vandalizing the flat of the American Ambassador's secretary and violence towards his wife Melinda, ensured his early return; his 'breakdown' was reported to the FO's personnel department. Once back in London he was treated by a psychoanalyst in Wimpole Street, while taking up a new position as the head of the American department at the FO. He continued to drink and made several public outbursts in various clubs, where among other things he announced himself as the 'British Alger Hiss' and accused Goronwy Rees, Burgess's friend and one-time Soviet recruit, of 'ratting on us'. Knowing that he was being followed and that his actions were under surveillance, he grew increasingly fraught and fatalistic about his future.[10]

Having returned to London from Washington on 7 May, Burgess now sought out Maclean. He had seen little of him in recent years (they had been on alternative sides of the Atlantic for much of the time), but now, over lunch at the Royal Automobile Club, where Burgess was a member, they plotted an escape route. Yuri Modin had been instructed to tell Maclean to defect, which he also urged on Anthony Blunt, who Moscow felt could easily be implicated. Blunt, by now in comfortable and successful career roles as Director of the Courtauld Institute and Surveyor of the King's Pictures had no intention of leaving. More of a concern was what to do with Burgess. His defection would inevitably bring more suspicion on Philby. The official instruction Modin passed on from Moscow Centre was that Burgess should accompany Maclean only part of the way. In reality, the danger of Burgess being spotted with Maclean even for a short time would need explaining, and it seems that Burgess himself had come to the conclusion that if he left with Maclean he would not be returning. Perhaps he did not relish the inevitable interrogation from the security services should he stay. Burgess's decision to flee had significant consequences for Philby and the 'Cambridge Four'. Burgess's final week in London was a testament to his breadth of contacts, as he dipped in and out of the capital's exclusive clubs, made hurried phone calls to W. H. Auden and Goronwy Rees (among others), enjoyed an Apostles dinner, as well as saying last-minute goodbyes to his family, lovers and close friends.

For their part, MI5 had been watching Maclean closely – using their own codename CURZON – and after authorization had been received from the Foreign Secretary Herbert Morrison, had arranged to bring him in for questioning on Monday, 28 May. The central figures at the FO who were involved in the investigation of Maclean included William Strang, the deputy undersecretary at the FO – and Cairncross's former boss – and Roger Makins, Strang's deputy; both felt MI5 were too pedestrian in dealing with Maclean. In a now well-documented series of events, on Friday, 25 May – his thirty-eighth birthday – Maclean left the MI5 Watchers at Charing Cross station, as he boarded his commuter train to Kent. Burgess drove up to Maclean's house in Tatsfield where he was introduced to Maclean's wife Melinda and the Maclean children as 'Roger Styles' and, after dinner, they made a hasty departure to the port at Southampton where they scrambled aboard a pleasure cruiser for Saint Malo. On arrival the next morning they stayed on board for breakfast and then took a taxi to pick up the train at Rennes for Paris. Back in London, MI5 had been unaware that Maclean had taken a day's leave on Saturday, 26 May, and were only alerted to his disappearance on Monday, 28 May, the approved date for his interrogation.

As MI5 attempted to track them – they had been alerted early on by border control at Southampton – questions were raised about Burgess, who hitherto had not been linked to Maclean in any of the earlier leaks, though his connection to Philby (who had been linked) would prove vital. The search was on for other known communists at Cambridge in the same period as Burgess and Maclean, and John Cairncross was among those investigated. Cairncross, of course, knew nothing of Burgess and Maclean's espionage activities or the circumstances of their departure. It was only after their disappearance that he started to reflect on the possible significance of some of his earlier contacts with them.

The initial cause of MI5's suspicion of Cairncross was the relatively flimsy case of finding the letter sent to him with details of relations between Nazi Germany and fascist Italy that had been signed off 'With Fraternal Greetings'. He had already seen this in his file while working at MI6. Nevertheless, the seriousness of the Burgess and Maclean disappearance meant that at their next meeting in June he was fully briefed by Modin on how to handle any subsequent interview with the security services. Given he had been unaware of the espionage activities of Burgess and Maclean, there was little he could add to the case of the two diplomats. However, his own position became more precarious, and in light of the growing publicity surrounding the case he feared for his future, including its impact on his recent marriage.

His fears were confirmed when he was called to interview in September and first encountered Arthur Martin, the MI5 officer who would remain involved with his case for several years. Martin quizzed him about the 'Fraternal Greetings' letter and asked him to explain his involvement with the communist group at Cambridge. Desplte Martin's aggressive tone, Cairncross was able to explain away his communism as a brief flirtation (which was true) and denied any knowledge of the letter. His answers, however, had not entirely convinced the security services, and in December he was called for a second meeting, this time with Jock Whyte who continued with the same line of questioning. The pressure on Cairncross was growing. He avoided further monthly meetings with Modin and destroyed his photographic equipment (which he had never mastered). Although Modin had earlier told him of a contingency plan to get him to Prague, he had no intention of taking such a journey and his main concern was for his new wife, who had no knowledge of his spying. None of his family or acquaintances knew of his work for the Soviets and, unlike the members of the Cambridge Four, he had no friends in MI5 on his side.

Guy Liddell, MI5's Deputy Director, who played a major part in the ensuing interviews with friends and acquaintances of the 'missing diplomats' as they were now referred to, knew Burgess and was a close friend of Anthony Blunt. His diary entries reveal his initial refusal to believe either of them was implicated. At first he attributed Burgess's disappearance with Maclean to 'helping a friend who was in sex trouble'. A month after their disappearance and despite being told by Goronwy Rees that Burgess had confessed to him years before that he was a 'Comintern agent', Liddell remained sceptical.

I find it difficult ... to imagine Burgess as a Comintern agent in the ordinary accepted interpretation of those terms. He certainly had been Marxian, and, up to a point, an apologist for the Russian regime, and would have been capable of discussing in a highly indiscreet manner with anybody almost anything he got from official sources. He would have done this out of sheer political enthusiasm without any regard for security.[11]

The prospect of Anthony Blunt being in any way connected to Soviet espionage was even more unpalatable. Over several lunches at his club and elsewhere over the ensuing months, Liddell remained convinced of his friend's innocence. On 10 July, for example (a time when Blunt was worried about being incriminated by Burgess's lover Jack Hewitt who had made indiscreet comments to the press), Liddell was reassured by Blunt's explanation.

> I took the opportunity of asking Anthony again about his views on Marxian doctrine and the extent to which at any time he had been associated with communist activity. He told me that in his early days at Cambridge he had been associated with a number of communists, many of whom were fellow apostles. He has always been interested in the Marxian interpretation of history and artistry, but he had never believed in the way in which the Russians applied it, nor had he accepted or been interested in the purely political aspects of the Marxian teaching. He was quite emphatic that when Burgess approached him, I think in 1937, to assist him in obtaining political information of an anti-fascist kind, he was firmly under the impression that Burgess was working for the government. Burgess had never said to him anything which would imply that he was working for the Comintern.[12]

Over the following months as Blunt felt increasing pressure, partly in fear of losing his role as the Surveyor of the King's Pictures and partly worried that Jack Hewitt might carry out his threat to commit suicide, Liddell told Tommy Harris, a close friend of both Blunt and Burgess since the 1930s, that 'if Anthony did not pull himself together he might well be jeopardising the whole of his career'.[13] He continued to believe, however, that Blunt's 'reticence' in coming forward with more information was due to his 'personal loyalty' to Burgess. Even after Blunt's memory had improved sufficiently enough by mid-November to produce papers belonging to Burgess, Liddell was unyielding in his defence of Blunt.

> I think in fairness to Anthony, I should say, as regards Burgess' papers, he was at some pains, I think genuinely, to explain that he had not deliberately withheld them from us, but had quite honestly

forgotten about them. ... He realised that in the circumstances of our interview a poor construction might be put upon their sudden production, but hoped that I would believe him when he said that there was no more in it than forgetfulness and a failure in the light of later events to estimate their possible importance at the time of receipt.[14]

Blunt held a key to Burgess's pokey and scruffy top floor flat in Mayfair, and carried out what he intended to be a clearing up operation on behalf of Moscow Centre. Unfortunately for John Cairncross, he missed Burgess's guitar case which contained a variety of correspondence. After handing over the key to MI5 so they could search the property, a document came to light which implicated Cairncross. This was Cairncross's fourteen-page handwritten summary of FO officials' views on appeasement and the German invasion of Czechoslovakia. On further inquiry by MI5, John Colville, his old lunch companion at the Travellers (and Trinity College contemporary), was able to identify Cairncross by matching the dates in his appointments diary with those of the notes, while the latter's spidery handwriting was recognized by one of the secretaries. This was clearly more serious than the 'Fraternal Greetings' letter and led to MI5 putting him under surveillance, and eventually calling him in for interrogation.

'There seems to be a strong case against John Cairncross, now in the Treasury and was at one time in Section V', Guy Liddell noted in his diary on 4 March 1952.

A piece of paper in his handwriting, giving notes on interviews in 1939 with various officials in the Foreign Office and other departments, was found among documents belonging to Burgess. As Cairncross is of the same vintage as Burgess and Maclean and knew them both, it looks very much as if he was at one time an agent of Burgess.[15]

Leaving aside the error in Liddell's identification of Cairncross as 'of the same vintage as Burgess and Maclean' – they had both gone down prior to his arrival at Cambridge – this unambiguous statement suggests a firm belief early on in his MI5 interrogations that Cairncross was a spy. There was no excusal for him on the grounds of 'youthful enthusiasm', his initial explanation for Burgess's communism, nor, as in his seemingly unshakeable defence of Blunt, matured over several lunches, was the flirtation with communism attributed to interests in art and literature. Liddell's view of Cairncross had not been informed by personal knowledge or friendship and was quite possibly reinforced by his assumptions about the type of Communist Party members – lower middle class? Scottish? – he was monitoring in his daily work. Negative reports from the civil service about their difficult employee may also have swayed Liddell's views. In any case, Cairncross was now a significant suspect and was under serious investigation by the security services.

Following the earlier interviews with Arthur Martin and Jock Whyte, he was visited at the Treasury on 31 March by Jim Skardon, the former metropolitan police detective who had been seconded to MI5 during the war and who had succeeded in extracting confessions from Alan Nunn May, Klaus Fuchs and William Joyce ('Lord Haw-Haw') among others. Skardon was renowned for his skilful questioning technique in which friendly chatter helped to secure the trust of his suspects before he delivered more penetrative quizzing. Asked about his friendship with Burgess, Cairncross told Skardon they met infrequently at social gatherings and parties in London attended by such a range of personalities that he felt flattered to be invited. He also recalled travelling with Burgess from Cambridge to London by train in the spring of 1937, shortly after they first met. He told Skardon that he regarded Burgess as a political 'gossip', and that his ostentatious display of his sexuality and flirtatious behaviour made him feel uncomfortable.

After the discussion of Burgess's character, Skardon then passed Cairncross a copy of the fourteen-page document that had been found among Burgess's belongings, advising Cairncross that he believed it to be in his handwriting. Cairncross was 'shocked' and 'practically speechless' (according to Skardon's written account of the meeting) on reading through the document.[16] In his attempts to account for it, Cairncross emphasized the political seriousness of the German occupation of Czechoslovakia after the Munich Agreement, and the wide-ranging discussions that followed in and around the FO. He denied that the meetings with FO officials summarized in the document were pre-planned, though was unable to give a convincing answer as to why his lunch companions were referred to as 'my informants'. He told Skardon that he regarded his conversations with Burgess as informal political discussions and was completely unaware that Burgess intended to use it for any other purpose.

> The thing that shocked him the most was that this document should have been found amongst Burgess's belongings. If he had ever thought about it all, he was sure that he had recovered it from him.[17]

As things stood, there was little evidence against Cairncross, but Skardon told him that in the event of more information of 'other or similar activities' coming to light there could be grounds for prosecution.[18] Skardon also told him that his superiors at the Treasury had been informed of the investigation and that he would not be allowed to continue in his job. Cairncross told Skardon that he was worried less about losing his job than the damage to his name that would result from a conviction. After their interview, which lasted just over an hour, Skardon and his colleague John Simkins updated John Winnifrith at the Treasury of Cairncross's position, and Winnifrith formally suspended Cairncross later that afternoon.

In between Cairncross's meetings with Skardon, 'C' (Stewart Menzies), the head of MI6, took Kim Philby for lunch at the Travellers to inquire whether he would like an advance on the bonus he had received following his resignation from MI6. 'C' was convinced at this time that Philby was innocent, despite his close associations with Burgess and Maclean and what seemed to be mounting evidence that suggested otherwise. Guy Liddell advised 'C' that 'the only thing to do in cases of this kind, where one knows an individual fairly intimately, was to sink one's personal views and allow those concerned to get on with the job, purely on the basis of the ascertainment of facts. Otherwise one was liable to get misled'.[19] Advice that was strangely at odds with his own assessment of Anthony Blunt.

At their next meeting at the War Office on 2 April, Cairncross told Skardon that he had spent the intervening days reflecting on the earlier discussion and wished to make a statement. His statement described his educational background, his attraction to communism while a student, entering the FO, his first meeting with Maclean (at the FO) and the meeting with Burgess, Louis MacNeice and Anthony Blunt in 1937 and his knowledge of others in Burgess's circle like Harold Nicolson. His casual friendship with Burgess, he explained, led to political discussions at the time of appeasement which had resulted in his summaries of FO attitudes towards Chamberlain's appeasement policy. In his statement, Cairncross explained that he was 'under the impression that (Burgess) was in a secret department'. He also stated that Burgess told him he had burned the documents.

Skardon now saw 'discrepancies' in Cairncross's account. He noted from their discussion the fear that Burgess would 'have a hold over CAIRNCROSS as it would enable him to blackmail CAIRNCROSS into providing further secret information'. For Skardon this 'almost certainly' confirmed 'a knowledge of the sinister possibilities of this association with Burgess. At the very least it demonstrates that whatever he may have heard about BURGESS being employed in a secret department, he was not completely satisfied that BURGESS was entirely loyal.' Or, more likely, Cairncross was instructed to put forward that explanation by Modin and Moscow Centre. Nevertheless, Skardon seemed satisfied with his answers. At the conclusion of the meeting, Cairncross asked for assurances about his departure from the Treasury, indicating that he hoped a 'formula' for a resignation could be found to avoid the more damaging publicity that would follow a dismissal. Skardon had some sympathy for this and told him he would be in touch shortly to arrange a further meeting and that if he had to call him at home he would use the name Seddon to avoid possible anxiety for Cairncross's wife, Gabi.[20]

The next meeting was set for the following week in the same room. Surveillance on Cairncross was maintained over the coming days which only increased their suspicion that he had been involved in subversive activity. On one occasion, Watchers retrieved the latest copy of *Communist Review* (the Communist Party of Great Britain's monthly paper), after he had deposited it in a wastepaper basket while being trailed in a public park. 'It is difficult to see how a man who describes himself as having given up his communist ideas and as having become a Churchillian would go on wasting his time reading such turgid material,' Guy Liddell noted.[21] There were plenty of reasons why Cairncross may have been interested in it. It wasn't all 'turgid'; Eric Hobsbawm and Christopher Hill and other members of the CPGB's impressive history group were occasional contributors on aspects of the British radical tradition, and there were also reviews of Ralph Vaughan Williams and other composers. But perhaps the most likely reason is that one of *Communist Review*'s main writers was his old Cambridge friend James

Klugmann, the man who had brought him to Soviet intelligence in the first place. By April 1952 Klugmann was deeply in the mire of Cold War politics. The previous year on Moscow's orders, following the Stalin-Tito split of 1948, he had written *From Trotsky to Tito*, an absurd apology for Stalinism in which Klugmann denounced his old comrade Marshal Tito (whose communist partisans he had helped connect with the allies during the war) as a renegade acting on behalf of British intelligence. Klugmann's tribulations would no doubt have interested Cairncross rather more than Chinese leader Liu Shao-Chi's manual of 'How to Be a Good Communist' that was covered in the same issue.

More serious developments followed in the coming days. Under increasing surveillance and by now very concerned at where the Skardon interrogations may be leading, Cairncross requested an emergency meeting with Modin, which he activated by leaving a chalk mark in a defined spot. Before setting off to meet Modin he had an early evening meal at the Travellers but 'as I was going down the steps to the street I noticed, out of the corner of my eye, a porter rushing to the telephone'.[22] Now aware that he was being followed, he took a taxi from the Travellers and by a complicated detour arrived at Ealing Common underground station, the first point of contact with Modin before they convened at Gunnersbury Park, on another branch of the District Line of the London Underground. At Ealing Common, he waited at the bus stop outside the station. However, Modin, who had been slowly making his way along a side street that led into the main thoroughfare, had spotted what he thought were two intelligence officers waiting at the bus stop on the other side of the road to Cairncross. Modin decided not to go ahead. Cairncross, however, continued on to Gunnersbury Park. Suspecting, correctly, that he had been followed, and unaware that Modin had turned back, he lit up a cigarette: as a non-smoker it was his sign to abort the meeting.[23]

What MI5 made from his explanation that he was at Gunnersbury Park for a rendezvous with a married French woman (who did not show up) is difficult to tell from Skardon's subsequent report of their next meeting on 9 April. Despite this anomaly, Skardon did not succeed in eliciting a damaging confession. Skardon pointed to the apparent contradiction in Cairncross's statement that Burgess may be involved in 'secret work' for the British government while at the same time fearing that he could be blackmailed by Burgess to provide further material.

Despite Skardon's pressing, Cairncross dismissed it as more akin to an 'unpaid debt' that he was anxious to recover. 'It was quite impossible to shake him on this, and he seemed to be quite unaffected by the direct attack made upon him,' Skardon noted in his report. Skardon then asked Cairncross about Burgess's known contacts, including Blunt, Moura Budberg, Alexander Halpern, Frederick Kuh, James McGibbon, Wolfgang Pulitz, David Layton and others. He was also asked about his brother Alec – an economics contemporary of Philby at Cambridge. If Skardon was not entirely satisfied with Cairncross's responses, he was unable to hit on more fruitful lines of inquiry.

> Throughout the interview CAIRNCROSS behaved as though he had nothing to hide, and eventually satisfied me that he was 'coming clean' at every point. … I have the very pronounced feeling that he is completely under control.

(In the margin of the MI5 file, someone, presumably an MI5 colleague, has added 'Of whom?')

At the conclusion of the meeting they discussed his plans for the forthcoming Easter break, and Cairncross indicated that he would be spending it with his wife in the Cotswolds and that he planned to take a holiday in Italy in June. 'I did not ask him to surrender his passport, for in the circumstances I do not think it is justified or necessary', Skardon concluded. Following the interrogation of Cairncross, Guy Liddell noted in his diary that Skardon had done a good job, a view shared by civil service and security service chiefs. 'We are lucky to have got rid of Mr Cairncross when we did', Sir William Strang, Cairncross's former boss (and friend), who was now leading the investigation into the disappearance of Burgess and Maclean, reported back to Anthony Eden, the Foreign Secretary. But it was Cairncross himself, having outwitted his adversaries in MI5, who felt most relieved at the end of the interviews.[24]

Over the next few weeks Cairncross avoided Modin until the latter managed to make brief contact with him. At this last meeting, they agreed that further appointments would be too risky. In his memoirs, Modin claims he passed Cairncross a parting gift of cash (as a wedding present), though the amount is not specified.[25] Cairncross was obliged to resign from the Treasury, but he was now free. His intended 'holiday' to Italy would become a long-term affair, and he would only return to live in Britain for the last month of his life, over forty years later. For now he had escaped the clutches of both MI5 and the KGB. He was free, too, from a civil service career for which he had been entirely unsuited. Years afterwards, he felt sufficiently free from its shackles to gently mock his old employer in verse.

A Civil Service Love Song

MADAM, for long it has been clear to me
That, as I'm sure will be appreciated,
In your own interest this affair must be,
At your earliest convenience, terminated.

It is with deep regret that I transmit
This indication that our ways must part,
But this decision cannot be reversed, for it
Has not been lightly reached. With all my heart

I thank you for, in our joint operations,
Having preferred me to more senior wooers,
Wishing you better luck, happier relations
Next time, Madam, I *was* sincerely yours

Sir, in your letter of the twentieth,
You served me notice that our ways must part,
Brief was our meeting, yet, while I draw breath,
I will record the minutes in my heart.

Expect from me no strong representations,
My love, unprecedented, still endures,
For, Sir, despite this rupture of relations,
I am – unwillingly – forever yours.[26]

Chapter 12
An Italian escape

Cairncross's enforced resignation from the Treasury had given him the chance of a new start, albeit one with the shadow of the past hanging over him. One of his immediate tasks was to try and explain to his new wife Gabi why he was leaving the apparent security of the civil service to step into the unknown and persuade her to leave her adopted country and start over. As a refugee she could hardly have relished another major move, even if his plan to launch an academic and writing career or seek out the possibilities of working for the new United Nations had its appeal. For the moment, Italy was just another holiday destination while the couple considered their future life together. Without knowing the circumstances of Cairncross's resignation, Lord Hankey was also surprised to hear his news, though offered support for his 'interesting' idea of a new career, while warning against impetuosity.

> I always tell people who are leaving a job … you should never leave one job until you have another in your pocket. … That much said, I need hardly say that I should be more than delighted if you decide to use my name as a reference for either UNESCO or Oxford for what it is worth and if the need arises I will do my best to help you.[1]

His brother Alec, when he heard of John's resignation from the civil service, was sceptical of his reasons for seeking a new start. At the time, however, he was – as usual – occupied with his own career. At the same time his brother was explaining to MI5 officers the reasons for his flirtation with communism at Cambridge (and hiding his Soviet links),

Alec was at an international conference of economists in Moscow, paid for by the Soviet Union. He and the other members of the visiting party, which included Sidney Silverman, the Labour MP, Lord Boyd Orr, the Chancellor of Glasgow University, and assorted academics, were there ostensibly to discuss trade between East and West. Unsurprisingly, they saw it as an opportunity to get a glimpse of Soviet society at first hand. As Alec later described his visit on the BBC's Third Programme, the Moscow he found was 'dowdy and depressing', with 'cheap but crowded' public transport. He alluded to the 'narrowness of Soviet culture', with little evidence of Western art in its galleries. When the group got on to the streets, they were questioned by Soviet citizens for their views on America, the prospect of a 'united Europe' and the rearmament of Germany.[2] In his memoirs Alec pondered over the purpose of the visit and what the Soviet Union got out of it. 'Was it all propaganda? Was it from weakness or self-confidence that we were invited? Was it in preparation for a post-Stalin regime? Or to break the partial blockade operated by the West?'[3]

Back in London, his brother was grateful that there was no need for his Soviet controllers to put any emergency escape plan in place. Instead of the prospect of suffering Soviet art, he was now drawn to the cultural and artistic opportunities offered by Western Europe. But he needed a job. Ideally, he would have liked to do more work for the BBC and find an academic post somewhere. His friend Douglas Parmée was by now a fellow of Queen's College, Cambridge, and already immersed in research for what would be a prodigious output of writings and translations. Cairncross himself continued making hopeful applications for academic posts, supported by the impressive services of Graham Greene and Lord Hankey as referees.

Despite the insecurity of his position, he had not at this point discounted remaining in the UK if the right job came along; he was not, after all, facing an immediate risk of prosecution, even if he knew it was always possible that his association with the spies and his Cambridge communist links would become more widely known. But a couple of articles in John Lehmann's literary magazine *Penguin New Writing* was the sum of his publications and not enough to convince the BBC drama department that his French translations were ready for transmission. 'It is staid, stiff and undramatic and the grandeur, the brilliant economy and the supple dramatic power of the original are lost', producer Helena

Wood commented after Cairncross had submitted his version of Racine's Andromaque.[4] Despite more lobbying of Rayner Heppenstall, the BBC's drama producer, he could not convince them to take up his ideas. This was the beginning of a battle with the BBC that would go on for the next decade or so until they finally took his work seriously. Heppenstall, writer, friend of George Orwell who had produced a version of *Animal Farm* for BBC Radio, was a fellow Francophile, though also a man of forthright opinions. He cut short their six-month correspondence by questioning 'whether there is very much point in your periodically writing to remind me of your existence'.[5]

Cairncross was in need of a new start. His proposed holiday to Italy had sparked a desire to return to the island of Capri, which he had visited previously and where he and Gabi had recently spent their honeymoon at Graham Greene's villa, Il Rosaio. He initially planned to stay for a period at Il Rosaio (rent-free) to get down to some serious writing and launch what he hoped to be a literary career. Capri's literary associations held much appeal for him, and its short-term residents in the past had included his favourite Austrian poet, Rainer Maria Rilke, who spent time on the island from 1906 to 1908 and was mesmerized by its charm and natural beauty. Capri was a renowned refuge for exiles of various sorts. Maxim Gorky, escaping from the repressive atmosphere of Russia in the years immediately prior to the revolution, spent seven years on the island, where he hosted Russian revolutionaries and established a school for socialists, which he considered to be an ideal refuge from bourgeois culture. Gorky would later return to the island with his mistress Moura Budberg, a future friend of Cairncross. If Cairncross had reached Capri in 1952 he might have met the exiled Chilean poet Pablo Neruda who resided for some months on the island after having to leave his own country under threat of arrest by the Chilean authorities. However, on this occasion, the Cairncrosses' plans came to nothing. Greene had already agreed to let his house to friends throughout the summer and autumn of 1952.

Therefore, when John and Gabi first set off for Europe in June 1952 they had only a vague idea of where they would finally settle and were still undecided on what to do with their Lansdowne Crescent flat. (In the end, they kept it on for several years.) Still in possession of the car bought for him by the KGB, it was left to his wife Gabi, a more experienced driver, to transport them through Europe. Gabi was still unaware of the reasons for his resignation and perturbed by the instability in their living arrangements. She knew he had strong literary and writing ambitions and had always been keen to travel, but they left London without definite plans. An uncertain summer and winter followed, during which he and Gabi spent some odd days and cold nights travelling through France. At the end of June they put up in a hotel in Paris, where they were joined by Gabi's mother. By mid-July, however, they had moved on to the Jura region, in eastern France, where they rented a pied-à-terre for a few weeks, before heading for Switzerland. Here, they waited for news of John's applications for lecturer posts to Oxford, Cambridge and Glasgow universities. These had been enhanced by a 'wonderful testimonial' from his old tutor Harry Ashton, but while in Jura they heard the sad news that Ashton had died, just a month after writing the reference.[6]

They reached Switzerland in August, where they met some of Gabi's cousins, who, on hearing rumours of her recent 'changes' from an old aunt, were expecting to find her pregnant. Gabi, Cairncross's elegant, sophisticated wife wanted a family of her own, and the early uncertainty over their future as they made their way through Europe cannot have made a comfortable beginning to their married life. With her own family spread between America and Europe, she was exasperated at having to vacate their London home to stay in 'these dreadful places'.[7] She had only just got to know her Cairncross in-laws and relatives, who had been quick to adopt her. Her niece Frances had visited them at Lansdowne Crescent, and she was looking forward to spending holidays with her new relatives in Scotland.

While they were in Switzerland, they also met Alec, now back from the Soviet Union and keen to understand more of his brother's decision to resign from the civil service. Initially sceptical, he was now 'shocked' at what he saw as his brother's 'irresponsibility' in leaving a job without another one lined up and, even worse, without any savings.[8] Still in the dark over the circumstances of John's departure from Britain, and not entirely convinced by his new career plans, Alec provided financial help. He would do this intermittently over the following forty years together with occasional moral support and advice and useful contacts for his brother's writing projects or policy consultancies.

Their decision to settle in Italy was made possible through friends and relatives of Gabi's, who came to their help and offered them rooms in their large house in the Monteverde Vecchio district of Rome, near the Villa Doria Pamphili, a seventeenth-century residence within a large landscaped public park on the Gianicolo hill. Franco and Jole Lombardi had been active in the Italian resistance movement during the fascist years. Gabi, who had got to know them on a previous stay in Italy, was related to their governess. She now introduced her husband to the family, at the beginning of what would be an enduring friendship. Franco Lombardi was a professor of German philosophy who because of his Jewish background and opposition to the regime was exiled under Italian fascism. After the fall of fascism, Jole became a socialist member of the constituent assembly which drew up the democratic principles of the post-war Italian Constitution; she was, at the time, the youngest parliamentarian and one of few women in Italian politics. Jole's brother Enzo Tagliacozzo was a history professor who was forced into exile after refusing to swear his allegiance to Mussolini by taking the *tessera*, the fascist party card, which the regime demanded of all professors and teachers. Tagliacozzo first sought exile in London, where he worked for Radio Londra, the Italian section of the BBC, which had been set up in September 1938 to broadcast to Italian citizens. As well as providing news and information denied to them by the regime, Radio Londra broadcasted coded messages to those in the Italian resistance.

After Italy entered the war, Tagliacozzo managed to find a place on the last boat leaving Britain for America, where he joined members of the Rosselli family, including Amelia Rosselli, the mother of the two Rosselli brothers who had been murdered by fascist agents in France in 1937. Once in the United States, Tagliacozzo worked as assistant to Gaetano Salvemini, the unofficial leader of the exiled Italian intellectuals, at Harvard University. With Davide Jona, Tagliacozzo and Salvemini published the anti-fascist review *Controcorrente*, a non-aligned journal which sought to challenge the appeasement of Italian fascism internationally. This brought them into conflict with Italian-American supporters of Mussolini, as well as right-wing Catholic groups and an antisemitic Boston Cardinal. *Controcorrente* was one of the leading journals among a plethora of publications produced by exiled Italians which sought to counter the spread of fascism by restating the ideals of liberty and democracy. Though it didn't espouse a party line, it held to a broadly liberal-republican philosophy rooted in the secular enlightenment tradition. These ideas were shared more widely by the

Mazzini Society, in which Tagliacozzo and Salvemini were also active. They were involved, too, in *L'Italia Libera*, a republican and socialist newspaper which sought to continue the work of Carlo Rosselli.[9]

John Cairncross found himself, therefore, in the fortunate position of starting his own exile with stimulating friends, who had experience of resisting fascism at close hand, and whose left-wing liberal-socialist principles he broadly shared and, indeed, had encountered while at the Sorbonne in the early 1930s. The Lombardis had similar cultural interests in music and literature and staying with them was certainly a much better start to their life in Rome than the Cairncrosses might have expected. Given Cairncross's own anti-fascist commitments and criticisms of British government policy towards Italy and Germany, they would have had much to discuss. The Lombardis introduced them to other friends and played an important part in helping Cairncross to build more interesting social circles than the ones he had left behind in London. The Tagliacozzos were living nearby (the Tagliacozzo brother and sister had married the Lombardi brother and sister), and Cairncross would be a regular visitor to their home, where early in his stay he provided English lessons for Signora Tagliacozzo, helping her to qualify as an English teacher, while at the same time enjoying 'high level discussions about literature'.[10]

If their new environment was agreeable, then their surroundings were also very pleasant. Villa Doria Pamphili had been close to a site of a major battle during the short-lived Roman republic in 1849, when Garibaldi and his supporters tried to resist the attempts of French troops to return Pope Pius IX. That might have appealed to Cairncross as much as the art nouveau and the Roman ruins in the English garden. Despite the uncertainty in their lives, at least these were ideal conditions to begin a new life. Porta Portese market in nearby Trastevere would be another favourite haunt for Cairncross, and he started a long habit of taking off early on Sunday mornings in search of second-hand books and prints and the odd necklace for Gabi.

Rome in this period was still recovering from the effects of war and German occupation – it had been bombed by Allies and Nazis alike. It was the 'neo-realist' period when Italian cinema captured the harsh social realities in the years before the Italian economic boom of the mid-1950s to the late 1960s. It was the time too of *Roman Holiday*, the film which starred Audrey Hepburn as a crown princess who sought release from the official constraints of her embassy by exploring Rome's narrow streets and ancient landmarks – the beginning of the actress's own love affair with the city.

Mostly, though, Italian intellectuals and writers sought to make sense of the new post-war world by grounding their art in the realities of poverty, unemployment and criminality through films like *Bicycle Thieves*, *Rome: Open City*, *La Terra Trema* and others. Among the mix of Roman and more recent ruins, there were the beginnings of new housing projects to cater for those left homeless by war as well as for those migrants from southern Italian towns and cities. This new housing included some of the apartment complexes in the Monteverde area along via Donna Olimpia, leading on to Pamphili Park. Pier Paolo Pasolini, who came to live in the area a year after Cairncross moved in, would set his novel *Ragazzi di Vita* in the surroundings of these buildings. Despite the glamour of *Roman Holiday*, the 'Dolce Vita' was still some years away and the city's darker side was still evident, in cases like the murder of Wilma Montesi which implicated the post-war Italian political class in a prolonged scandal while 'offer[ing] a grand narrative of a city that was struggling to find a new sense of itself'.[11]

Nevertheless, post-war Rome was a city in which it was possible to live well, and Italy as a country held many attractions for the Cairncrosses. They found its way of life, its food, climate and hospitality more congenial than the austere Britain they had left. They both spoke fluent Italian which gave them access to its facilities and the ability to negotiate Italy's complicated bureaucracy while also enabling new and lasting friendships. It also meant that seeking work was less onerous than it might have been, and Gabi quickly found employment as a trilingual secretary in the Food and Agricultural Organization of the United Nations (FAO). John took on a mixture of roles as translator at the FAO, consultant at the Banca Nazionale del Lavoro at its offices in Via Veneto (the street immortalized a few years later by Federico Fellini's *La Dolce Vita*) and occasional contributor to the foreign press. He relished his part-time work as a foreign correspondent and penned stories for *The Economist*, *The Observer* and *The Glasgow Herald*, while continuing his association with the Canadian Broadcasting Company (CBC). Alec had worked briefly for *The Economist* in 1946 under Geoffrey Crowther, whose editorship transformed the magazine by increasing its circulation and introducing talented writers and journalists. John Cairncross's links with *The Economist* were with its veteran correspondent Cecil Sprigge and his wife Sylvia, herself a former war correspondent in Italy for the *Manchester Guardian*. Cecil Sprigge had been the founding director of Radio Italia at the BBC during the war where Cairncross may have first met him, or may have been introduced to him through Enzo Tagliacozzo. Both Sprigges were long-time experts on Italy (Cecil Sprigge was first appointed as a Rome correspondent in 1923), and they were also well connected to Italian intellectual circles, with Cecil a close friend of philosopher Benedetto Croce. By the time Cairncross arrived in Rome, Sprigge was coming to the end of his period as a correspondent and Cairncross was happy to pick up bits of journalism where he could.

Cairncross was proud of his association with *The Economist* and hoped it would be the start of a new career as a correspondent. He was 'flattered' by the warm reception of his early articles, as he attempted to make sense of the bewilderingly complicated contours of Italian politics. He subscribed to the view of a friend that 'it is as difficult to put the whole of Dante on a postage stamp as it is to explain the Italian situation in five minutes'. However, he was praised for his astute observation that the '*immobilismo*' of the government of Mario Scelba, a Sicilian Christian Democrat, had been such an obstacle to economic development that it was likely to be a short-lived experiment.[12] His work for *The Economist* consisted of full-length articles and pieces that could be used in editorials. He also sent in several articles that were not published, but for which he was paid a retainer fee. As was *The Economist*'s custom, his articles were published without a byline.

His fortunes at *The Economist* changed, however, following the arrival of Andrew Boyd as its foreign editor in 1955. Boyd, not one to hold back his views, started to question some of Cairncross's forecasts. These had 'not made it easy to draw on your material as a basis for editorial comment', the forthright Boyd told his part-time Rome correspondent. Boyd wanted more 'simplification instead of so many intricate and sometimes unnecessarily oblique references to events and personalities whose importance is not easy to gauge here'. He also regretted that 'on more than one occasion you have made a mountain out of a molehill'.[13] In Cairncross's long replies (the length of his letters often double the size of an average article) he defended his political forecasts, pointing out that other colleagues had thought them 'sound'. Cairncross winced at the 'unjustified slight on my professional ability', quibbled over payments and, with some justification, reminded Boyd that the Italian political situation was one of 'convoluted intricacy. Nothing in Italy means what it says. Everything is a façade.'[14] As if to demonstrate the point, his last article was a report on the San Marino election in August 1955, a spectacle in which the Christian Democrats unusually promoted the emancipation of women and their communist–socialist opponents were accused of bringing forward the election date to catch out the 'reactionaries' still on their summer holidays.

The previous year he had been sent by the Canadian Broadcasting Corporation (CBC) to Trapani in Sicily to cover the Easter celebrations, a ritual that had existed since Spanish occupation of the island four centuries earlier and consisted of 'The Procession of the Mysteries', (different artistic representations of The Passion and the death of Christ) being carried on a float through the streets of the city, to the sounds of evocative music and emotional weeping.[15] While in Sicily, he interviewed (for the *Boston Globe*) a young woman from a poor suburb of Syracuse who during her pregnancy the year before had claimed to have seen the weeping Madonna. This was an event which had brought hundreds of thousands of pilgrims to the city and had received the endorsement of the miracle by the city's archbishop, while the communists attempted to discredit the whole phenomenon. For Cairncross, it was a 'fascinating human drama', which in its repercussions had intensifed 'the struggle for the soul of Sicilians between the Vatican and the Kremlin'. It was 'an Italy that had almost disappeared', he recalled later, 'and one which I found fascinating'.[16]

His pieces for *The Observer* were probably arranged through Wayland Young, then its Rome correspondent. Young had a deep interest across the arts as well as a particular interest in political scandals, which resulted in books on the Wilma Montesi and John Profumo cases and commentary on the *Lady Chatterley's Lover* trial. He also shared Cairncross's interest in the history of sexuality in Western societies. Young, later a Labour peer as Baron Kennet (who defected to the Social Democratic Party after its formation in 1981), was renowned for outspoken and heretical positions, which would also have chimed with Cairncross. In addition to eliciting the odd article and piece of research from Cairncross, it is likely that Young, who was well connected and enthusiastic for new ideas, helped him discover more of Rome's literary salons.[17]

Here, Cairncross quickly felt at home, finding the stimulating and more open salons agreeable while occasionally flattered by the respect afforded him as a British scholar with a wide of knowledge of European literature. Italy's intellectuals of the early 1950s remained strongly influenced by the experience of fascism and the need to rebuild not only Italy's democracy but also its cultural life. Many had played a role in the resistance movement, and the Italian Communist Party (PCI) as the largest influence in the partisan struggle grew to become a mass party of two million members. As such it retained a hold over most of post-war Italy's cultural life, with leading film directors, writers and artists in its ranks. With his ambivalence towards ideology and activism, he found a looser milieu more appealing, notably in the group around *Lo Spettatore*. This was a monthly magazine founded in 1948 by Elena Croce, editor, translator of German literature (and daughter of the liberal philosopher Benedetto Croce) and her husband Raimondo Craveri. Craveri was an author, banker, economist and one of the founders of the Partito D'Azione (Action Party), another of the anti-fascist movements inspired by the liberal socialism of Carlo Rosselli. Craveri and Elena Croce did more than run a magazine; they hosted a cosmopolitan salon of scholars and writers steeped in the tradition of the European Enlightenment, but who now sought a radical edge to Italy's post-war cultural predicament.

Craveri and Cairncross became friends. They had much in common. During the war Craveri had been a member of ORI, a non-communist partisan group which organized secret missions in the north of Italy and sought to be a bridge between the British and Americans and the Italian Committees of National Liberation (CLN). In the autumn of 1943, Craveri set up a 'clandestine network of radio transmitters, couriers and centres of information which helped the Allies and also greatly facilitated the difficult task the Committees of National Liberation had in giving cohesion to the independent autonomous initiatives that spring up'.[18] Some of Craveri's fellow members of Partito D'Azione, including Ugo La Malfa, became prominent post-war politicians. After the war Craveri, who himself published books on Voltaire and political economy, sought to break down the barriers between the communist and Catholic traditions by inviting Franco Rodano, a Catholic communist, as well as liberal writers and non-Italian intellectuals, to contribute to the magazine. *Lo Spettatore* was more political than some of the other cultural magazines of that time, while it was more eclectic in the range of its articles, reviews and commentary.

In many ways Craveri, like Cairncross, was a bourgeois radical, a stalwart opponent of fascism who was too suspicious of orthodox ideologies to commit to a party line. Craveri, like Cairncross, admired seventeenth-century antiques and artwork, with a particular interest in Persian ceramics. As a successful businessman and banker, his professional work was in the sphere of political economy and in the early 1960s would employ Cairncross at his political consultancy. These common interests as well as their experiences in different wartime intelligence roles would have given them much to discuss. Some mystery has been attributed to Craveri's precise wartime roles, given his work at different times for the Office of Strategic Services (OSS), America's wartime intelligence agency, as well as leading the ORI partisans, but his contribution to the resistance struggle was significant and anti-fascism remained a defining part of his outlook. His wife Elena Croce provided the main cultural input, using her connections with writers and philosophers and her experience in editing and publishing, to draw in contributors.

Intellectual stimulation apart, Cairncross's occasional journalism was not sufficient or regular enough, and he gradually found a more sustainable income from translating and editing. The UN had proved fruitful in this regard, and from 1955 he began a long association with it which continued for over twenty years, the longest of all his spells of employment, even if it extended over different contracts and consultancies. As Gabi was already working for the UN as a trilingual PA, it made sense for them to move to Switzerland once he had the chance of more translation work. Switzerland held other attractions and possibilities. His work on Molière had progressed, and he had completed his investigation into the origins of Tartuffe, but to-date had enjoyed no luck with British publishers. He thought there was a better chance with a small Swiss publishing firm that had been recommended to him. In the spring of 1955 the Cairncrosses drove through Italy (stopping off in Milan so they could see an Etruscan exhibition), then on to Lyons, before arriving in Montreux, where they stayed in the resort of Orgevaux. Here they were joined by Alec and his wife Mary before his brother took up a new post in Washington as director of the Economic Development Institute at the World Bank. Gabi had recently returned from an enjoyable time with her Cairncross relatives in Scotland and the north of England, which she was visiting for the first time. They still had their place in Holland Park, and she returned regularly in their first years away, though she now found London 'overwhelming' after Rome. While she was in London she also felt obliged to carry out errands for John, as he himself was unenthusiastic about returning to Britain. She was still unaware of the real reason for his reticence to accompany her, which he normally put down to a lack of tlme: 'With every mail, John sends another letter with ideas of what I could do now that I am here – find some books in Charing X Road, contact some people, get information etc etc.' Although she often had the company of her mother, who was then staying in their London flat, she valued the time she spent with Alec, Mary and their children on picnics and visits: 'I feel richer for having made friends with your children and enjoyed every moment with them. ... I do hope we will be together in the future, more often than in the past. It does seem a shame to be so far away.'[19]

It was not only Gabi who John relied on to pick up books for his research. Prior to their departure, Alec was also asked to drop in at Lansdowne Crescent to retrieve some books on seventeenth-century French literature which would enable the completion of his brother's book on Molière. Switzerland was a more hopeful prospect for both work and publishing and over the next year they gradually moved their base from Rome to Geneva, returning to the Conches area outside the city which they had got to know during their early months travelling in Europe. However, while John now had the chance of more regular translation work at the UN in Geneva, Gabi was still filling in with temporary jobs at the UN in Rome. Here, she was introduced to some leading economists and administrators over for official visits and sometimes acted as their unofficial guide to the old city. On one occasion, she found herself showing John Kenneth Galbraith and his wife the sights of Rome. Galbraith, regarded as an expert on agriculture and development, had just returned from a spell as adviser to the Indian government (where he later would return as an ambassador under John F. Kennedy). She was impressed with his 'encyclopediac mind' as one who 'wanted to have all the information available'.

Lake Geneva had its attractions over living in the city, even if Gabi found the cost of living more expensive than in Rome. It was 'pretty relaxing', John told Alec, 'which is just as well. One is tempted to link it with Calvinism on weather grounds alone. (It does rain a lot)'.[20] His work at the UN in Geneva had prospered with the help of an old friend, Tania Alexander, whose husband Bernard was a leading official at the United Nations High Commissioner for Refugees (UNHCR). Tania was the daughter of Moura Budberg, the extraordinary Russian aristocrat, whom Cairncross had got to know in London in the early 1940s. It was likely Cairncross had met Tania at her mother's salons. Like her mother, Tania was 'a very cultivated woman',[21] of a similar age to himself. In London she had built a promising career in editing and publishing, and her enthusiasm for Russian and German literature was a point of common interest between the two, while Cairncross would no doubt have admired her access to writers. They had kept in touch since he had left London, and she was now able to welcome him to Geneva. In late 1956, she invited him and another new UNHCR employee, Declan Walton ('the first Irishman to walk through the doors of the UN looking for a job'), for early evening drinks. At this time the UNHCR had had to deal with floods of refugees leaving Hungary for Austria in the aftermath of the Soviet invasion, and Walton, who was a German speaker, had been given the task of going to Vienna to liaise with the Austrian government, where he remained under the supervision of Bernard Alexander. Tania thought Walton and Cairncross had similar interests and introduced them. They became firm friends. 'He was the only person at the UN I could talk to about German literature. I rather took to him', Walton recalled (Figures 6–10).[22]

Figure 6 Entering the Foreign Office. Reproduced by kind permission of the Syndics of Cambridge University Library.

Figure 7 At the Treasury in 1948. Reproduced by kind permission of the Syndics of Cambridge University Library.

Figure 8 John Cairncross with Gabi (and in-laws) at their wedding in 1951. Reproduced by kind permission of the Syndics of Cambridge University Library.

Figure 9 With Gabi in Piazza Navona, Rome, in the early 1950s. Reproduced by kind permission of the Syndics of Cambridge University Library.

Figure 10 Relaxing in their spacious house in Bangkok. Reproduced by kind permission of the Syndics of Cambridge University Library.

Chapter 13
Professor Cairncross

Since his departure from Britain, Cairncross had been determined to give more time to his scholarship. The failure to get an academic post had been a setback but did not deter him; he knew that his chances of succeeding without major publications were slim. He had had the idea of a book on Molière since Cambridge when, under the guidance of his tutor Harry Ashton, he became intrigued by *Tartuffe*, Molière's play which pointed fun at the *faux dévots* – those hypocrites who feign religious virtue and piety as a way of ingratiating themselves with people of influence. Encouraged by Ashton, Cairncross believed that the original version of *Tartuffe* was a *complete* play of three acts rather than a fragment of a later five-act production, which became the accepted version of the play. After embarking upon a serious investigation of the available sources, dealing along the way with the various secondary interpretations of Molière's work by generations of scholars, he maintained that the earlier three-act play had been replaced with the five-act version as a direct consequence of the attacks made on Molière by the religious authorities and leading elements of the French aristocracy. Following *Tartuffe*'s first three-act performance in the presence of King Louis XIV in Versailles in May 1664, a tirade of criticism and controversy followed, as leading clerics denounced it for the harmful effects it posed for the church and its potential threat to the social order. Despite the King's sympathy for Molière (he had praised the play as a light-hearted comedy), the archbishop of Paris declared that he would excommunicate advocates of the play, including those who read, performed and even attended its performance. Under such pressure, the King himself forbid its public performance In its existing form. The play had been subsequently revised in light of these attacks and under the threat of prosecution.

Cairncross was convinced that Molière's original and complete three-act play – the *Urtartuffe* as he called it – more accurately reflected the playwright's portrayal of the hypocrisy of those who used religion to curry favour with ruling elites. The *Urtartuffe* also suggested Mollère was more radical in his views, notably his critique of religious elites, than he had been credited by many *Molièristes*. Molière's work was satire and he was rightly renowned as a master of comedy, but his ideas should also be considered for their critical interrogation of the manners and customs of emerging bourgeois society. One of the aspects of Molière's thought which had appealed to Cairncross since he had studied *Ecole des Femmes* at university was the more progressive role he envisaged for women. This was another aspect which had upset the clerics.

Cairncross had developed an earlier taste for the investigative side of research through the experience of working with his brother Andrew on their book on Shakespeare's attitude to money, intended for a French publisher. This was a project they had started when he was still in the civil service and was one of the writing commitments he cited in his attempts to explain his resignation to Alec in 1952. The brothers invested a significant amount of time in the preparation of the chapters, with John taking on the joint tasks of analysing the significance of money in that era and translating the work, with Andrew Cairncross providing insight on the playwright's life and thought. However, the two Cairncross brothers could not agree on where the primary focus of their collaborative work should lie. John felt his contribution – including the translation – was worthy of most credit, while Andrew thought that, as the Shakespeare authority, his contribution should be more prominent. Consequently, and despite completing two different draft manuscripts, *Shakespeare and the Age of Gold* was never published.[1]

One of the difficulties he faced when researching Molière was that there was no existing contemporaneous documentary evidence to explicitly support his propositions. Most of the contemporary documents he examined made no mention of an incomplete earlier play, while he was also sceptical of the claims made by Molière's actor-manager, La Grange, who maintained that it was an incomplete version. Cairncross believed La Grange's testimony was unreliable as his Private

Register, which kept details of the plays, was often amended with hindsight. Instead, Cairncross undertook painstaking analytical work to demonstrate that the *Urtartuffe* was a complete version. This largely depended on demonstrating that the original play consisted of Acts I, III and IV only, and that Acts II and V (which included a warm praise of the King) were out of step with the other acts, contained less elegant writing and were therefore likely to be later additions. This analysis he put together in concise, pithy and compact exposition amounting to no more than eighty pages and enhanced with a preface by the eminent French scholar Raymond Picard, a valued friend in subsequent years.

However, finding a publisher for his book *New Light on Molière* was not an easy task for an unpublished author without an academic home, and it was only after his move to Switzerland that he succeeded, with the help of Eugénie Droz, in publishing it in 1956. Droz, in addition to running her own publishing house in Geneva, was a noted Romance scholar and prolific writer and editor, well acquainted with the works of Molière. She was enthusiastic and took on the book. The reviews of his first book were favourable and must have given him much pleasure (and relief to his publisher) while vindicating the time spent on his research. The *Times Literary Supplement* (*TLS*) praised his book as 'an ingenious piece of detective work'.[2]

Buoyed by this success, he committed more time to scholarship and settled into a regular routine of working late after his daytime job at the UN. His UN work provided his regular income, but he had also found it more stimulating than most of his civil service roles. He had quickly moved from translating to composing policy briefings, editing papers and attending meetings and conferences. He had made good contacts in the Geneva and Washington offices, and it seemed that his earlier wish for a job which enabled him to travel would finally be realized. In 1957 a new opportunity arose for him at the UN to become the chief editor of the Economic Commission for Asia and the Far East (ECAFE). This took him and Gabi to Bangkok, where they enjoyed a good quality of life with sufficient time for him to get on with his writing and even attend academic conferences. After a month in a hotel they were provided with a large house in spacious grounds, with varnished wooden shutters, teak furniture, 'a beautifully tiled bathroom with shower and a tiny square bath' and two servants to help them with the upkeep and their occasional entertaining. The work itself started at 7.00

am and finished at 4.00 pm, with official transport taking him to and from his office through the congested traffic composed of trams, buses (made from converted lorries) and 'pedicabs', driven by taxi drivers dressed in shirts and straw hats.[3] Gabi enjoyed their new affluence and the freedoms and status it afforded as the wife of a leading official and, with a keen interest in Thailand's history and culture, took a part-time job in the tourist office.

The work itself he found interesting as he did his 'extremely pleasant and stimulating colleagues'. He saw his role as the chief editor as important in addressing vital questions on agricultural development, such as utilizing mineral resources for electricity and irrigation. He believed in this work and regarded it as central to the objective of raising living standards. However, news of his appointment had come to the attention of MI5 in London who notified A. F. Maddocks, a diplomat based in the Far East, to keep an eye on him during his time there. Maddocks's wife knew Erica Propper, a friend of Gabi's, and attempted through Mrs Propper to establish more information about the Cairncrosses. However, all that could be ascertained was that Erica and Gabi shared a Jewish background in Germany and had known each other since their time there.[4] MI5 had not kept Cairncross under surveillance since his departure from London, and they found nothing in Bangkok to suggest he still had any Soviet contacts. Nor was his work of a sensitive nature as far as the security services were concerned. They retained their interest in him, however.

Cairncross enjoyed Thailand, describing it as 'a land of enchantment' and developed a great affection for the people and their attitude to life. He was particularly impressed by their 'tolerance' which he regarded as their 'most notable and enduring characteristic'.[5] He used the long evenings to begin what became an abiding though ultimately unfulfilled research project on the history of seventeenth-century Siam. He would work on this for many years but never succeed in finding a publisher.

More fruitful, however, were his next projects on French literature. Following his struggles to get his first Molière into print, he had more trouble in finding a publisher for his Racine translations, and it was once again thanks to Eugénie Droz that his *Phaedra* saw the light of day in 1958. This followed another rejection from the BBC, after he had tried once more to get them interested in a dramatized version of *Phaedra*, Racine's dramatic tragedy, but despite some praise for the quality of its translation and appreciation of the enormous task involved – 'how can one hope to render Racine into an English text?'[6] – Cairncross's offering was deemed unsuitable for its drama department. The Droz book edition, however, was very well received, and was followed by another encouraging review in the *TLS*, which disclosed to its readers that

> Mr Cairncross's blank verse translation of Phaedra will surprise those who maintained that Racine is untranslatable. He contrives far more successfully than any of his predecessors to reproduce the conciseness and the succinctness of the French.
>
> What is equally important is that he manages to bring to his translation the sinewy tautness of the English blank verse rhythm.
>
> It is not merely the best English translation known to the present reviewer; it is far more impressive than anyone would have dared to hope.[7]

When Cairncross's friend Declan Walton, by this time the UNHCR representative in Morocco, opened his copy of the *TLS* while breakfasting on his terrace, it came as a bit of a revelation: 'So this was the John Cairncross I had come to know.'[8] As Cairncross flicked through his own copy of the *TLS* he might, in passing, have expressed some relief that he did not face the constraints experienced by communist writers, such as Howard Fast, whose book *The Naked God: The Writer and Communism*, was reviewed in the same issue. Fast, who had joined the American Communist Party during the war, when there was much support for the Soviet Union as an ally, had been blacklisted under McCarthyism which forced him to self-publish, and he spent time in jail for refusing to cooperate with the House Un-American Committee. For his work as a 'communist writer', he was awarded the Stalin Peace Prize in 1954, but in 1956 broke with the Soviet Union over Khrushchev's Secret Speech and the invasion of Hungary. For that he was accused of 'Jewish bourgeois nationalism' and of being a renegade, and it was these dual constraints on his intellectual integrity that he recounted in his book.

> The commercial book publishers of the United States had hustled me out of their offices because I was a communist; the Communist Party had established its discipline because I was a writer. I sat down … and wept, because it was the end.[9]

Despite the constraints of working for Soviet intelligence and the circumstances of his enforced resignation from the civil service and subsequent departure from Britain, Cairncross's writing had actually renewed his intellectual integrity. It had offered him escape, but also a sense of achievement and restored his self-esteem. This time, moreover, his scholarship was quickly seized on by other publishers. 'Had a nibble from Penguin asking if I would do another two [in addition to *Phaedra*] in principle', he told Alec. 'This is precisely what I offered Penguin six years back.'[10] Penguin would eventually publish his *Phaedra*, along with other Racine plays, in one of its 'classic' series.

The year 1958 also brought some sadness with the death of his mother, to whom he had been close in his early years and who, from a distance, had supported his academic ambitions. There had always been some distance between him and his father (who had died in 1947), but his mother had been the driving force behind her children's education and took pride in their various achievements. He had dedicated *New Light on Molière* to her. His sister Elsie, who had remained in Lesmahagow, had spent considerable time looking after her parents, and he now offered her a holiday at a small place he had purchased inexpensively, with the help of a family legacy, in the ancient coastal city of Terracina, some 50 miles from Rome. Another of his occasional retreats, he felt Terracina would help Elsie 'to get away from a deadening and imperious routine'.[11]

He now entered the most productive writing period of his life. He even had time to publish a poetry collection, *By a Lonely Sea*, in which he brought together translated works of French, Italian, German and Spanish authors with some of his own original verse. This work was the result of long hours of study, which had begun when he was still in the civil service, had continued while in Rome and completed in the more relaxed surroundings in Bangkok, where he worked on his translations late into the evening. If the majority of his selected poems were literary works he had known since university days, some had been enabled by his more recent time in Italy, notably the works by Emilio Greco, the Italian sculptor and Umberto Saba, poet and writer. To these he added some new translations as well as the two he had originally published in *Penguin New Writing*. In addition to a translation of Greco's poetry – which included the poem 'Syracuse', reminiscent perhaps of his visit to that Sicilian city a few years earlier – Greco allowed him to use one of his noted drawings for the cover of the collection. When Cairncross first arrived in Rome, Greco had a studio at the Villa Massimo, at the German Cultural Institute (Accademia Tedesca), and it is likely that they had friends in common. Cairncross's interest in Pinocchio, the basis of a later incomplete publishing project, may also have its origins here, as Greco's *Monument to Pinocchio* was completed in Cairncross's early years in Rome. Saba, a poet from a Jewish background in Trieste who had spent the last years of the Second World War fleeing from the threat of expulsion, had finally been recognized for his poetry during the 1950s, but died in the year Cairncross took up his post at ECAFE. Among Cairncross's own poems was *The Escapist's Ballad*, his own way, perhaps, of coming to terms with his recent past, which ended typically with a Molière-like flourish.

In the valley of the silent sun
The world spins blindly on till time's undone.

Contradictions flower and fade
In the mind's defenceless shade,

Paralyse and tear apart
The frantic instincts of the heart.

World of error, world of terror,
Gleaming from refracted mirror.

Laughter's hand alone can bind
The ligaments of heart and mind.

By a Lonely Sea was published in Hong Kong in 1959. It benefited from a foreword by Edmund Blunden, the renowned poet and author, to whom Cairncross had sent the manuscript unsolicited, without them being previously acquainted. Blunden commended it as 'the work of a poet whose gift of languages enabled him to render into English with sense and subtlety lyrics and sonnets that have become famous in their original speech'. Cairncross's gratitude to Professor Blunden and others for recognizing his work – his translations rather than his own offerings would always be his *métier* – went alongside his debt to his wife Gabi, who had encouraged his writing, had introduced him to important friends and family connections and who had also borne the task of typing his work. He dedicated the book to her: '*To Gabi. You Who Are Music, Colour, Fire*'.[12]

These publishing successes now took priority. 'I have decided not to renew my contract,' he told Alec towards the end of his second year with ECAFE. 'The two years have been valuable educationally and in allowing me to finish my books. But if I take another UN job it will have to be at a much higher level.'[13] In fact. he did extend his time in Bangkok by another year until the autumn of 1960, by which time the couple had decided to return to Rome, where they felt most at home and which offered an environment flexible enough to provide both regular work and the intellectual stimulus he needed for his writing. Their departure from Bangkok was put in some doubt, however, by a serious car accident at the end of September. A Dutch friend was driving Cairncross back to their beach bungalow in his new Porsche when it collided with a six-wheel truck travelling in the opposite direction. Cairncross had a lucky escape, though suffered serious enough head and leg injuries to keep him in hospital for some days.

Before making their way back to Europe the Cairncrosses spent four months travelling extensively through South East Asia taking in Indonesia, which they found to be 'organized anarchy' and where it seemed impossible to prosper without being part of a 'network' of contacts. However, he was struck by the freedoms afforded to the people – notably the women – in a society he had expected to be more religiously constrained: 'One hardly has the impression that Indonesia is a Moslem country.' They thought Nepal 'fantastic' for quite different reasons. Staying in a village near Kathmandu, with 'no modern implements of any kind', they were intrigued to find its one main street packed with women weavers. They were followed everywhere by curious local children, pulling at Gabi's stockings. They 'might have been on another planet'.[14]

The couple returned to Rome in February 1961, where they took a top floor apartment at the end of Viale dei Quattro Venti, a main thoroughfare running through Monteverde and not far from the Lombardis' old villa. They were still close to Pamphili Park and could appreciate its features from their long terrace. Gabi's mother, missing her daughter and in ill-health, had joined them from the United States and after a 'fight with customs' at the new Fiumicino Airport (which had opened only the previous month), helped them settle in. She was 'marvellous for her age, voluble, happy', Cairncross reported to his brother, while Gabi herself was now looking forward to resuming their life in Rome and returning to FAO where her work was appreciated.

> Rome is a pleasant city and we feel very much at home here, especially with all our friends, intellectual stimulus (lots of musical people in our circle).[15]

He had omitted to tell his brother about a new development in his personal life. While in Indonesia he had formed a short-term attachment to a young married woman from Sumatra. The circumstances of the relationship were delicate – he was concerned for her safety if their affair became known – but Gabi became aware that he was seeking new love interests. Gabi correctly perceived that it was part of his wider search for more freedom. He was enjoying the intellectual excitement of being a published scholar and had used his time in the Far East to speak at conferences and build his academic contacts. On his return to Italy, he resumed his enjoyable literary discussions with his coterie of friends and UN colleagues in Rome. He found them a useful sounding board for testing his new theories and arguments. In addition to more FAO work he also took on some policy writing for Italconsult (a management consultancy which specialized in international projects) working under its director, his friend and ex-partisan Raimondo Craveri. At the time when he was looking to expand his research and publications, he could not have had a better and more sympathetic boss, to whom he dedicated his new book on Molière, published in French by Nizet as *Molière: Bourgeois et Libertin*. Here he expanded on another of his arguments first conceived in Harry Ashton's tutorials that Molière should be seen as a freethinking radical whose satirical works were underpinned by a critique of seventeenth-century French society. In particular he focused on Molière's critical attitude towards religion, evident in *Tartuffe* (particularly the original Urtartuffe) but notably in *Dom Juan*, where he saw in the actions of Molière's libertine the author's own contempt for the constraints imposed under religious orthodoxy. In *Dom Juan* Molière's empathy for the plight of women is particularly clear in his portrayal of the pressures on them to conform to prevailing manners and morals, with only education offering respite. Cairncross also cites as an example of Molière's radicalism the early chapters of *The Misanthrope*, which he interpreted as being partly autobiographical: the last two chapters were written in the aftermath of the banning of *Tartuffe* and in the more pessimistic period Cairncross had described in *New Light on Molière*.

This new book, his 'French Molière', was closely followed by his Racine which Penguin had finally agreed to publish in their Classics series. For this edition he added Iphigenia and Athaliah to Phaedra, and the status of this publication encouraged him to think again about applying for university posts. This would mean dispensing with UN jobs and consultancies. These had been fulfilling in their own way, enabling him to travel and discover new cultures, but he was increasingly of the view that his future career was to be in writing and research.

By 1963, it had also become evident to him and Gabi that their relationship was faltering. He had made it clear that he wanted more 'freedom' and was interested in new relationships, while Gabi, by now tired of doing the bulk of his typing as his writing ambitions expanded, was growing pessimistic about the future of their marriage. It was clear to Jeannette Walton that she found John 'difficult' at times.[16] Gabi admired his intellectual gifts, though remained sceptical about his various ambitions to earn a living through writing. She was also frustrated at what she saw as his inability to take criticism and to be too easily provoked when differences of opinion were aired. He was engrossed in his work, which now consumed most of his evenings. 'We hardly go out', he informed Alec.[17] Gabi cannot have been happy, as she was now clearly behind his writing commitments in the order of his priorities.

This meant that when he was offered a temporary post working for the Pakistan Planning Commission in Karachi from February 1963, he travelled alone. He enjoyed the culture of the Indian subcontinent (though he was shocked by its casual racism) and the freedoms enabled by his position, which in providing both flexible working hours and ample remuneration allowed him to enjoy embassy receptions and parties of the kind he might have experienced as a foreign diplomat earlier in his career, had he been deemed fit for 'representation' by his bosses. Towards the end of this posting, he was contacted by Lester Crocker, his friend from student days at the Sorbonne, who was leaving his post as head of Romance Languages to take up a deanship at the same American University, Western Reserve in Cleveland, Ohio. Crocker had been impressed by Cairncross's recent publications and thought his friend would make an excellent replacement. Raymond Picard was one of his referees for the vacant position, but Cairncross needed one more and, lacking in academic contacts, not for the first or last time turned to his old friend Graham Greene.

> I am being asked to accept a chair at a joint called The Western Reserve University, Cleveland, Ohio by the newly appointed dean, an old buddy of mine whose former chair I would fill (Romance Languages). By now I am resigned to the idea of becoming respectable and not just of writing the books I want to write. And I have decided … that it is time I did something about my private life which has been pretty empty since I left Bangkok. The years are passing much too rapidly to be left unused.[18]

Greene, who had just returned from Haiti and Cuba, happily obliged, sending Crocker a paragraph recommending his 'colleague and friend', who 'has not only the qualifications of a scholar but also the ability to convey his own enthusiasm for the subject to others'.[19]

Cairncross's rather disdainful description of his new position – the 'joint' that might host him for 'two years or until I get bored, whichever is the shorter' – was perhaps a deliberate attempt to play down just how much it meant to him in front of his illustrious friend. He now had the prospect of a full-time academic position, something he had long cherished, and the opportunity to experience the United States for the first time. He worried initially that the US authorities would be aware of his previous difficulties with MI5 and block his visa application. However, he was pleasantly surprised that this was not the case and had sufficient confidence in the prospect of a new career that after returning from Karachi he made a brief stop in London to do some research at the British Museum before heading back to the American Consulate in Rome to finalize the paperwork. Before he left he saw Gabi, who, while he had been in Pakistan, had held out hope of a reconciliation. However, on meeting him again she seemed convinced that he had already decided that 'fleeing' from 'home, wife and mother-in-law' was a prerequisite for his research and writing. She had recently read a new edition of Cyril Connolly's *Enemies of Promise* and, in a perceptive remark to Alec, suggested that the author 'seems to describe John in the chapter "The Charlock's Shade."' Connolly writes, 'A writer is in danger of allowing his talent to dull who lets more than a year go past without finding himself in his rightful place of composition, the small single unluxurious "retreat" of the twentieth century, the hotel bedroom.'[20] 'According to this', Gabi lamented, 'I haven't got much hope!'[21]

'If he slips out of the bedsitting stage, he'll probably be ready for a young attractive new experience', she added. No doubt Connolly's suggestion that 'marriage can succeed for an artist only where there is enough money to save him from taking on uncongenial work and a wife who is intelligent and unselfish enough to understand and respect the working of the unfriendly cycle of the creative imagination', also grated with Gabi.[22] As a wife who had 'great faith in his gifts', she had grown tired of his touchiness and sensitivity when any of his ideas were questioned. 'What is annoying is that any kind of criticism – however correct it may have proved – coming from me is regarded as a sign of bad faith, lack of confidence in his ability and intellect. Is it another Cairncross trait that they cannot take differences of opinion from a person near to them?' she asked her brother-in-law.[23]

Cairncross arrived in Cleveland, Ohio, in February 1964. Western Reserve University did not disappoint, and he quickly felt at home in his academic environment. He would have been delighted to read the welcome from the Reserve Tribune, the student newspaper, which described him not only as a 'distinguished scholar' but, on account of his experience and interests, one whose 'academic and political background [was] rivaled by few men in the world today'. His new colleagues included Jacques Lusseyran, who taught French literature. Blind since childhood, he set up a resistance group at the age of seventeen following the German invasion of France. Arrested for these activities two years later, he was sent to Buchenwald concentration camp and was one of the few survivors of the camp when it was liberated in 1945. Frank Rosengarten, who taught in the Italian section, was an expert on aspects of the Italian resistance and a translator of Antonio Gramsci's letters from prison. Ruth Malhauser was one of several younger colleagues in Cairncross's department who were in the formative stage in their academic careers. At the time of Cairncross's arrival, she was working with Lusseryan and another colleague on Albert Camus's last fictional work The Fall (La Chute).

Soon after his arrival, he took on three teaching responsibilities himself: a seminar on seventeenth-century France, 'Advanced Studies in French Literature' and 'Dissertations', where he recommended that students address unresolved existing questions – much as he had done with Molière – rather than necessarily seeking out new topics. He enjoyed his teaching, where his style of lecturing from only minimal notes was popular with students, as was the time he made available to them to discuss their work. He also relished being in the United States at an important time in its history, less than three months after the assassination of John F. Kennedy and in the midst of the civil rights movement. In Cleveland, he witnessed demonstrations against segregated schools and the accompanying violence and remarked to Greene on some of the predicaments of travelling through the university quarter back to his hotel at night. Two years later this area would be hit by the Hough Riots, which took place in a mainly African American district close to the university.

He admired too the lack of inhibition among the student generation in their attitudes to sex and relationships, while hinting to Greene of the chance of a new love interest with a younger colleague. (He admired, even perhaps envied, Greene's success with women but never came close to emulating him in that regard.) Cairncross found Cleveland's cultural amenities to his taste, at a time when George Szell was music director of the Cleveland Orchestra, the local cinema was featuring a series of Ingmar Bergman and Akira Kurosawa films and the city's impressive museum hosted enough exhibitions to sustain even his appetite for art. He was plainly enjoying his academic life and the freedoms it offered and in April was happy to be asked onto the morning 'Opinion' slot on local TV to talk about his research on Thai history, something he had previously regarded as a hobby. He told the local paper, the *Cleveland Plain Dealer*, that the future of Thailand was bound up with the United States and the outcome of its war with the communists in Vietnam: 'They grow the best rice, have a stable government and they've been a faithful ally of the United States.' Describing his affection for the 'land of smiles', he was keen to share with the Americans his enthusiasm for its people. 'The Italians have the great art of living in the present. That's true even more of the Asians who value especially the human factor.'[24]

Beyond the university, his research continued to be well received with impressive reviews of his Racine. 'Salute John Cairncross, who has done the impossible', Donald Davie declared in his *New Statesman* review. 'Believe it or not, Racine is in English at last, and in English verse.' Cairncross had eschewed both the 'lazy literalness' and 'vulgarity' of previous translators in bringing restraint and subtlety to Racine's texts. 'The sexual double-entendre is doubtless present, true enough, in what Phaedre says' (Davie writes), 'but to bellow it from the house-tops is not the way to deal with it'. After years of toiling, following dead ends and receiving rejection slips, Cairncross would have been delighted with Davie's concluding remarks:

> One is saddened but not surprised to learn that the BBC and every British publisher in sight kept Cairncross's version out of print for fifteen years, and that it was a Swiss publisher who saw its merits. At least Penguin Books took the tip eventually. It's to be hoped that they now have John Cairncross following up these versions of Iphigenia, Phaedre and Athaliah with translations of the rest of Racine.[25]

The *TLS* review of his 'French Molière' was less favourable, however, though hardly merited the scale of the author's intemperate response. The anonymous writer who reviewed *Molière: Bourgeois et Libertin* alongside two other books on the French playwright noted Cairncross's sympathy for the radical interpretation of Molière's ideas, commended him for his analysis of *The Misanthrope* (observing that Cairncross had successfully reapplied the analytical tools he had introduced in *New Light on Moliere*), while at the same time questioning whether his conclusions were adequately supported by evidence. He also queried the book's title and suggested that 'he is inclined at times to lean too heavily on the work of [the Molière scholar] Professor Antoine Adam'.[26]

Cairncross's reply, published in the *TLS* letters column two months later, was a lengthy rejoinder to what he saw as an attack on the credibility of his argument, painstakingly rebutting every critical point and providing extensive counter-arguments to support his original case. He started off by saying that the review 'contains some strange statements as to the contents and purpose of my book', and then provided a comprehensive defence of his argument, underpinned by a tendency to exaggerate the claims of the reviewer, whose suggestion (for example) that he had overly relied on the work of Antione Adam might imply to the 'uninformed reader' 'that I have slavishly copied his writings'. His earlier treatment by publishers and the limitations of existing Molière scholarship remained a sore point, and he felt it necessary to remind readers (and the reviewer) of the enthusiastic reception of his earlier Molière and Racine in the same publication. The reviewer was given space in the same edition to respond to Cairncross, and he stood by his original points while refuting Cairncross's claims: 'I said nothing which could possibly suggest that Professor Adam was a minor or controversial writer or that Mr Cairncross had "slavishly copied his writings".' He went on:

> It was of course no part of my intention to dissuade your readers from reading Mr Cairncross's work and I do not think that anything I said could reasonably have had this effect on anyone interested in Molière. Mr Cairncross appears to be a victim of the don's compulsive desire to be 'right' in a sphere in which it is totally impossible for anyone to be sure of being right.[27]

However, by this time he was already aware that his 'don's life' was coming to an end almost before it had properly begun, and when he was at the peak of his writing and scholarship. The hurt he felt at the *TLS* review was no doubt amplified by other events. Indeed, by the time the review appeared he was already making preparations to return to Rome. His past had caught up with him once more.

Chapter 14
Confession and exile (again)

As soon as he had been offered the post at Western Reserve University, Cairncross had worried that there would be problems over his visa application once the American authorities contacted the British security services. MI5 were made aware of his intentions to take up the post and in discussions with their counterparts in the FBI agreed with their decision to allow him a visa on the basis that it would provide the opportunity to interview him further. It was believed that the statements he had made twelve years earlier did not amount to the full story. New information had come to light following the defection of KGB agent Anatoliy Golitsyn in December 1961 and in his subsequent debriefings with the CIA director James Jesus Angleton, when Golitsyn revealed to the CIA that the Soviets had recruited a 'ring of five' British spies from Cambridge University. Though Cairncross was not among those named (and of course was not a direct contemporary of the others), Golitsyn's revelations prompted MI5 to reconsider the cases of those known to have had communist sympathies at Cambridge in the 1930s. As they had never been entirely satisfied with Cairncross's earlier statements, he was once more under suspicion.

The defection of MI6's former head of counter-espionage Kim Philby in early 1963 added to the urgency of MI5 investigations. Philby had come under scrutiny following the disappearance of Burgess and Maclean in 1951 and was forced to resign from MI6 shortly after when initial suspicion from the FBI was followed by an interrogation from

MI5's Dick White. Philby had reached the top of MI6 and continued to receive the backing (combined with a £4,000 pay off) from senior colleagues and friends in the organization for the next decade, despite being named in parliament as a spy and amid growing attention from Dick White and Arthur Martin at MI5. The 'Philby Affair' remained a matter of acute embarrassment for the British security services and, according to papers released in 2015, Sir William Strang, Cairncross's old boss (in 1938) and at the time of the disappearance of Burgess and Maclean the FO's most senior official, suggested in December 1952 that 'if we want to avoid embarrassment, the best course would be to let him (Philby) slip away'.[1]

After leaving MI6 Philby took on various jobs, including correspondent for *The Observer* and *The Economist* in Beirut (the year after John Cairncross had relinquished similar roles for those same publications in Rome). When Flora Solomon, a Russian friend of the Philbys from the 1930s, objected to the anti-Israel slant of Philby's *Observer* articles she added that Philby had previously been a communist who had tried to recruit her as a spy, effectively confirming Golitsyn's claims. Following a fateful meeting in Beirut with his old friend and MI6 colleague Nicholas Elliott – in which Elliott passed him a list of suspected spies (which included Cairncross) – Philby made his escape on a Soviet freighter heading to Odessa.[2]

Unsurprisingly therefore Cairncross's arrival on 11 February 1964 on flight PAA 103 was closely observed by the American authorities and at customs he was told he would be needed for further questioning once he reached Cleveland. On Sunday, 16 February, he was visited at his hotel by MI5's head of Soviet counter-espionage Arthur Martin, one of the officials who had interviewed him in 1952. Martin was already in the United States where, immediately prior to seeing Cairncross, he had interviewed Michael Straight at the Mayflower Hotel in Washington, DC. In this meeting, an outcome of collaboration between the FBI and MI5, Straight had repeated to Martin a confession he had made six months earlier to the FBI: namely, that he had been recruited as a Soviet agent at Cambridge by Anthony Blunt. Straight's confession occurred as he was on the verge of being appointed chairman of the National Endowment of the Arts by the J. F. Kennedy administration (and for which he would have faced an FBI check). Therefore, by the time Martin reached Cairncross, he already knew of Blunt's role in espionage.

Following his meeting with Straight, Martin's approach to Cairncross was made with the full cooperation of the FBI.[3] In the first meeting Martin suggested to Cairncross that he 'had not told him the whole truth' in his earlier interviews and that frankness on his part would be in his best interests, though 'no promises' could be made on the outcome of any confession. Notwithstanding the stress of undergoing further interrogations, Cairncross's heart must have sank as he considered the implications of this new development for his career prospects as an academic. Nevertheless, he agreed to get it off his chest and confess his espionage to Martin. He started by describing the role of James Klugmann and 'Otto' in his recruitment once he had joined the FO. Martin asked him about the different Soviet controllers he had served (five in total) and where his current loyalties stood. The assumption on Martin's part (no doubt shared by MI5 colleagues) was that Cairncross had remained a communist with pro-Soviet leanings, and although Cairncross attempted to explain his actions as based on a strategic rather than ideological decision (on the grounds the Soviets were a wartime ally), this did not convince Martin or stimulate much of a conversation on the international crisis of the 1930s. Their discussion of politics seems to have been limited to exchanging different views on the current international situation (in which Martin indicated a distinct lack of enthusiasm for newly liberated former African colonies), but Cairncross at least felt his interrogator had some sympathy for his predicament, even if he could not offer any guarantees.

His decision to confess at the beginning of his interrogations (a series of interviews which lasted the duration of his time in Cleveland) was made on a calculation that to refuse to cooperate would only lead to more uncertainty and prompt removal from his new position with ramifications for his university and his standing as a scholar in their eyes. He later insisted that his confession was not made from a position of strength, but 'a gesture of despair whereby I was accepting ruin'.[4]

Immediately after his first interview with Martin, the British cabinet discussed the affair. It had come at a critical time in the troubled relationship between government and the security services, which had been rocked by a series of spy scandals, including the exposure of the Portland Spy Ring, the prosecution of George Blake (who was sentenced to forty-two years for spying, which included revealing details of the MI6 and CIA tunnel under the Berlin Wall during Operation

Gold) and John Vassall, the civil servant in the Admiralty who passed
naval secrets to the KGB after they had blackmailed him on grounds
of his sexuality. The previous year had brought more problems for the
government of Harold Macmillan with the conclusion to the Profumo
affair and the aftermath of Philby's defection.

Following Michael Straight's confession and the naming of Anthony
Blunt as his recruiter, they were given another headache. Blunt was
then in the 'apotheosis' of what was already a distinguished career.[5]
After being appointed Surveyor of the King's (later Queen's) Pictures
in 1945, he had been knighted in 1956 and had recently been made
Slade Professor of Art History in Oxford. He was an acclaimed authority
on Poussin and the previous year had bought a rediscovered work of
that artist. He was a popular and respected figure among academic
colleagues and students at the Courtauld Institute, where he had been
Director and Professor of the History of Art since 1947. In 1964 he
was also still recovering from the loss of his close friends Guy Burgess
and Louis MacNeice the previous year, and from the shock of being
denounced as a spy at the Travellers Club by a fellow member, the
espionage writer Donald Sutherland. In the same period that Cairncross
was fielding questions from the FBI in Room 309 at the Commodore
hotel in Cleveland, Blunt was being interrogated by MI5 in London.
It took him much longer to admit to his espionage. Finally, as his
interrogator Arthur Martin recalled,

> He sat and looked at me fully for a minute without speaking. I
> said that his silence had already told me what I wanted to know.
> Would he now get the whole thing off his chest? I added that only
> a week or two ago I had been through a similar scene with John
> Cairncross who had finally confessed and afterwards thanked me
> for making him do so. Blunt's answer was: 'give me five minutes
> while I wrestle with my conscience.' He went out of the room, got
> himself a drink, came back and stood at the tall window looking out
> on Portman Square. I gave him several minutes of silence and then
> appealed to him to get it off his chest. He came back to his chair
> and {confessed}.[6]

Unlike Cairncross, however, Blunt's espionage was never brought to
the attention of the prime minister, though the Queen was informed.

Following Cairncross's first interview in Cleveland, Alec Douglas-Home, who had succeeded Harold Macmillan as the British Prime Minister, convened a meeting at 10 Downing Street on Thursday, 20 February to discuss the affair. Among those present at the meeting were Rab Butler (foreign secretary), Henry Brooke (home secretary), Sir John Hobson (attorney general), the acting director of public prosecutions, Sir Burke Trend (cabinet secretary), Sir Charles Cunningham, Sir Bernard Burrows, and Timothy Bligh, the principal private secretary (PPS) to the Prime Minister Alec Douglas-Home.

This meeting, one of several over the coming weeks which discussed the Cairncross case, attempted to clarify the legal situation in regard to possible extradition and prosecution, assess any political ramifications should the case be made public and ensure that relations with the FBI continued to run smoothly. The meeting concluded that 'there was general agreement that Cairncross would be allowed to remain in the United States', but also that 'the United States would be reluctant to permit a self-confessed spy to stay indefinitely on American territory, and it must be assumed that the university of Cleveland [*sic*] would not be prepared to confirm Cairncross's appointment to their staff'. The dilemma of possible prosecution and whether the British government was prepared to pursue such a course of action (which must have remained on Cairncross's mind throughout) continued to provoke discussion and uncertainty within government circles. The meeting 'agreed that we could not afford to connive at his evading our jurisdiction or to appear reluctant to have him sent back to the United Kingdom if this could be arranged'.

On the other hand:

It was not clear whether he could in fact be returned to this country. The offence was not extraditable, and the United States Government might therefore be reluctant to deport him to the United Kingdom, even if they had power to do so (which was itself uncertain). Nevertheless they might find means of returning him to us.

Even if he were returned to this country, we should not necessarily be able to secure his conviction. The confession which he had made in the United States had been volunteered in return for certain inducements; and it would not therefore be admissible as evidence. Moreover [it was] doubtful if court was likely to endorse action in

respect of espionage which must have ceased at least 12 years ago
– the more so since it could be represented as having been directed
to the benefit of a country, which for a large part of the period in
question, was an ally of both the United Kingdom and the United
States.[7]

In light of this dilemma, the meeting decided that

> for these reasons we should not at this stage close our minds to
> the possibility that the most expedient outcome of the affair might
> be for Cairncross himself to decide to leave the United States for
> some third country without ever returning to the United Kingdom –
> as he was perfectly entitled to. But we should equally keep open the
> possibility that the right course might now be to send a police officer
> to the United States, who would seek to extract from Cairncross
> a confession under conditions which would make it admissible
> evidence.[8]

These uncertainties continued over the following weeks, as further
interviews continued between Martin and Cairncross and, subsequently,
with the FBI. Initially, the meetings took place in his room at the Commodore
hotel; later the FBI agreed to move to another hotel to avoid their presence
coming to the attention of the university authorities. Occasionally, the
interviews had to be fitted around his lectures on seventeenth-century
French literature, but they managed to find an acceptable arrangement
that suited both parties. At no point during his interrogations did his
colleagues at Western Reserve University have any inkling of the fate of
their head of department. For him it was a brief return to an earlier secret
life, but he was sufficiently well-trained in keeping up appearances with
those closest to him to prevent any unwanted questions.

Relations between Cairncross and his interrogators were cordial and
cooperative. Following one session, one of his FBI interviewers returned
home with one of Cairncross's literary translations after expressing
an appreciation of poetry. The FBI files record that 'Cairncross was
completely cooperative and gave the impression of trying to recall all
pertinent details regarding his espionage activities for the Soviets'.
According to the FBI, Cairncross expressed gratitude for the way he had
been treated and even offered to work with them against the Soviets.

Back in London, the dilemma of what to do about him continued to exercise the British government in further cabinet meetings and in memos between the Cabinet Secretary Burke Trend, Douglas-Home's PPS Timothy Bligh and Roger Hollis, the Director General of MI5. Once Cairncross had made it clear that he had no intention of returning to the UK, their options were more limited, and they informed the FBI that they did not seek to pursue the matter further through the US immigration department. At the same time, they would continue to investigate through Arthur Martin the possibility that Cairncross could be persuaded to return to the UK of his own accord to make a statement that might be admissible in court. The contact between Martin and Cairncross (and later Peter Wright) would continue for the next decade during which he would be allowed to return to the UK while he cooperated, without knowing for certain if charges were to be brought against him.

Behind the scenes, Bligh and Trend were worried about possible leaks to the press and put together a set of possible questions and answers for the prime minister and foreign secretary to come up with, if needed. For example, had they been 'imprudent' in questioning Cairncross in the United States (rather than waiting to question him on home soil)? The response should make clear that they couldn't miss the opportunity of interviewing him 'under favourable conditions' for the first time since he left the Treasury in 1952. If they were asked why they hadn't interrogated him as he passed through London on his way from Pakistan to Rome to pick up his visa, it should be pointed out that no new information had come to light at that point and therefore there was no reason to hold him for further interviews. They would uphold the view that, on security service advice, 'if he were questioned in the United States he would be more willing to discuss his past and to provide us with information which we could not otherwise obtain'.[9]

These were still 'inconclusive discussions between ministers' on what to do about Cairncross. If they were moving towards the view that they could not extradite or prosecute him under these conditions, then this is something that they were reluctant to make clear to him. There would be no question of offering him immunity for information provided, and he would be given no reassurances that he would not face arrest if he decided to return to the UK, a point clarified to him by the FBI who had now taken over the interrogation.

Ministers were also thinking through the possible ramifications that would result from any publicity surrounding the case, and in this regard, Burke Trend advised the prime minister that another matter would have to be considered. At the time of his brother's interrogation in Cleveland, Alec Cairncross was the government's chief economic adviser, a situation which had implications both for him and the government. As Burke Trend put it to the Prime Minister Alec Douglas-Home,

> Disclosure of the facts would be bound to call into question to some extent, the position of Cairncross's brother. Quite apart from the distress and embarrassment which this would inflict on an individual whose integrity we have no reason to question, we have to ask ourselves what would be the probable result in terms of public policy in the widest sense if it became known that the government were employing, as their Chief Economic Advisor, a man who was the brother of a self-confessed communist spy. This is a harsh but crude way of putting it; but that is how I fear it could, and probably would, be represented.[10]

Alec, of course, had to be informed, and he was later summoned to a meeting at the Treasury. He assumed that it was in connection with the likely change of government and the implications it would have for his role. As he wrote later, 'The revelation came to me as perhaps the greatest shock I had ever experienced.'[11] Alec told his interviewers that not only did he have no knowledge or suspicion that his brother had worked for the Soviets but he also had no idea that he had even been part of the communist group at Cambridge, despite sharing rooms with him for a year.

Although Alec had been sceptical of his brother's reasons for leaving the civil service in 1952, as well as critical of what he saw as the irresponsibility of his actions so soon after his marriage, he assumed it had been solely because his career had not progressed and he wanted to pursue his research and writing. He had always supported him in this, both financially over a long period and by putting him in touch with political economists for help with consultancies and policy briefings. As the nearest in age, they had shared childhood experiences, early friendships, lodgings and confidences as they grew up, and he had thought they had remained close. He had great admiration for his younger brother's intellectual capabilities and had been proud of all his achievements at school, university and not least when he topped the civil service and FO exams. He also felt very protective towards him, as a younger brother. He now felt badly let down. 'My father was very, very hurt, because he felt he could have helped John.'[12]

By the time Alec had had his 'rough ride' at the Treasury, Alec Douglas-Home had already decided, on the advice of Burke Trend and others, to take no further action. However, for John Cairncross, the problems were only just beginning. The FBI told him that he must leave the United States by 29 June and so, two days before the deadline, he took a flight from Cleveland to New York, where the FBI escorted him on to an Air France flight to Paris that had been chartered for the use of French academics and teachers. His future thrown into doubt, once more he sought escape in Rome. Before he reached Rome, however, he had to meet Arthur Martin and Peter Wright for another debriefing in Paris. He was now doing his best to cooperate with his inquisitors in providing names of other civil servants who had been communists at Cambridge or at Bletchley Park. Martin and Wright also turned up in Rome and continued to remain in touch with him for the next decade. Both were to some degree outsiders at MI5; they did not share the public school backgrounds of some of the hierarchy which at least gave them and Cairncross some measure of common empathy.

On arrival back in Italy, he wrote to Lester Crocker in July to tell him that it was unlikely he would be returning at the beginning of the next semester because of ill-health. Initially, he did not make it clear that he was leaving permanently, and the university expected that he would return. In his reply, Crocker told him that 'he was disturbed to learn that you're ill. Of this I had no suspicion, although I knew you were a bit tired.'[13] His colleagues held out hope that he would be able to carry out limited duties: for example, teaching his graduate course on a part-time basis, with Ruth Malhauser once again put in temporary charge of the department. By mid-September, however, it was clear he would not be returning: 'We shall all miss you and now everything must be replanned, but our main wish and hope is that your ailment is less serious than you seem to think; and that your recovery will proceed at a further pace than you presently think.'[14]

On his return to Rome he initially stayed with Gabi, who by this time had moved to a smaller apartment in Via Felice Cavalotti, still in Monteverde Vecchio and near to the Tagliacozzos. However, by October he had found another apartment in Parioli, a posher, northern suburb of Rome on the other side of the city. Gabi knew by now that there was little chance of any reconciliation. They had been apart and living in different countries for well over a year. 'I suppose knowing his feelings', she wrote to Alec, 'this was the only solution and in fact we both find it hard to live together as we did in summer but I have certainly not yet found a balance in myself and a long-run solution; it will no doubt take some time and this is the hardest moment'.[15] In the space of a month, Alec had had to come to terms with the fact not only that his younger brother had been a Soviet spy but also that John's marriage was now finally over. In addition to all the discomfort it had brought to his Treasury position – though with no lasting damage to his career – he was expected to offer a sympathetic ear to the personal troubles of his brother and sister-in-law.

In 1952 Gabi was unaware of the real reasons for Cairncross's resignation from the civil service. It is unlikely that he ever told her the whole story though quite feasible that she might have got the idea that he had been a spy once they had developed friendships with former Italian partisans who had experience of wartime intelligence work. In any case their separation in 1963–4 came at a convenient moment for him in this regard – the burden of making a further confession to his wife at this time was partly relieved by their decision to go different ways.

Although Gabi had continued to work on FAO projects in Rome, including their 'Freedom From Hunger' campaign, her chances of further progress in the organization beyond administrative and secretarial work were thwarted by not having a degree, though she felt her other qualifications – previous campaigning work, language skills – merited more consideration. She did not get the new FAO position she sought, however, and the following year she decided to return to London, to take up a more fulfilling role for the Anglo-Jewish Association (AJA). This new role involved fundraising for music and art scholarships for Jewish students and representing the association at international meetings and conferences. Gabi and her husband would remain friends and continued to offer support for each other in troubled times.

With his academic career abruptly ended and his marriage over, John Cairncross was now faced with rebuilding his life once more. He received more encouraging news from the BBC. His dealings with the corporation had hitherto been difficult, and he often felt they were not taking his ideas seriously, sometimes leading to fractious exchanges. His Penguin Racine, however, had brought him more recognition, and he now had the advantage of a sympathetic ear in the BBC drama department. Martin Esslin, of Hungarian and Jewish descent, but brought up in Austria until he left when it was annexed under Nazi Germany in 1938, had recently come to prominence as the author of the influential essay, 'Theatre of the Absurd', which looked at the rising influence on drama of the existentialist themes of Albert Camus and others. Esslin, obviously unaware of Cairncross's own existentialist crisis, wrote to ask if he could commission his *Andromaque.* He told Cairncross that only his translation of Racine could serve their purposes – praise that renewed some pride and morale. Esslin commended Cairncross's 'highly successful translation', while gently suggesting that the idiom in one or two passages 'is a little too contemporary and colloquial':[16] a suggestion which Cairncross unsurprisingly refuted. 'Racine, the real Racine, *must* be modern and alive', he replied to Esslin.[17] Relations between the two thrived, however, and soon after Esslin wrote to tell him that 'I am trying to get Peggy Ashcroft to play Andromaque. I have given her a copy of the script, but I have not yet had a reply.' Peggy Ashcroft did not materialize, but the production, which was first aired on the Third Programme on Sunday, 25 April 1965, was well received. Sheila Allen, at the start of what would be a glittering career, was in the lead role and Esslin was happy with the outcome. He thought Allen 'might have been slightly too angry at the beginning, but at the climax of the play I think she is very moving indeed', he related back to Cairncross. Esslin had hoped that Cairncross would be able to join him for rehearsals in London, but the latter, who was reluctant to travel to the UK unless MI5 had endorsed his visit, made an excuse and investigated ways of listening to the broadcast in Italy. He was able to read the reviews, however, which were generally favourable, though he found the one in *The Listener* 'rather snooty'.[18]

This was the beginning of a fruitful rapport with the BBC as more interest in his translations followed. Andromaque was later repeated in the Radio 4 'Monday Play' series, and although his translation of Corneille's *Le Cid* was refused by Radio 3, he succeeded in placing his translations of Racine's *Berenice* and *Athaliah*. This was largely due to the encouragement of another friendly producer, Charles Lefeaux, a veteran of BBC Radio whose previous productions had included the Dick Barton Special Agent series. With the help of Lefeaux – who had been warned that Cairncross 'was not an easy man' on account of his inclination to see most editorial queries as a slight on his authority and judgement as a translator[19] – *Berenice* was performed in 1969 and *Athaliah*, with Irene Worth in the lead role, broadcast on Radio 3 the following year. This time Cairncross had even hoped to visit London for the rehearsals, intending to combine it with an assignment, under MI5 auspices, to confront James Klugmann about his role in recruiting him to Soviet intelligence. He got to see Klugmann the following year but had to pull out of the rehearsals with another excuse. In any case, he did not relish visiting 'strike-ridden England', he confessed to Lefeaux. There was quite enough political uncertainty in Italy.

Chapter 15
Hot autumn

Much had changed in the twelve years since John Cairncross first arrived in Italy. Its transformation during the so-called economic miracle which began in the late 1950s had turned a mainly agricultural country into a leading industrial power, with its strength in car production, clothing manufacture and the production of all manner of consumer gadgets and appliances combining to drive unprecedented growth. The industrial triangle of the north, which had attracted large-scale emigration from the south of Italy, had gradually expanded into wider areas and was reflected in the modernization of the country's infrastructure and transport systems. It had benefited from early membership of the Common Market since the Treaty of Rome in 1957, enabling access to the customs union, common agricultural and transport policies and its social fund. Cairncross had witnessed some of these changes at first hand during his time at the Banca Nazionale del Lavoro and, most notably as a consultant at Italconsult, working under Raimondo Craveri.

However, from the late 1960s Italy faced new challenges in the form of political and social unrest from groups who felt excluded from the new prosperity. Its 'hot autumn' of student protests and trade union strikes in 1969 – a culmination of rising discontent which matched *les évènements* in France the previous year – was followed by a challenge to the legitimacy of the state itself, in the form of terrorism (of left and right) and emerging evidence of a secret 'shadow government' composed of business leaders, politicians, military leaders and newspaper editors. Systemic mafia-backed corruption was another concern, and the violent attacks of the Cosa Nostra returned to the streets of Sicily. This decade, often summarized as the 'years of lead', culminated in the kidnapping and murder of former prime minister Aldo Moro in 1978.

John Cairncross often considered leaving Italy during periods he thought were particularly serious, but in reality it remained his adoptive country – one he loved and which he felt offered both more freedom and stability in troubled times. From the late 1960s his life took on another mix of insecurity and intrigue as he felt obliged to maintain a dialogue with Arthur Martin, Peter Wright and their MI5 colleagues. Over the following years he was permitted at certain times to visit the UK for further interviews in addition to an (unsuccessful) attempt to extract a confession from James Klugmann, his original recruiter. At the same time he had to return to the UN and establish himself as a regular employee at its FAO offices, while continuing to pursue his research in his spare time. And he was now alone.

At least he had a new start in Parioli, in Rome's northern district. With its plush apartment blocks and gardens, it was a step up from Monteverde (which had expanded significantly through the new public housing schemes) and offered a quieter and more exclusive respite from the city and his day job. During the war, Parioli had been frequented by fascist officials and apparatchiks but by the 1960s its elegant streets housed intellectuals, film directors and fashion photographers. It was close enough to the centre for him to reach the FAO's offices at Circo Massimo easily by bus, and the main Termini train station was only a ten-minute drive. His fourth floor one-bedroom apartment, in a secluded spot away from the main road, had a small kitchen and a large terrace, overlooking the gardens of the Villa Balestra. Though modest in size, there was enough room for his books, his Van Gogh sketches and his Thai rubbings. He still enjoyed the occasional escape to the country. After he and Gabi separated, they sold their small holiday house in Terracina which enabled him to take on a small farmhouse in Cortona, Tuscany, as a weekend retreat. It had its own olive grove and two hectares of land and was the kind of property that in later years would become the ideal second home for scores of the English middle classes. For him, however, it would be another promising investment that never came to fruition.

At FAO, he took on a variety of roles, initially assisting the director of the Economic Analysis Division. He quickly slipped back into his work as an editor, knocking together material for policy briefings and papers on aspects of rural development, population and the global food crisis. He renewed his friendship with Declan Walton, who had moved to Rome to work on the World Food Programme and then in 1968 moved to the FAO as *Chef de Cabinet* of the director general. They would meet regularly for lunch in the staff canteen, which served good food at reasonable prices in the Italian *tavola calda* tradition. Here they would leave work behind and talk about German literature and poetry, recalling their favourite verses. On one occasion, reciting the last stanza of Rainer Maria Rilke's poem *Herbsttag* ('Autumn Day'), Cairncross ran out of steam, and Walton was delighted to be able to complete it.

> Wer jetzt kein Haus hat, baut sich keines mehr.
> Wer jetzt allein ist wird es lange bleiben,
> Wird wachen, lesen, lange Briefe schreiben
> Und wird in den Alleen hin und her
> Unruhig wandern, wenn die Blätter treiben.

> (Who now is homeless ever will be so.
> Who now is lonely ne'er will find a friend,
> But sit up, read, write letters without end,
> And in the sombre alleys to and fro
> Restlessly wander as the leaves descend.)[1]

This stanza, with its emphasis on the wanderer's search for fulfilment, offered a pessimistic take on the condition of the intellectual. Walton likened it to something Cyril Connolly had written in the last volume of his literary magazine *Horizon*, partly summing up (though he did not then know it) his friend's ongoing predicament:

> It is closing time in the garden of the West and from now on an artist will be judged only by the resonance of his solitude or the quality of his despair.

Walton offered a willing ear for Cairncross's literary ambitions and would sometimes be given manuscripts to read as well as a collection of his already published work, sometimes inscribed with dedications. ('To Declan and Jeannette, who are preternaturally keen on the works of Jean Racine', read one.) He was always interested in his friend's various publishing ventures and was intrigued to learn that he had been granted access to the Vatican archives to research the Jesuits in Asia. Cairncross's research was now the major priority in his life, and he continued to correspond with academics, attend conferences, solicit recommendations and enter into battles – sometimes acrimonious – with publishers and editors, notably over his ultimately unsuccessful attempts to publish Phaulkon, which continued to gather dust despite being revised and retitled. Over thirty years of work and endorsements from Greene, Hugh Trevor-Roper and others were not enough to convince either mainstream publishers or even the university presses that the book had a readership.

At times he found writing a 'solitary existence', as he confided to friends and relatives, but he had the strength of character to persevere as other events once again threatened to engulf him. In 1967 the *Sunday Times* 'Insight' team ran a series of articles about Kim Philby, whose disappearance in 1963 and reappearance in Moscow as a defector six months later was the cause of much critical discussion of MI6's handling of espionage matters, including from its counterparts in American intelligence. This study, subsequently published as *Kim Philby: The Spy Who Betrayed a Generation*, had followed a plethora of spy novels and Cold War thrillers from John Le Carre, Len Deighton and Ian Fleming, and was regarded by MI6 bosses as further evidence of inaccuracies, 'misconceptions' and 'journalistic self-righteousness' in misleading the public over the role and activities of the secret service.[2] One immediate response to the *Sunday Times* investigation was from Philby himself, whose *My Silent War*, written under the authority of the KGB, was published the following year. Graham Greene, his old MI6 colleague, had also been sceptical of the accounts of journalists and authors who had little real experience of Britain's secret services or Philby's role within them. 'What a fuss at the moment about Kim!' Greene remarked to Cairncross as the press coverage intensified. A year later, however, he penned a surprisingly warm foreword to Philby's book, in which he agreed with the depictions of their former secret service colleagues, while recalling Philby's affection for his staff over their long lunches and drinks together in the pubs of St James. He expressed admiration too for Philby's commitment to a cause, while noting the 'chilling certainty in the correctness of his judgement, the logical fanaticism of a man who, having once found a faith, is not going to lose it because of the injustices or cruelties inflicted by erring human instruments'.[3] This unexpectedly positive endorsement of Philby's book may retrospectively be seen in a different light, as four further meetings between Greene and his old colleague in Moscow in the 1980s are now regarded as having being instigated by Sir Maurice Oldfield (then head of MI6 and another friend of Greene's) with the hope that Philby, even at a late stage, might turn.[4]

The ensuing articles and debates came at a time when the security services were reassessing the Cambridge spy circle (and even held suspicions of an Oxford ring). There was tension within MI5 between Peter Wright, who was apt on occasion to follow his own whims and given to conspiracy theories, and others in the hierarchy. Cairncross, still worried about his eventual fate, had kept in touch with Wright and other MI5 officers while they hoped he could produce the names of other possible spies. Their concerns were not just historical; over one hundred Soviet agents were estimated to be active in Britain in the 1960s and 1970s, though the material they provided was mainly of poor quality.[5]

Unlike Anthony Blunt, Cairncross was never given confirmation of immunity from prosecution in exchange for his cooperation. In Paris, on his return from the United States, he was told by Arthur Martin and Peter Wright that 'he was free to come to the UK'.[6] However, this was regarded by their successors as an erroneous instruction which wrongly implied immunity had been granted. No such agreement had been made by the attorney general, though the latter did make clear that Cairncross 'could be assured that if he comes to the UK to assist in a particular operation, he will not be prosecuted in respect of the espionage committed by him'.[7] These occasional visits enabled him to visit friends and family. He would usually put up at a modest price at the Crescent Hotel in Cartwright Gardens, Bloomsbury, helpfully close to several second-hand bookshops. Occasionally, he would stay with Gabi in Hampstead. Her work for the AJA under its president, Maurice Edelman, a Labour MP (and another Trinity College graduate in modern languages), was more rewarding than her previous FAO role, and she was much admired by her colleagues. Later, she would travel to Strasbourg as an AJA observer to the Council of Europe meetings, and she kept up her contacts and friends across the continent.[8]

In his meetings with MI5 he provided some names of people he knew at Bletchley and in the civil service. Then, on the authority of the attorney general (following a suggestion by Peter Wright), he was 'invited to come to the UK to confront the man who had originally recruited him'.[9] He had not seen James Klugmann for over thirty years. Their lives had taken very different paths. After Klugmann's adventurous SOE career, in the post-war period he had devoted his life to the Communist Party, managing to follow party orthodoxy at the key moments while retaining the admiration of its members for his lucid and engaging educational classes. By the time Cairncross met him for lunch at a London hotel he was a declining figure in the party, distrusted by its leadership and – despite remaining an inspiring mentor for younger proteges – was regarded as too weak to help the growing alternative 'Eurocommunist' cause.[10] Like Cairncross, Klugmann had rarely spoken about his own involvement with the NKVD, though in his case communist faith and the party he served would have ensured him some protection. In the aftermath of the Philby investigations, Klugmann also attracted press interest and feared an approach, though could hardly have expected it to come from his old friend. Over a good lunch they had time to reminisce about their old tutor Harry Ashton, their time at Trinity, and current intellectual interests, though given Klugmann's enduring loyalties – he was writing the CPGB's official history at the time – and Cairncross's aversion to orthodoxies, these would now have diverged considerably. Once lunch was over, to Klugmann's consternation, Cairncross (who was still irked by his deception in 1937) broached the possibility of MI5 cooperation; a perturbed Klugmann declined the offer, denied any involvement with Soviet agents and promptly curtailed the prospect of any further meetings between them. Given that Cairncross had spent thirty years brooding over Klugmann's involvement in his original recruitment, any affection for his old friend would have dissipated over the years, and it is unlikely he would have been able to entirely hide his contempt for the veteran communist. He had already told Martin that he 'would have no hesitation in bearing witness against him', if he managed to help bring him to trial.[11]

Peter Wright, who had initiated the meeting between the two, was, along with Arthur Martin, continuing to keep a close watch on Cairncross. In 1972, while on a visit to Paris to meet Lester Crocker, Cairncross was convinced that he was being followed and kept under surveillance by MI5. David Rubin, then a young scholar at the University of Virginia whom Crocker introduced to Cairncross over tea at the Cercle interallié during this visit, found him to be a 'nervous wreck'. Years later, after his public exposure, he explained to Rubin the reasons for his concern.[12] Peter Wright was regarded with growing contempt by Roger Hollis and the new generation of MI5 officers. He was 'a man with an obsession … quite mad and certainly dangerous' for his conspiracy theories and reckless judgements, according to Stella Rimington, one of the new counter-espionage replacements for Wright.[13] Rimington was set to work on the Cambridge spies and was present in what turned out to be the last official interrogation Cairncross faced with the security services, carried out in Ministry of Defence offices in Whitehall. Rimington remembers him as a 'thin, grey, stooping figure, coming in out of a dark night, always wearing a mackintosh',[14] while he remembered her as a 'very personable young lady … dressed elegantly in trousers'.[15] The interview, which was secretly recorded and led by one of Rimington's senior colleagues, produced little: presumably because MI5 continued to pursue the line – in their view, one insufficiently examined by Wright and Martin – that Cairncross was fully aware he was part of a ring that included Blunt and Burgess. According to Cairncross's account, they even believed that he had been 'shielding' Blunt in his earlier 1952 interview with Martin – an assumption he regarded as an 'uproarious idea!'[16] Unsurprisingly, given the distance between them and Cairncross's obstinacy, it became (in the words of Rimington) an 'intellectual sparring match' and nothing further accrued from their discussions.[17]

Cairncross was by now a veteran of intellectual sparring matches in his various dealings with publishers and reviewers, but he was pleased when Penguin took his translations of Corneille for their Classics series. After Racine, he had relished the opportunity of taking on Corneille whose 'robust and often oratorical style' he found even more challenging. His translations of The Cid, Cinna and The Theatrical Illusion owed much to long conversations with his friend Raymond Picard, and he drew extensively on the latter's Two Centuries of French Literature. By the time Cairncross's Corneille was published, however, Picard was in his final illness.

Another writing project which came to fruition was his history of polygamy. This assignment had been long in the making and had its origins in the second-hand bookshops of Paris during that awkward summer of 1952, when he and Gabi were deciding where to spend the next part of their life. Then, he came across an eighteenth-century study of monogamy which, in its conformity to Christian values, surprisingly hinted at a whole hidden literature of opposing heretical views. This set him off on a trail through bookshops and libraries in search of this 'largely underground tradition of Christian polygamy', providing him with the intellectual challenge and the requisite detective work on which he thrived. Various espionage experts, flicking through his publications, have generally attributed this work either to interests In the 'sex-pol' writings of Willhelm Reich, which it was believed he inherited from Arnold Deutsch, or to be taken as evidence that he was as much a 'womanizer' as the other heterosexuals in the Cambridge ring. In fact, his study of polygamy brought together different strands of his interests across the history of religion, European attitudes towards non-Western cultures and the contribution of freethinkers who questioned the prevailing consensus on sexual morality and the moral foundations of modern societies. His work on Molière had stirred interest in debates between 'libertins' and exponents of religious orthodoxy as well as the hypocritical attitudes towards women held among the privileged hierarchies. Alongside the polygamists, he also discussed the ideas of the utopian socialist thinker Charles Fourier who was only now being taken seriously – some of his major work was not published until the 1960s. Cairncross saw Fourier's ideas as rooted in the secular traditions of the French Enlightenment, while Fourier's vision of a new society was as much a critique of 'patriarchal polygamy' as it was of 'bourgeois morality' – an inhibition imposed on both sexes.

> Now that it is possible to see him in perspective, he emerges as a remarkably coherent visionary whose nearest analogy is with the English poet Blake. He flatly rejects the idea of sin and the necessity of frustration. Man is basically good and he is made for joy. The driving force in life is passion in the widest sense. Hitherto, the passions have been constrained. They should on the contrary be developed. ... His design for living presupposes a plentitude of sense and mind, a smooth and effortless integration of man in society of which there have been only rare glimpses in the past, as when Tahiti was first discovered by European navigators.[18]

Fourier's utopia, according to Cairncross, was 'avowedly polygamous' where 'men and women are both free to take several partners simultaneously'. This no doubt resonated with the hippies of late-twentieth-century Europe (though had little to do with the privations of his own single life). But it also appealed to aspects of his latent feminism, evident in what he held to be freethinking outlooks on marriage and the relations between men and women, with memories of the 'Flying Fornicator' at Cambridge and the male hierarchy in the civil service offices never entirely erased. As the book was going to press (this time fully indexed, footnoted and with an extensive bibliography with Routledge), he was co-authoring, with two women colleagues, an FAO booklet on 'The Missing Half', an assessment of the conditions of women in rural areas who were suffering from both economic hardship and patriarchal oppression.

In his review of *After Polygamy Was Made a Sin* for the *Sunday Times* ('How Many Wives at a Time?'), Cyril Connolly concurred with Cairncross's analysis of the puritanical basis of Christian polygamy in the way it denounced adultery and promiscuity while preferring wives to concubines, 'for without wives neither sex can enter the kingdom of heaven'. He wonders why the author did not include Percy Shelley or William Godwin, 'both of whom preached and practised a certain plurality', but despite some omissions

> Mr Cairncross more than makes up by his unearthing of many obscure but extremely significant defenders of polygamy, an idea which is anathema in most Christian communities and quickly brings down the wrath of the state.[19]

The book was welcomed on a lighter note by polygamist friends. The philosopher Freddie Ayer, an acquaintance from the 1940s, wrote to tell him that he 'enjoyed the book greatly and thought very highly of it. It seems to me that you have fully achieved your aim of employing your considerable scholarship for the diversion of the reader.'[20]

After looking forward to 'the dirty book by Claymore', Graham Greene was fascinated on reading the published version, in particular by his friend's treatment of Johann Leyser, a seventeenth-century German protestant theologian sacked by the church for promoting polygamy. Greene was 'amazed at the amount of research you must have done and how you found the time for it'.[21] Later, he was happy to recommend the work as a 'book which should be read by all polygamists'.

Greene was less successful, however, in getting the book accepted in translation by his French publisher, Laffont. Despite Greene's recommendation and the help of a mutual friend in Paris who delivered the copy (Cairncross never trusted the Italian postal service) he was left frustrated and annoyed at his treatment. On arrival at Laffonts, Cairncross felt patronized to be addressed in English and was assured that no copy had been received.

At least *Polygamy* had given him renewed hope that he could devote more time to writing, as he neared his mid-sixties and the prospect of an FAO pension. With this in mind, he sold his Cortona farmhouse and put all his savings into the purchase of land for a small house on Capri. Capri had always been his ideal place of escape, and his affection for the island and its literary connections had grown over the years after spending time at Graham Greene's villa. He initially intended that his own Anacapri property, situated further towards the sea (in Via della Grotta Azzurra), would be an inspiring place to work. In the event, he lacked the financial security to retire and write (confirming Gabi's earlier doubts) and never spent a prolonged period in the house. Instead, he kept it as an investment; however, even that proved to be disastrous, and within two years of purchasing it he was already looking for a buyer. He had unknowingly made the purchase without securing land rights, and he soon discovered that part of the steps and passage leading into the small house was jointly owned by a third party, a French lady who had been in Capri for some years. These were potential pitfalls for future buyers and five years of the seven years of his ownership of the property were spent trying to sell it.

The house had become a burden and was not in any case serving its original purpose, as in order to keep the place on he had to continue working on FAO consultancies after his official retirement at the end of July 1975. As he told Greene, his choice was 'between living OK (and not really using the place) and selling it and living fairly fat and carefree, and above all, in a position to do my writing. Sad, but that is the way. Money has come too late to me, or let's say I never had the shrewdness to pick up a bargain when I had a little.'[22]

Despite his financial difficulties and frustrations, his life in Rome continued to offer compensations through some stimulating friendships and interesting circles. Vikram Shah, who was *Directeur de Cabinet* in the office of Edouard Saouma, the Lebanese Director

General of FAO, found 'an intellectual clicking' when he first met Cairncross. Shah enjoyed their conversations on French and American writers, and he and his American wife Tina would regularly invite Cairncross for dinner at their home in EUR, Rome's residential and business district. Cairncross 'liked the fact that I'm an Indian with a British part and a French part', and they talked at length about his time in Bangkok and the legacy of European colonialism. Occasionally, Shah and his wife visited Cairncross in Parioli, where they found the apartment of a 'typical bachelor' and bibliophile, 'where each available space was full of books, heaps of books all over the place'. He would supply the wine, and Shah and his guests would normally bring food. Sometimes they would be joined by his Parioli neighbour who worked for Swissair, and who shared some of their cultural interests.[23]

Another occasional lunch companion was Paul Ress, a journalist friend of Graham Greene's, who had previously been working for *Time* magazine. On Greene's request, Cairncross had helped find a job for Ress in the FAO's press department, and they continued to meet in Rome before Ress moved to Switzerland for a better post. At the time, Ress was in a relationship with Edith Sorel, a translator and journalist who had worked with Che Guevara and Fidel Castro and been a useful contact for Greene when he was working on *The Honorary Consul*, his thriller set in Paraguay. Though mainly based in Paris (she had been entrusted with delivering Cairncross's *Polygamy* manuscript in the ill-fated episode with Laffont's), he enjoyed the company of Ress and Sorel which brought him closer to Greene's literary circles.

His pride that he was somebody who mattered in Greene's life was further enhanced by the arrival in Rome of Norman Sherry, Greene's biographer. It was Sherry's first visit to Italy, and while he elicited Cairncross's thoughts on Greene's life ('he seemed specially pleased with some tentative theories I outlined', John remarked to Alec[24]), Cairncross 'nursemaided' him around the city. He gave him a day-long tour, embellished by his now wide knowledge of Rome's history and culture, before dispatching him to Capri to talk to more of Greene's friends.

By the mid-1970s Italy's political situation was deteriorating sharply with more student protests, terrorist atrocities and a 'historic compromise' between the Christian Democrats and the communists, Italy's two main parties. The Italian communists (PCI) enjoyed growing popularity abroad for their distance from the Soviet Union and the innovative local government in Emilia Romagna and elsewhere, and after peaking at around 34 per cent of the national vote in the 1976 General Election, they were now close to power at home. Though Cairncross had some sympathy for the PCI's ideas, he had long maintained a strong ambivalence towards the possibility of political change in Italy since composing his articles for *The Economist* in the 1950s. He held little faith in the very Italian slogan *convergenze parallele*, under which it was hoped that the traditionally opposing forces of Christian democracy and communism could somehow be reconciled around an idea of progressive democracy and in which, inevitably, the rival parties and their apparatchiks would divide responsibility. At other times, he was very worried about where the intensifying crisis at the heart of the Italian state would lead. 'I'm not sure about staying on here', he wrote to his sister Elsie in May 1977. 'The situation is all right just now, but how long will it last?'[25] It was a prescient observation given that months later Italy would spiral into its worst post-war crisis with first the kidnapping and then murder of Aldo Moro, and the collapse of the historic compromise. Few other alternatives seemed viable. He briefly considered Greece, but after spending a short holiday there admiring its beautiful architecture, its history and culture, he was put off by the 'deluge' of tourists in Athens and the 'so-so food'. Crete was 'overrated', and he found the Greeks 'charming but rich in misinformation'.[26]

Earlier in the summer he had made one of his occasional visits to the UK to attend a Trinity College reunion, along with Alec, Douglas Parmée, David Layton and a few other contemporaries, including his old FO colleague Jock Colville. The Trinity dinner had been poorly organized, in his view, with the dining arrangements falling so below his expectations he wrote to the bursar to complain. His infrequent visits to the UK no longer included meetings with the security services, though they offered no guarantee that he would not face a further investigation. On one home visit during leave provided (and paid for) by FAO on his retirement in 1976, he enjoyed his first visit to Scotland in many years and was briefly reunited with his sisters, the 'aunts', who still lived in Lesmahagow. In general, however, he had no intention of returning permanently to the UK. He found it 'terribly dear, seedy and uncivilised' and always felt much more at home in Rome.[27]

And Rome was where he would stay as the Italian crisis ensued. The possibility of leaving – he contemplated Geneva at one point – had, in any case, been postponed by his unresolved property and financial problems. In the late 1970s, his life in Rome was enlivened by a fruitful collaboration with another former member of the liberal anti-fascist milieu. Frances Keene was a translator and teacher and a prominent member of New York literary circles, who visited Rome every year. She had a long association with Italy. During the Second World War she had worked as an assistant to Gaetano Salvemini and had edited a collection of writings (*Neither Liberty nor Bread*) by the main exiled Italian intellectuals. She had also worked undercover against the fascists in Florence for the American security service OSS. In the late 1970s she collaborated with Bruno Zevi, a prominent Italian architect and historian, on his independent TV channel, Teleroma 56. After Keene met Cairncross through mutual friends in 1977, she invited him to take part in a programme she was hosting on the work of an Italian artist. In subsequent programmes he would appear in discussions with participants as diverse as the Italian actress Elsa di Giorgi and a Polish professor of industrial psychology – sometimes helping out with translations for the benefit of Italian viewers.

One of the guests he met through Keene was Allan Evans, a twenty-three-year-old American musician, who was scheduled to play gospel, blues and ragtime guitar on one of the programmes. Despite an age gap of forty years, they became firm friends, with Cairncross making an immediate impression on his younger companion.

From the first moment I responded to John as if he were a long-lost older friend who was not only eager to ferret out a 23-year-old's perspective but to share anything he could about music and the many subjects that opened onto.

This included lunch at Ranieri's, the historic restaurant near the Spanish Steps, to help Evans, a sound archaeologist, with his research on Vladimir de Pachmann (1848–1933), a pianist from Odessa (and acquaintance of Liszt), whose archive, formerly kept in Rome, had now vanished. As he was introduced to Rome's hidden treasures, some way off the official tourist trail, Evans was struck by Cairncross's 'insightful grasp of the city's layered history, culture, its unique customs'. It seemed 'as if I were being instructed through a process of osmosis'.[28] Having discarded thoughts of leaving Rome, John Cairncross, for his part, felt as close to his adopted city as he had ever been, until the arrival of two unwelcome visitors on an early December morning.

Chapter 16
Public exposure

It was always a matter of regret for John Cairncross that some of the defining moments of his life were bound up with the predicaments of Anthony Blunt. At Cambridge, the Modern Languages Club meetings he attended in Blunt's rooms (above his own) were subsequently turned by later erroneous accounts into 'tutorials' in which, along with Leo Long and Michael Straight, he was cultivated in the ways of Marxism and Soviet espionage. In fact, even on the question of French literature Cairncross and Blunt were a 'major mismatch', with Cairncross's 'idiosyncratic critical approach altogether foreign to Blunt's school manual approach'. According to Professor David Rubin, his readings of Molière and others had 'nothing in common with the screeds of vulgar, reductive and simplistic Marxists'.[1]

In 1951, after Blunt's 'hoovering' of Burgess's flat (following the latter's disappearance) failed to uncover Cairncross's summaries of government and FO positions on appeasement, it seems plausible that over several lunches Blunt alerted Guy Liddell – or more likely did not demur from his friend's suggestion – to Cairncross's probable involvement in espionage. Then, in 1964, in simultaneous interrogations in London and Cleveland, they both confessed to working for the Soviets, though the outcomes of these meetings held different consequences for their career prospects. Blunt was given immunity, while Cairncross was left in a mire of uncertainty. Now, in late 1979, their intertwining fortunes came to public attention for the first time after the biographer and broadcaster Andrew Boyle published his book *The Climate of Treason*, which contained strong hints that Blunt ('Maurice') had been part of the Cambridge spy network. In the prelude to publication, Blunt had instructed lawyers amid rumours of his involvement, while *Private Eye* named him as the 'fourth man' shortly after the book appeared. In the ensuing controversy – its escalation coinciding with the BBC's production of John Le Carre's *Tinker Tailor Soldier Spy* – Prime Minister Margaret Thatcher, who had only taken up office six months earlier, was obliged to make a statement in the House of Commons. On 16 November, in response to a question from Labour MP Ted Leadbitter, she confirmed Blunt's espionage, and the following week parliament debated the affair.

In opening the debate, Thatcher clarified that in 1964 after a total of eleven security service interviews in which Blunt had denied any involvement in espionage, he was offered immunity from prosecution in exchange for a full confession and cooperation with their investigations. This had been authorized by the then attorney general and acting director of public prosecutions, and the home secretary (but not the prime minister) had been consulted, and the Queen was informed that the surveyor of her pictures had confessed to being a Soviet agent. Thatcher also confirmed that since 1967 successive prime ministers and home secretaries had been told about Blunt. The debate which followed Thatcher's opening statement largely focused on the claims of an establishment cover-up and the question of whether there needed to be more accountability of the security services to ensure that ministers and parliament – and ultimately the public – were kept fully informed of their activities. Labour MPs were particularly vocal in their criticism of the 'establishment', with Willie Hamilton, a consistent parliamentary critic of the monarchy, couching his arguments in narrow partisan (and homophobic) terms. It was 'one more instance of the conspiracy of British Governments against the governed', he claimed.

> If she [i.e. Thatcher] is looking for the fifth, sixth man … she does not need to look for them in the Labour Party, in the comprehensive schools or even among the British Leyland shop stewards. Let her look for them among the ex-public schoolboys, those with homosexual propensities, those who voted Tory at the last election and those in social groups 1 and 2.

Tony Benn raised the level of debate marginally to call for a Freedom of Information Act, though his suggestion that there should be 'democratic control of the Security Services' received little enthusiasm ('one might as well store cognac in a colander', was one Conservative response). Unusually, the debate brought contributions from three honourable members who had held prime ministerial office, and it was left to one of these, Jim Callaghan, to attempt to contextualize the activities of the Cambridge spies.

> Insufficient attention has been paid today ... to the atmosphere of the 1930s. ... I should point out that there was a terrible feeling in the 1930s that we were facing a prospect of either fascism or communism and that people had to choose. I was never bitten by the bug, but I can understand those who were. At the risk of incurring the displeasure of Conservative members I must say that it was the craven attitude of the government of the day, in the face of the Nazis, which led people to reach that conclusion. Had there been a different attitude towards the Nazis in the 1930s by the government of the day, I do not believe that some of those people would have gone where they did.[2]

But this was a lone voice, and the general tenor of much of the criticism, echoed by the press, seemed to be driven by theories of homophobic perversion and establishment conspiracies and sometimes delivered in anti-intellectual tirades.[3] Attention inevitably turned to other possible traitors. 'How many [spies] are still alive and roaming around?' Hamilton asked.[4]

Barrie Penrose and David Leitch, who had been part of the *Sunday Times* insight team which investigated Kim Philby ten years before, were quick to take up the story. They had been tipped off about another Soviet spy by Jock Colville, who did not name Cairncross but provided sufficient clues to the spy's identity for it later to be confirmed by a former FO secretary who had recognized his handwriting in the material passed to Burgess. In fact, Colville's alleged claim that 'a top civil servant – one of the best brains at the Foreign Office – worked secretly for Moscow by passing information to Burgess' was not a particularly accurate one. Cairncross was not a 'top civil servant'; he may have come top in his FO exams, but his knowledge was hardly utilized in his roles, and he was unaware that what he passed to Burgess was sent on to Moscow. Nevertheless, it was enough to leave the scent for ambitious journalists in search of a good story, and in the days between Thatcher's statement and the parliamentary debate on Blunt, Penrose and Leitch published Colville's 'revelation' of 'yet another Soviet spy'. Now, five weeks later, they tracked Cairncross to his Rome apartment. After their first call in the early hours of the morning went unanswered, they returned a few hours later to find him up and about after breakfast. Though shocked by their arrival, he agreed to the interview and confirmed the 'revelation' that he had passed to Burgess his notes on British government and FO attitudes on appeasement in 1939, prior to the outbreak of war. In their front page *Sunday Times* story his interviewers reported his 'confession' that he was a member of 'the notorious Cambridge University Communist cell in the nineteen thirties and that he later supplied diplomatic and political material to Soviet agent Guy Burgess'. This was a poor representation of the interview given that he explicitly denied being an agent and had no knowledge either, when passing on his handwritten summaries to him, that Burgess was one. The 'I Was spy for Soviets' headline was misleading as at this time they had no knowledge of his own meetings with Soviet controllers, and the only line the two journalists were pursuing was the Burgess connection. The interviewers had even failed to uncover Cairncross's time at MI6, much to Graham Greene's surprise (and amusement).

The knowledge that Cairncross was now to be publicly exposed as a suspected Soviet agent was a profound shock and triggered a wholly different level of distress. News that his uncle had been a spy came as a 'complete surprise' to David Cairncross, who was on holiday in Barcelona when the story broke. Then working as a clerk for the Foreign Affairs Committee in the House of Commons, he was quietly reassured that there would be no implications for his own career. At the same time, the misrepresentations in the *Sunday Times* irked his uncle, and he attempted to correct them in a BBC interview the following day. For the first time he went public in explaining his actions, which he entirely attributed to his opposition to appeasement. He had not passed material to Burgess in any official capacity, 'but as you know, one can elicit information if one has certain skills, which he undoubtedly had'.[5] It would take another ten months, with the help of his brother and the Press Council, for him to have his correction to the Leitch and Penrose article published by the *Sunday Times*.

His niece Frances Cairncross, then the *Guardian*'s economics correspondent, was contacted by the *Sunday Times* who wanted to reach her father. Alec, of course, had been told of his brother's espionage in 1964, and despite everything had remained protective and supportive of him. He now told the *Sunday Times* that he was 'not 100 per cent surprised by the news',[6] but offered a lengthier explanation to the *Guardian*, recalling his 'astonishment' on hearing of the confession in 1964 and revealing that he was 'still in the dark about what he did. John has never said a word to me about this and I have never said a word to him. I do think he was very silly. I don't know what went on in his mind but I can understand that many people were driven to desperate action at that time.'[7]

Andrew Boyle, who did not mention him at all in *The Climate of Treason*, told *The Observer* that Cairncross was of minor significance and just one of six diplomats under investigation by MI5 after the disappearance of Burgess and Maclean. However, Cairncross's status was immediately equated with Blunt, and it was seen as another establishment 'cover-up'. This was the view of the Labour MPs Dennis Canavan and Bob Cryer, who sought more answers in the House of Commons on the assumption that Cairncross had been granted the same immunity as Blunt, with Canavan repeating a familiar claim (in *The Scotsman*) that there was 'one rule for the establishment'.[8] In a written question on 17 January, Bob Cryer asked the attorney general 'if he will refer the case of Mr John Cairncross to the Director of Public Prosecutions, with a view to seeking extradition from Italy and prosecution under the Official Secrets Act'. In rejecting that request the attorney general replied that 'even if there were admissible evidence, which there is not, extradition is not available from Italy in respect of offences of this nature'.[9] Cairncross would later note the irony of being represented as the beneficiary of an establishment cover-up, as he came to believe that he himself was a victim of one.

The shock of his public exposure threatened to disrupt his Rome life, and he swiftly took himself off to Switzerland for an extended Christmas break. Press pictures taken by Barrie Penrose show a beleaguered and strained John Cairncross, apparently awakened from his 'hermitic' existence by inquisitive investigative journalists. Initially, he feared for his security, concerned about the tenure at his Parioli condominium, as well as the impact it might have on his work and friendships. At his lowest point, he even hinted to his nephew David that he was considering ending his life, tentatively inquiring about Exit, the pro-euthanasia association.[10] He needn't have worried about the reaction in Rome. Those Italians who got to know of it were more fascinated than disturbed by having a spy among them. Declan Walton, who like other friends 'didn't have the slightest clue' about his espionage, received a few phone calls and was shocked to hear the news, but their friendship carried on as normal.[11]

In fact, despite the obvious stress that resulted from being pictured on the front page of the *Sunday Times*, the journalists and molehunters had little to go on beyond Cairncross's connection to Burgess. It was still a long way from the 'Fifth Man' revelations in 1990, and although there was suspicion of a more significant role, no evidence was produced. When Marjorie Wallace, another *Sunday Times* writer, broached with him the possibility that he was the 'Fifth Man' (from the vantage point of one of Rome's buses), Cairncross was able to deflect the question with typical obfuscation before returning to his commentary on the history of the city. It was another decade before the end of the Cold War would precipitate the opening of archives and the revelations of former KGB officers would identify a more serious connection between Cairncross and the other Cambridge spies.

Cairncross briefly considered legal action against the *Sunday Times* but decided that would only inflame publicity and, as he was hardly likely to be given a sympathetic hearing, made do with a letter correcting what he saw as the report's inaccuracies. In Switzerland, he carried on with his translations of La Fontaine's Fables, deciding that *Le Savetier et le Financier*, a story of how a cobbler's simple life was turned sour by the burdens and responsibilities of wealth following a chance meeting with a financier, was suitably ironic for the corrosive values of modern times. No doubt pondering over the erosion of the cobbler's independence and security enabled him to assess his own current predicament, born from a dependent affiliation from which he had found it so difficult to extricate himself.

He was soon back in Rome in a more upbeat mood. 'Here in Italy nobody cares a damn about it all', he reported to David Rubin. 'I'm back and gradually resuming normal life.' He also told Rubin that he was going ahead with the sale of his Capri property – a place he had barely used – which would free him to 'buy a little place as a refuge should things take a turn for the worse here'.[12] The Capri house had now become a significant burden. Despite being an Anacapri neighbour, Graham Greene had never been inside the house, and he was as curious about its property status as he was surprised about plans for its early sale: 'Wasn't it rather unwise to build a house without the rights of passage?'[13] Nevertheless, on request, he suggested some writer friends who might be interested in the property.

Cairncross finally sold the property in 1982, ending what had been a very complicated transaction. He could not have imagined that the whole saga would result in an even more disastrous aftermath, as his attention turned to investing the proceeds of the sale – effectively the sum of his life savings. His various investments over the years had failed to bring him the financial security he needed, and he was frequently reliant on short-term loans from Alec. Tired of worrying about bonds and shares, he decided to invest his money in ancient Roman coins. (He already owned a small collection.) He had been passed details of a collector in Milan and made arrangements to stop off there to purchase the coins in cash (as well as attend an exhibition of Etruscan rock carvings) on his way to Paris (via Turin) by train. In need of medication, he arranged to purchase Swiss medicines (not available in Rome) at a border town in Italy easily reachable from Milan. Leaving his luggage in Milan and cashing his cheques for the equivalent of £26,000, he bought a ticket for Chiasso – his destination for the medicines – which was not, as he thought, like Ponte Chiasso, on the Italian side, but was an Italian-speaking Swiss town the other side of the frontier. On arrival at Chiasso, he made his way to the exit through a doorway which he expected to lead him to an Italian luggage area, only to be confronted on entry by customs officials. After finding the large quantities of cash in his bag, they promptly arrested him. A succession of Italian governments had maintained strong laws on currency smuggling, and he knew immediately the seriousness of his situation. He was detained, first in Como, and subsequently in Rome, and charged with currency offences for which he was given a one year sentence and a fine of £40,000, plus legal costs, with his proceeds from the Capri property confiscated.

The complexities of the Italian judicial system meant that he was not detained more than a few days, though he faced a long trial and the threat of expulsion from Italy. He appealed successfully for the right to remain in the short term and began what turned out to be a four-year-long process of successfully contesting the charge. An immediate problem he faced was that with his history of espionage and dealings with the security services he could not turn to the British Embassy for help. Following this second outbreak of unwelcome publicity, some elements of the British press were quick to make the connection between his spying and the sinister-sounding ordeal at Chiasso. Alone, and at his most vulnerable, he turned instead to trusted friends, some of whom visited his temporary prison where they found him depressed, though well looked after and helping out as a translator for fellow inmates with immigration worries. Friends regarded the reasons for his arrest as incomprehensible, though the circumstances which took him there recognizable as the actions of an absent-minded professor: 'He was a strange mixture. Very careful of money and investments but also lackadaisical. All that money and being stopped at the frontier was typical.'[14]

In organizing his defence he wrote to his most loyal friends explaining the latest 'misadventure' and requesting references for good conduct. As before, his correspondence, closely typed on blue airmail envelopes, managed to combine a summary of his latest troubles with enthusiasm over new writing projects. He wrote to Greene:

> It would help immensely … if I could get a statement to the effect that I (have) a blameless record (judicially speaking) and reputation for balance and prudence, totally unlikely to have indulged in anything so mad as circumstances appear to suggest. … If you could lend your great weight by writing me a letter, I'd be immensely grateful. I may say that I couldn't have thought up such a fiendish trap had I spent a week at it. Since my only aim is to be able to live on here where I am perfectly happy (and have just renewed my lease), and since my imprudence was obviously going to be magnified in light of the previous scandal, I had every reason for extreme prudence, which is the exact opposite of the appearance of my action … I had in fact hoped to have a revised copy of my poetry translations (including Baudelaire) ready for you.[15]

Greene had already heard about the 'unfortunate adventure' from the press and reassured his friend that he 'didn't believe a word of it'.

He then submitted a short statement in his support: 'I have known John Cairncross for forty three (43) years, we have worked together during the war, and have been friends ever since. He is a man of complete honesty on whose word I would absolutely rely.'[16] Other statements came from Lester Crocker and FAO colleagues. By the end of this complicated saga, with friends and family offering different interpretations of the circumstances leading up to his arrest in Chiasso, it is impossible to come to a settled conclusion on the reason for his actions. Was he in search of medication, did he intend to buy ancient coins or had he judged that his money would be safer in Switzerland rather than Italy?

His lawyers began the long process of appealing the sentence and recovering his money. The absence of official backing from the British Embassy remained a problem and was amplified by his previous notoriety. Without any British 'establishment' support to count on, he turned instead to the Italian equivalent. His long stay in Italy had given him first-hand insight into the murky world of Italian politics. Under its *partitocrazia*, the Christian Democrats presided over a series of coalitions as the leading party of government, benefitting from the privileges and favours this bestowed, at a time, following the Moro affair, when the Italian state was in crisis, with its deep-seated corruption and threat posed by secret organizations like P2 and the Sicilian mafia. Cairncross had long abandoned any hope of Italy changing – even when the popular Italian Communist Party came close to power in the 1970s – but was also aware that to survive in desperate circumstances Italians often chose to 'play' the system. He knew that Italian justice cases were not only long drawn out sagas but also often decided by the ability to exert influence in key areas of politics. Giulio Andreotti was the grandmaster of Italian politics, seemingly permanently embedded in one ministerial role or the other. At this time he was the minister of foreign affairs and therefore on Cairncross's radar as he sought to take his case to the highest levels, with the help, as always, from his brother whom he now badgered to get in touch with British officials in Rome. 'Andreotti can fix anything', he told Alec, 'and I'll get Italian friends to approach him from the other side'.[17] Whatever the impact of such an approach, the saga dragged on for another eighteen months before he finally received confirmation that his case was to be included in Francesco Cossiga's June 1986 Presidential Amnesty for Economic and Financial Crimes.

His continuing financial troubles ensured that he was tied to the FAO for the time being, which meant that his long-term plan to be writing full-time remained unrealized. It took him years to retrieve his money from the Capri sale, and he was still reliant on subsidies from his brother. Now in his early seventies, his health showed signs of deteriorating. Already deaf in one ear his eyesight was failing, and he needed an operation for cataracts. He was also more watchful over his food. Years in Rome had given him a discerning palate, and he had a good knowledge of some of the best and cheapest trattorias in Trastevere where he was warmly welcomed by the owners as 'Dottore'. He preferred seafood to red meat, and FAO lunch companions like Silvia Balit (Enzo Tagliacozzo's daughter) now found him choosing the vegetarian options in the *tavola calda* at work. To FAO colleagues he was a warm and likeable personality, 'a jolly fellow around the office', Kay Killingsworth, who sometimes gave him a lift back to Parioli, remembered.[18] David Cahn, a relative of Gabi, who got to know him while an archaeology student at the Swiss Institute in Rome in this period, has affectionate memories of his friend who always had a 'slightly confused manner' and an endearing habit of 'pushing up his enormous glasses, which were constantly slipping down his nose'. They would sometimes eat or take coffee together, and Cahn recalls his liking for *frullati* (smoothies).[19] Despite advancing age and the onset of ailments, he continued to attend parties and gatherings and enjoy the company of younger people.

It was at one of these parties, on Rome's Via Appia, the ancient Roman road that connected the capital to the south, that he met Gayle Brinkerhoff, a young American opera singer. From a military family and with a bachelor of music degree in voice performance from Indiana University, Brinkerhoff moved to Europe to further her musical training at the Hochschule für Musik und Darstellende Kunst and the Viennese State Opera Studio for young artists. She worked professionally for several years in Austria and Switzerland where she performed many leading roles for mezzo soprano.

In the early 1980s she moved to Milan where she studied with Maria Carbone, the Italian operatic soprano. When Carbone moved to Rome Brinkerhoff followed her there to continue her studies. Once in Rome, she shared a flat with friends, shopped cheaply at the markets and worked hard at her singing. One evening in 1984, Lisa, her flatmate (and another singer), invited Gayle to her joint birthday party which she was sharing with her aunt, an FAO colleague of Cairncross's. Among the twenty or so assorted guests, in a setting which reminded her of one of Federico Fellini's films, Gayle and Cairncross found themselves next to each other on the terrace and got talking about aspects of French and German poetry. It was clear that despite the big age difference they shared some common interests. She was impressed by his manners and gentle nature, which helped ease her own shyness, and was struck too by his lucid and eloquent speech.

> He was charming and had a way of listening intently: he didn't make you feel like an idiot, he didn't try to dominate, put people down, he always tried to find common Interests. In a way he was more than charming: gracious almost. ... He was pretty down-to-earth and certainly no snob, intellectual or otherwise.[20]

After that first meeting she thought little of it and returned to her work, but Cairncross pursued her through mutual friends and eventually obtained her phone number and asked her out for dinner. It took several months before they regarded themselves as a couple. Not everyone in his wide circle welcomed their blossoming relationship given the forty-year age difference. Older women friends of Cairncross were jealous of his new partner, while others had doubts over how long it would last. Some of Brinkerhoff's flatmates were shocked. Some friends, of course, found other reasons to question her new romance. 'Do you know who he is?' she was asked by one friend, who recounted to her the public furore over his espionage. Brinkerhoff's response, repeated numerous times in the forthcoming years, was 'I couldn't care less'; she considered his past life as something beyond her comprehension: 'It didn't resonate.' When they were together they avoided any discussion of his espionage: 'He didn't want to talk about it. He wanted it to go away finally.'[21]

She brought significant changes to his life. She felt he 'had lost his way' and had become 'a bit of an oddball'. Despite his numerous friends, he was 'isolated in his inner life'. After breaking with Gabi and his brief affair with the Indonesian woman, he had been on his own apart from a close attachment to a Filipino woman who briefly shared his apartment in the early 1970s. His one-bedroom flat in Parioli had been reduced to a bedsit arrangement and was without a fridge or a proper cooker, and there was a strong smell of the camphor he used to protect his books and prints: 'He didn't even have a washing-machine and used to wash his clothes in the bath-tub and hang them out to dry, badly creased over the railings of the large terrace.'

It was clear to Brinkerhoff that he needed help in coping with some aspects of modern living. She brought more order to his small Parioli flat, providing a new bed, putting up more bookshelves and installing a proper stove in his tiny kitchen. He cut an eccentric figure and still wore his Thai culottes and sandals in early morning visits to the *tabacchaio* or *edicola*, but over time, under her influence, he also started wearing jeans and sported a variety of elegant headwear.

For his part, he welcomed this unexpected development in his personal circumstances. 'By the way, I've acquired a delightful young girlfriend', he announced to David Rubin, briefly interrupting their discourse on French literature,

> with whom I propose to make another trip to Paris. After long years in the desert, I'm happy and rather astonished at the enthusiasm of my partner which is possibly even greater than mine. I am also getting on well with a whole circle of young people here and to some extent in Paris. No generation barriers which I think is most gratifying and, again, rather surprising.[22]

They enjoyed going to concerts and occasional social gatherings along the Tiber or sitting down together to a simple dish of pasta. Sometimes she would drive him the 80 miles or so to Bolsena, to spend a weekend with his friend Basil McTaggart, an expert on the Etruscan ruins in that old city. Mainly, though, they worked at home as Gayle was in a formative stage of her singing career – of which he was a proud advocate to friends and relatives – and he was absorbed with ongoing writing projects, including a new book on Molière. He had long acquired the habit of refining his translations late into the night and would sit on their long terrace working, sometimes continuing in bed.

The weekend trips came to a temporary halt after they volunteered to take on a puppy from a litter of Saluki hounds. A British–American friend of Gayle needed to find a home for them, and initially they found space for one; in future they would get to own four. This new arrangement offered some semblance of family life, and the dogs would take on a big commitment in subsequent years. Owning a dog also extended

Cairncross's already wide circle of friends. Their apartment in Via Spadini was handily placed next to the grounds of Villa Balestra, a popular dog-walking area in Parioli, where its prosperous residents would meet and chat in the mornings. This group, made up mainly of women, had in the past included the actress Audrey Hepburn, who lived in an attic apartment nearby, and was now unofficially orchestrated by an exiled Russian aristocrat, 'Principessa' Elena Wolkonsky, who had spent her youth in France and Italy after the seizure of power by the Bolsheviks. After many years in Rome she had achieved a reputation as a cultural figure and conversationalist; a lover of poetry and frequenter of Rome's salons, Wolkonsky was also determined to keep the Russian literary tradition alive among the small orthodox community.[23]

Also among this circle, accompanying his dog, was the photographer Fiorenzo Niccoli, who got to know the couple well. He was from a generation of Roman photographers used to mixing in the intellectual milieu of journalists, writers, costume designers and film directors. Long summer evenings and nights would be spent in Piazza Navona until 3.00 am–4.00 am talking about culture, film and fashion, a tradition that he regretted was in decline by the 1980s. He regarded Cairncross as a like-minded figure, a historian and philosopher, with a very good knowledge of Italian literature, and he relished their meetings. They invited each other for dinner at their small apartments – Niccoli's decorated from floor to ceiling with photographs and books – and on occasions Cairncross would be introduced to journalists from the magazine L'Espresso (where Niccoli worked) or to other writer friends. They discussed the poet and dramatist Massimo Bontempelli, the writer Alberto Moravia and Italian cinema. Niccoli was impressed with his friend's range of interests and fondness for the culture and language of his host country: 'He spoke a very elegant, old-fashioned, classical Italian, not everyday Italian.' Apart from the odd ironical comment, they rarely spoke about politics and never about espionage; it was only many years later that Niccoli got to know about his friend's past. It would not have disturbed him or altered their friendship, as in his view 'Italians live and let live'.[24] He admired the man, whom he regarded as kind and stimulating company. Despite the age difference he was also struck by the closeness of the couple's relationship, which was held together by a protective concern on both sides.

Taking in more dogs meant that their extended family needed a bigger home. Prompted by the possibility of his landlord raising the rent or taking over the apartment altogether, they decided that it made sense to think about a long-term move. However, there was no prospect of renting – let alone buying – a bigger apartment in Parioli or elsewhere in central Rome. He had always thought of returning to France at some point, and there were advantages in being there for Gayle's musical career. In the autumn of 1989, when the Berlin Wall was being pulled down – 'Marxism is clearly doomed as an economic system. I never thought much of it', Cairncross had written to David Rubin in 1987[25] – they now discussed the possibility of settling in Provence. They envisaged a peaceful time together, and a belated retirement for him with his books. They were not looking back, and he hoped that the question of his espionage, which they had barely discussed, would not mar the remaining years they had together. 'Why should we seek remembrance of things past?' 'Do they not, uninvited, haunt us still?', he would say to Gayle, citing the Austrian dramatist Franz Grillparzer (Figures 11–15).

Figure 11 With his books in Via Spadini, Parioli. Reproduced by kind permission of the Syndics of Cambridge University Library.

Figure 12 With dogs Sidam and Stella in Rome. (Credit: Fiorenzo Niccoli.) Reproduced by kind permission of the Syndics of Cambridge University Library.

Figure 13 With Gayle at the Abbaye du Thoronet (the Cistercian Abbey of Thoronet) in Provence. Reproduced by kind permission of the Syndics of Cambridge University Library.

Figure 14 At home in Provence as the story breaks. (Photo by Pascal Parrot/ Sygma/Sygma via Getty Images.)

Figure 15 Writing his own account of the 'Fifth Man' – a task he never completed. (Photo by Jean-Pierre REY/Gamma-Rapho via Getty Images.)

Chapter 17
The Fifth Man

Leaving Italy after so long was a wrench. It had been his home off and on for nearly forty years, a stretch that exceeded the time he had lived in Britain. Rome had been a place of exile, but also one of liberation from MI5 (and MI6), the KGB and the civil service. It had given him the space to think and write – even if some of his intellectual projects never came to fruition. His anti-fascism had enabled him to ease his way into influential circles which helped keep him in work and build lasting friendships. His work, if sometimes more insecure than previously, was more rewarding. He thrived on new challenges, and his scholarship, his editing work and UN secondments provided him with a stronger sense of purpose than he had been able to enjoy during his ill-fated civil service career.

Since he arrived in 1952 he had seen Italy transformed from a mainly agricultural economy and young democracy rebuilding after fascism to a modern industrial nation, with the fast-moving changes in fashion and lifestyles coexisting uneasily with ongoing political inertia. Occasionally, he had been more than an observer of these changes, in his journalism for *The Economist*, and in his consultancies for Italconsult. Though he sometimes found the heat unbearable in the summer, he had always shared the Italians' capacity for good living, which was enhanced by his knowledge of its language and enriched by his curiosity about its history and culture. Despite the potential for upheaval in his life and friendships and the general personal stress arising from his public exposure in the *Sunday Times* and the aftermath of the currency saga, his status in Italy was largely unaffected. He retained his important friendships and continued to enjoy convivial lunches and dinners, where he was admired for his eloquence and his authoritative knowledge of literature, poetry and history. In short, he felt he belonged in the country which had adopted him and – far from the 'unclubbable', prickly Scot in the civil service – always relished the opportunities Rome afforded for social gatherings. Unsurprisingly, giving all this up for the South of France came as a shock to friends. It was like the Pope leaving Rome for Avignon, Frances Keene remarked to Allan Evans.[1]

Initially, Cairncross and Gayle had the idea of buying a property in France, but this proved to be beyond their finances, and in any case he was not regarded as a good prospect for a mortgage. However, they found a good-sized house to rent in the village of St Antonin du Var in Provence, and by the beginning of 1990 they had moved all their belongings, including his vast book collection and their two dogs. Graham Greene offered to help him with residency status and looked forward to seeing more of him. Now that Cairncross had given up his FAO consultancies and rounded off his pension, he was still looking for translation work, though as usual he had enough to occupy his time. He was still revising his Phaulkon, adding more original seventeenth-century manuscripts and documents to illustrate the differences between Thai and French colonialist positions, but was still struggling to put it into a form that would appeal to publishers.

He had also started another quite different project. The publication of Peter Wright's controversial memoir *Spycatcher* in 1987, together with further accounts of the whole 'Cambridge spy' saga, had jolted him to think again about the 1930s and the possibility of offering his own version. It was clear that the issue was not going to go away, and he now recognized that the best way of addressing his role in it would be to embark on his own historical retrospective account of the circumstances which influenced his choices. Though his friendships had not been seriously affected by his public exposure in 1979, he realized that the affair had 'puzzled friends to see a fairly normal in appearance, normal (if at most times eccentric) character mixed up with the KGB'. As well as correcting what he saw as significant errors in prevailing interpretations, it was a chance to try to explain to friends and family his own motivations for acting as he did.[2]

In Cairncross's view, the problem with the existing discussion of the Cambridge spies – including Peter Wright's *Spycatcher* – was the inadequate account of the historical context which led up to the Munich crisis. Drawing on the work of A. J. P. Taylor, Correlli Barnett and others, he now revisited the years leading up to the Second World War. Before anything else, an understanding of the decisions facing him and others of his generation depended on reassessing the tensions and divisions within the FO, which he had seen at first hand. In his view 'there was virtually a civil war between appeasers and resisters to Nazi Germany', with the real prospect of a 'collaborationist' government, while there remained a significant threat of invasion in the early years of the war.[3] He regarded the failures of British diplomacy as the crucial factor in the rise of Nazi expansionism, and in sharp contrast to those in government who thought Nazism could be contained as long as it wasn't unduly antagonized, Cairncross's experience of travelling and studying in Europe told him that an organized resistance movement was a likely option as the crisis developed.

Prompted further by the fall of the Berlin Wall in 1989 and the prospect of a united Germany, he had started putting some ideas together during his last months in Rome for what he intended to be a pamphlet, 'Munich and After', written under the pseudonym, David Jardine. He felt this nom de plume was necessary for him to be treated seriously on the back of all the adverse publicity in the wake of the Blunt affair and his own public exposure. As he became more absorbed in his reading, which extended to British diplomatic history since the nineteenth century, he replaced this idea with a prospective book outline. The book would have two parts, with Part 1 on the German question and appeasement and Part 2 on his own decision to work as a Soviet agent. However, this would be another – and not the last – of his unfinished works. In June 1990 they received a visit from Sheila Kerr, who told him that she had been working on a thesis on the Cambridge spies. She requested an interview for a TV documentary, which he declined.

Then, following an episode Gayle Brinkerhoff later likened to a scene from Monty Python, he was dramatically forced to revise his publishing plans. One early September morning, after Gayle had parked their Renault van after a shopping trip to St Antonin du Var, they were approached by a figure waiting for them among the nearby vines, who then followed them in through the gate. This was Christopher Andrew, a Cambridge academic and espionage expert, who asked Cairncross about the Battle of Kursk. They invited him in for a late morning aperitif of *kir* (made from white wine and cassis) and sat together at a table under a tree in the garden. Andrew told him he was writing a book and making a TV programme for which he would like to interview Cairncross. (Unknown to the couple, TV cameras were hidden in the surrounding vineyard.) Cairncross once again declined the interview; in retrospect Cairncross's cooperation for the book would have been superfluous as it had already been written and would be published the following month.

In early October, they were called by a friend who had heard a report on the BBC World Service that a book on 'the Fifth Man' was about to be serialized in the press. They prepared themselves for the ensuing media coverage, which far exceeded anything he had faced before. Christopher Andrew and Oleg Gordievsky's book, *KGB: The Inside Story* was published with serialization in *The Times* and accompanied by the Granada programme 'The Fifth Man' as well as a BBC Timewatch edition, and followed by extensive newspaper coverage. Gordievsky was a former KGB agent who had defected to Britain in the early 1980s. It was his recollections of what he had seen in the KGB archives and what he had picked up from conversations with KGB colleagues that formed the basis of the claim that John Cairncross was the 'Fifth Man'. The identity of the 'Fifth Man', to follow Maclean, Burgess, Philby and Blunt, had been a curiosity for many years, with numerous other candidates on a long list, including Victor Rothschild, Alister Watson, Leo Long, Michael Straight and even MI5's director general Roger Hollis, and the book claimed to have resolved this mystery. The couple, who had hoped for a peaceful time in France to enable them to carry on with their respective work (Gayle was in the crucial stage of a singing career), now found themselves besieged by the international press. He was seventy-seven years old and in declining health, and she had been preoccupied in arranging auditions. Now all their time would be spent on organizing his defence in the press, as the story broke and journalists started appearing at their door or on the phone, and at one point their landlady accommodated eleven of them at her nearby hotel. They turned many press requests down, while they felt that some of the ones they allowed had sensationalized his account. One exception was the interview he did with Yvon Samuel, the author and *France Soir* columnist, who lived nearby.

Most of the coverage focused on the 'Fifth Man' allegation. Gordievsky's claims were made from a period spent working in the KGB archives on an 'in-house' history of the KGB and through recollections of conversations with Dmitri Svetanko, a former head of the British desk. The claims of the existence of a Cambridge Five group had been made several times before, including, of course, by Golitsin in 1961. Cairncross even revealed that he had been included as one of a *Pyatchorka* – a list of five prominent agents – that had been issued after the Battle of Kursk in 1943. More details of the Cambridge spies, including the identity of 'Otto' and the quantity of documents Cairncross and others passed on to him and subsequent controllers, would only come to light in the late 1990s, with research carried out in Moscow by Nigel West and others.

It is clear that John Cairncross was a very significant spy for the Soviets and generally held in high regard by Moscow Centre. Evidence produced after he died confirms that he did not reveal the full extent of his espionage work, downplayed some aspects and ignored others entirely, notably in the post-war period, though the importance of the material he passed then is open to debate. There is also the inevitable doubt attached to the words of former spies who, in working in a clandestine way, have routinely broken trust, and have admitted to holding back details or having previously denied an involvement in espionage only to admit it later. Being identified as 'the Fifth Man in the Cambridge spy ring' had a profound effect on his last years. It also produced much inaccurate information about his life and left misleading impressions of his personality – about what motivated him to act in the way he did and the nature of his contacts with the other members of the so-called ring. Like the others, he was not recruited at Cambridge, but unlike them he worked independently; he did not know the others were spies, did not consult with them about espionage and had no involvement or even prior knowledge of the disappearance of Burgess and Maclean. Although he joined the Trinity College communists, he was not an 'ideological communist', in the sense of being an admirer of the Soviet Union, did not subscribe to Marxist economics and did not promote workers' struggles.

The press coverage which followed his public exposure as the 'Fifth Man' (including columns by distinguished public figures) only propounded many of these myths. Andrew and Gordievsky's *Inside the*

KGB contains several inaccuracies (sometimes prefaced by the use of 'probably' or 'doubtless'), including the following: 'In 1930, at the age of seventeen, probably already influenced by the political traditions of Red Clydeside …'; 'While at the Sorbonne during 1933-34' (he actually arrived in 1932) he 'probably made contact with Münzenberg's World Committee for the Relief of the Victims of German Fascism'. In fact, he met liberal anti-fascists, exiled from Italy. It claimed erroneously that Blunt was his 'college supervisor', whose 'aloofness from the harsh realities of the class struggle' 'jarred' his young pupil. In fact, as we know, what 'jarred' was the junior research fellow's limited knowledge of French literature. The claim made in the Andrew and Gordievsky book that he was the 'first atom spy' was quite a leap from his status as private secretary to Lord Hankey. His association with the other members of the so-called ring continued to inform commentary on his case and attribute to him characteristics and viewpoints he did not share. These are apparent in the interventions of a triumvirate of 'Lords': Lord Robert Armstrong, his former civil service colleague, Lord Dacre (who as Hugh Trevor-Roper had praised his Thai manuscript) and Lord Annan, the distinguished educationalist, who endorsed John Costello's suspicion that Cairncross might have blackmailed Alan Turing during his time at Bletchley Park, thereby adding further fuel for the scriptwriters of *The Imitation Game*. It was Dacre's article, 'The Real Harm Done by the Fifth Man', an otherwise intelligent appraisal of the effects of the Cambridge spies in promoting Stalinism as a credible alternative to liberal democracy, that was in fact least applicable to Cairncross: 'Their intention was to destroy Western civilisation, which they held to be doomed and replace it with Stalinist communism, which they supposed to be perfect, or at least perfectible.'[4]

In other reviews, *Inside the KGB* came in for sharp criticism as Gordievsky's evidence was pulled apart. In *The Spectator*, Phillip Knightley warned of the need to treat the 'recollections of defectors' with caution. Oleg Gordievsky was an 'ideological defector', who, after his disillusion with the Soviet Union, became 'the mirror image of Kim Philby', in working for the 'opposite side to bring down the system'. In this ideological role, according to Knightley, Gordievsky assumes free reign to label anyone not on the right as 'crypto communists'. That enabled him to include Harry Hopkins, the American Democrat and former adviser to Theodore Roosevelt, as 'the most important of all Soviet wartime agents in the United States'.[5] In similar terms, he would later denounce Labour leader Michael Foot, whose consistent anti-Stalinism since the beginning of the Cold War was easily verifiable to anybody who cared to look.[6] Hopkins was an 'unconscious agent', according to Gordievsky,[7] while Foot was at different times an 'opinion creator', an 'agent' and a 'confidential contact'.[8] Foot, a leading opponent of appeasement and friend of Orwell and Koestler, successfully sued the *Sunday Times* for alleging, on the back of Gordievsky's claims, that he had been "an agent of influence for the KGB". Another problem with Gordievsky's account was his tendency to change or embellish his story: in 1992 he told *The Independent on Sunday* that 'no one in the Labour Party was co-operating with Moscow or helping the Russian Embassy in London', only to return to the claims about Foot and others in later books. Some of his stories were 'self-serving; some partially true, some plain wrong', according to Richard Norton-Taylor, the *Guardian*'s former security affairs editor.[9] Even at one of the book launches for *Inside the KGB*, Francis Wheen recalled, Gordievsky admitted that he had no documentary evidence for labelling Cairncross as the 'Fifth Man'.[10] However, its purpose had been served, the 'Fifth Man' had been named, and it was more material for what Cairncross called the 'spy entertainment market'.

After a month of being on the receiving end of press requests, Cairncross reluctantly agreed to travel to Paris to take part in the BBC's *Newsnight* programme, on the understanding that he would be able to make an accompanying statement. It was perhaps naïve to expect the BBC to comply with their request for a statement under such circumstances, and he and Gayle arrived in Paris unprepared for the inquisition that was to follow. The interview was included as part of a wider discussion and debate on the validity of the 'Fifth Man' claim, involving Christopher Andrew who joined the programme from Washington and a sceptical Chapman Pincher in the *Newsnight* studio in London. The programme also included interviews with Phillip Knightley, one of the original *Sunday Times* 'Insight' team, and Robert Cecil, a former FO colleague and biographer of Donald Maclean. In his introduction, Peter Snow, the presenter, asked whether Cairncross was the 'missing link' in the Cambridge spy ring. Dressed in casual jacket and pullover and wearing shaded clip-on sunglasses to protect his eye problems, his academic posture and tendency to question the validity of every question he was asked, combined with what he perceived as the constraints of the Official Secrets Act, resulted in one of the least convincing interviews in the history of British broadcasting. Asked to reject accusations of espionage, he referred to the 'very delicate' nature of the issues: 'They are allegations which I would no, not discuss, no, would put them in a certain light, shall we say, but that is something, because that involves certain other issues which are beyond my capacity and not for me to discuss.' And to a question of receiving commendation from the Soviets for his role in the Battle of Kursk: 'This is a purely hypothetical question of a situation which we are only postulating and not accepting as the basis for discussion. As I said it is very difficult to go very further on this point.' He did, however, refute Andrew's and Gordievsky's claim that he was the first atom spy. 'Where is the evidence for that?' he demanded to know. In response, Andrew, from the Washington studio, waved a copy of a SAC minute – at which Cairncross was listed (mistakenly) as one of its joint secretaries. In Andrew's later authorized history of MI5, a scholarly tome of over 1,000 pages, Cairncross is not included in the long sections given over to the atom spies. In this same *Newsnight* programme, Robert Cecil clarified that in the period in which Cairncross worked for Lord Hankey the only atomic knowledge to which he would have had access was the decision that Britain had decided to go ahead with the bomb.

It was his response to the accusation that he was a 'traitor', where the normally soft-spoken Cairncross raised the tempo of the interview. He pointed the finger at Chamberlain, as 'the great traitor to Britain' who 'led the country down the garden path, blundered into war, betrayed Czechoslovakia; that's what I call treason'. This was the only time in the programme that the conversation turned to the issue he most wanted to discuss: 'Munich and after'. *Newsnight* was not a good experience, and some members of his family back in the UK were unhappy with his decision to do the interview, fearing it would stoke up further unwelcome publicity. In Lesmahagow, the 'aunts' had been disturbed by the 'Fifth Man' revelation, which brought local reporters to their door:[11] 'They were deeply shocked and offended when it was made public. It was a very bitter blow to hear him being called a traitor.'[12] While some felt he should have declined the BBC's advances, Cairncross himself believed that he had been 'lynched' by the press.[13]

The continuing furore over the 'Fifth Man' meant he revised his publication plans. 'I'm reconsidering all my priorities … in the light of the developments which have made me now, at any rate, notorious in the States,' he wrote to Lester Crocker, his friend and former university colleague in Cleveland. He embarked on another new book which would deal with the latest allegations, while allowing him to explain in full his reasons for choosing to work for Soviet intelligence. These would constitute his memoirs. It was provisionally entitled 'An Agent for the Duration' ('The Fifth Man that Never Was') and he sketched out three sections: 'An Unremarkable Civil Servant' (which dealt with his FO/civil service career), 'The Road to Disaster' (which focused on Munich and after) and 'He Calls Himself a Writer' (which would cover his literary interests). This was an ambitious project with an intended twenty-seven chapters. He thought it was necessary to treat the issue of his espionage as part of a wider historical investigation into the whole appeasement question, which had been absent from the 'Fifth Man' debate. This plan won the support of academic friends, who shared his view that the history of the 1930s needed to frame his analysis, notably the conflicts in the FO, the political failures in dealing with the threat of Nazism and the choices facing those who sought to change the policy of appeasement.

For what would be the last time, he turned to Graham Greene for support. He was worried about the effect the publicity in France would have on his residence status, and Greene, who had long experience of dealing with the French authorities, was able to reassure him on some matters to do with obtaining his *carte de séjour*, which would give him the right to stay in France. Greene welcomed his new book project and shared his friend's view that not only had he been misrepresented in the accounts of espionage writers – few of whom, Greene noted, had experience of working for the security services – but he had also been badly treated by MI5 itself. Cairncross felt that the attacks on him by 'establishment' figures in the press – including the triumvirate of lords – was for MI5 a useful way of distracting attention from the criticisms it had received for its handling of the 'moles', and deflect claims (later shown to be groundless) that Roger Hollis, their own director general, had been a Soviet spy. Cairncross told Greene that he felt he had been 'offered up as a sacrificial lamb'. He also expected better protection from the security service given that he had cooperated with them since 1964. Still without firm assurances that he could return to the UK without fear of arrest, any attempt to visit now would be the subject of intense press scrutiny. Greene put him in touch with his friend Colonel Ronald Challoner, the consul general in Nice, whose knowledge of the intelligence services Greene thought could be useful to his friend as he worked on the manuscript. Greene did what he could to help with his and Gayle's residency applications, while advising him to keep a low profile following the BBC interview. Greene also recommended his own literary agent to help get the account published. His last letters to 'Claymore' during late 1990 and early 1991 were often dictated by his niece, Amanda Saunders, because of the rapid deterioration of his health. In April 1991 Greene died of leukaemia, in Switzerland, aged eighty-six. Greene's death was a big shock to Cairncross: 'It hit him very hard. It was the only time I saw him unable to cope, putting his head in his hands.'[14]

Greene's support for Cairncross after his public exposure as the 'Fifth Man' was not only from sympathy for the plight of a friend in trouble. He also empathized with Cairncross's predicament, influenced of course by his own experience of working for MI6, as well his later dealings with Philby. Greene had drawn on this experience in his novel, *The Human Factor*, published in 1978, which returned to the themes of individual conscience, divided loyalties and the moral and psychological pressures on those who have chosen to spy for another country. Castle, the main character, was an MI6 officer who had passed material to the Soviets in exchange for help in getting his black lover out of Apartheid South Africa. He was a non-Marxist with no time for the Soviet Union and had acted on a combination of personal feeling and hatred of the Apartheid system. Once this had been accomplished, Castle, on his return to the UK, had married Sarah, his lover, and settled down back in MI6 offices, waiting for retirement and hoping that his espionage would not come to light. This precarious existence had some similarities to Cairncross's own situation, motivated as he was by one main cause, acting alone and unable to share with anyone other than his controller the nature of his secret work. *The Human Factor* was published a year before Cairncross's first public exposure, and there is no evidence that he had told Greene of his espionage before this. However, Greene may have had an inkling of it, or might have heard rumours about Cairncross from friends in intelligence. In any case, Castle resembled Cairncross more than Philby, who was often thought to be the model.

Cairncross's friendship with Graham Greene was the most important of his life. It is difficult to gauge the strength he took from their constant correspondence and their meetings over the years, but Greene's support had been invaluable in dealing with his various crises. There was also mutual respect between the two former MI6 agents. At their last meeting at Greene's apartment in Antibes the year before he died, Gayle, meeting Greene for the first time (as 'John's girl'), picked up the rapport; 'they shared something, a point of view, more than respect'.[15] Reflecting on his long friendship with Greene for an intended (but unpublished) obituary, Cairncross recalled a lecture Greene had given in 1969 entitled 'The Virtue of Disloyalty'. In this talk, on the occasion of receiving the Shakespeare Prize at the University of Hamburg, Greene warned against what he called the 'strenuous bugle note of loyalty', arguing that the vocation of a writer was to draw on disloyalty 'as an extra dimension of understanding'. Writers in essence were dissidents, who needed 'to see the virtues of a communist in a capitalist society and the virtues of a capitalist in a communist society'. At such times – and he used the 1930s as his example – some citizens may also have to choose the 'virtue of disloyalty' for the future of civilization.[16] Despite obvious differences – Greene was a Catholic and Cairncross a secular humanist – Cairncross concluded there 'was an underlying similarity in our approach to life. We were both not only dissidents but unconventional characters who defied or ignored public opinion.'[17]

As Cairncross continued with his memoirs in the face of more attacks – 'The Face of a Traitor' was one *Mail on Sunday* headline – he recognized himself as an exiled dissident. He regarded his earlier 'disloyalty' as 'virtuous' in the cause of furthering anti-fascism. In resisting the attacks launched on him by the 'establishment', he would have 'to be a piece of grit in the state machinery', as Greene had described the ultimate act of virtuous disloyalty. It seemed to him that journalists, espionage writers and commentators had already made up their minds about the 'Fifth Man'. They had 'got it all wrong', as he was wont to repeat to friends and family.

I reflected on why I, who was a radical, a libertarian, a pragmatist, and a loner, as well as a decidedly straight character, had now been stamped as an ideologue, a fanatical communist, a member of the KGB almost since my arrival at Cambridge, and a close associate of a patrician and partly homosexual group with which I had never had any contact and whose political ideas and values were diametrically opposed to mine.[18]

Molière, once again, was another source of comfort for him. His *L'Humanité de Molière*, an edited collection of essays (published in 1988 on a low print run by his first publisher, Nizet), enabled him to make the case for Molière as a humanist. Molière was also a radical and, to some degree, 'subversive' of religion and convention, which together with the humour that ran through his work had often helped Cairncross deal with his various troubles. Cairncross's single-mindedness saw him through the recurring pressures brought by his notoriety and sustained what in the circumstances was a prodigious output of translating and writing, backed by extensive archival research. Arguably, it was this single-mindedness, and what some perceived as intellectual arrogance, that had originally put him in the predicament. He had been contemptuous of the position of the British government towards fascism (which included its attitudes to Mussolini and Franco as well Hitler), had little faith in the FO's ability to make effective policy and decided that he could have more influence in taking decisive action himself. This self-confidence in his own judgements was reflected in other contexts: in his arguments with the BBC drama department, in endless tussles with publishers and editors and in his rivalry with other *Molièristes*. For those unmoved by hierarchies or uninhibited by uniformity and who appreciated long discourses on history and culture, he was a charming and humorous friend. For others, more reluctant to be distracted by his academic interests or insufficiently appreciative of his knowledge and expertise he could be a difficult person to deal with: 'He didn't suffer fools gladly.'[19] The one time he was criticized for not being single-minded was when he continued to pass documents to the Soviets after 1945. Some felt he should have shown more initiative and got out then, while the later conventional explanation was that he had sold his soul to Stalinism.

He had of course tried to get out by applying for academic jobs, pursuing a business opportunity and haggling for more BBC work. He also feared the possibility of blackmail from the Soviets, if he should stop, while the poor regard in which he was held by his civil service superiors precluded any attempt to negotiate with them. He tried to explain his dilemma in an unpublished preface for an early draft of his memoirs.

> Had I reported my experiences to my superiors, as is the current wisdom ... one can imagine how I would have been treated if my offences had been tried in the Cold War, when I would have always been cast as a dedicated communist and traitor.[20]

News that his former controller Yuri Modin had confirmed Cairncross's 'Fifth Man' identity and was in the process of writing his own account kept the issue in the news and provided Cairncross himself with more material. It was the high season for revelations from ex-KGB figures, as the Soviet system they had served came to an end, a spectacle witnessed by the couple in their French living-room. 'We're all delighted with events in Russia', he told Alec.[21] Alec remained supportive of his younger brother at his greatest hour of need, and he and his family visited them in Provence. John was grateful for his brother's help and often spoke proudly to his friends of Alec's achievements, notably as the government's chief economic adviser, master of St Peter's College, Oxford, and chancellor of Glasgow University, suggesting at one point to Graham Greene that he might refer to his 'famous brother' as 'Claymost'. Alec, who of course had spent part of the 1930s lodging with his brother in Glasgow and Cambridge, agreed that the best way of dealing with the accusations was to emphasize the particular historical context of that period: at one point they discussed extending the analysis from appeasement to the Battle of Britain. Cairncross sought other academic advice from his friends Professors David Rubin and Lester Crocker, while he put together a reading list of historical accounts of the interwar period. The writing process was interrupted both by his indifferent health and by the challenge of computers. His habit was to type out broad themes on his Olivetti typewriter at the kitchen table – a process made more difficult by his poor eyesight – and then annotate with handwritten comments (sometimes with suggestions from Gayle) before proceeding further. He continued to work in this way even after they had bought a computer, with Gayle now doing the bulk of the word processing from his typewritten drafts.

Though they were happy in this arrangement and the extra space for their dogs, fenced in after one of them was killed (and not, as one press report suggested, as part of a guard-dog protection unit), France had not been as welcoming as they had hoped. There was little of the idyllic French hospitality immortalized in Peter Mayle's *A Year in Provence*, published the year before they arrived. Despite both having good French and his long immersion into French culture, it was not easy to make friends locally. Unlike the Italians, who if they considered his espionage at all, viewed it with amused curiosity, the French were less conciliatory towards their new British neighbours once news of the *cinquième homme* reached the press. Politics was also unpromising. The dramatic victory of the right-wing parties of Jacques Chirac and Valery D'Estaing in the 1993 legislative elections didn't augur well. 'Both in politics and everyday life', he wrote to Alec, 'both of us want to get out of here. We would have gone (back) to Italy had things been a little more stable.'[22]

In fact, he had not finished with Italy. Italy and Italian culture was still on his mind, and he had been planning another important translation. His translations, after all, formed his lasting contribution to scholarship.

> John was a high class versifier. The translations are better than his original pieces. His handful of La Fontaine fables was as good as almost anything in English (except Norman Shapiro's). John's Racine is a masterpiece and of his Corneille versions, nothing beats his L'Illusion comique. In the 80s and 90s I lectured several times at Oxford, Cambridge, and London. The last piece I took on tour compared John's Phèdre with Robert Lowell's, much to the American's detriment. The audiences of Racine specialists agreed that John's translation was much better (e.g. more semantically symmetrical with the original, if less musical).[23]

Since the BBC first dramatized his translations of *Andromaque* and *Athaliah* for radio listeners in the 1960s and 1970s, London and Edinburgh theatregoers since the 1980s had been treated to his *Berenice* and *Britannicus*. 'The wonder of the evening', Michael Billington, the *Guardian*'s theatre critic, raved of the performance of the former at the Lyric, Hammersmith, 'is that with the aid of John Cairncross's blank-verse translation, it absorbs one totally in the Racineian world in which passion bursts through the atmosphere of formal severity like a bright coloured figure shattering a paper hoop'.[24]

His new work was to be a translation of *The Adventures of Pinocchio* for Oxford University Press (OUP). He had undertaken some Italian translations in the past, and indeed his first published work was his translation of Umberto Saba for *Penguin New Writing* in 1950. He had also demystified the doctrines of Vilfredo Pareto for the use of American economists. However, his new commission was on a different scale entirely. OUP, well aware of his work on Racine in the Penguin Classics series, was enthusiastic. He thought he could adopt a broadly similar approach to Carlo Collodi's original work, in which 'the special magic and poetry in Pinocchio must be recreated without having recourse to affected or "*recherche*" expressions. This means that the task of preserving the work's unique charm is more difficult than it looks and means that the translator must draw on a certain literary skill so as not to fall into an artificial fairy tale style.'[25]

Carlo Collodi (born Carlo Lorenzini) was from a humble Italian background but benefited from a good education, which enabled him to work at the Libreria Piatti bookshop in Florence, a place with a reputation as an unofficial nineteenth-century salon for intellectuals and writers in the period before the Italian Risorgimento. Influenced by these literary circles and Giuseppe Mazzini's ideas of republicanism and democracy, he joined a Tuscan battalion in the First Italian War of Independence against Austrian Occupation in the 1848 rising. Subsequently he launched *Il Lampione*, a satirical newspaper with a light political touch, and later *Scaramuccia*, a theatrical journal named after the boastful clown who was a regular feature in Italian *commedia dell'arte* and similar to Molière's character Coviello in *The Bourgeois Gentilhomme*. In subsequent years, Collodi earned a living through journalism and publishing, maintaining his literary and political connections in the aftermath of Italian unification before *Pinocchio* was published in 1883.

It is easy to see how Collodi's style appealed to Cairncross. Though *Pinocchio* was a nineteenth-century work, he was struck by some similarities with Molière's earlier plays which drove his interest as he embarked upon this new challenge. The combination of humour, political satire and social criticism was there in Collodi as it had been, in a different context, in Molière two centuries before. Collodi was writing at a time of great change and upheaval in Italian society and working with new techniques – such as the 'verismo' of the Sicilian novelist Giovanni Verga.

Cairncross could easily identify with Collodi's broad liberal republicanism. A similar outlook provided much of the intellectual origins of the thinking of the exiled intellectuals, the Rosselli liberal socialists, the Mazzini Society republications he encountered, initially in Paris and subsequently during his own exile in Rome. That tradition, lost in the Cold War polarity between Italian Christian Democrats and Italian communists, would be buried in the Berlusconi era.

Moving back to Italy, therefore, made a lot of sense. However, he was struck down by serious illness shortly after he had agreed with OUP to do the Pinocchio translation. His health had been deteriorating, and in addition to eye, ear and teeth problems, he had been diagnosed with high blood pressure. In the late summer of 1993 he suffered his first stroke which put him in hospital until January 1994. This brought a lot more work for Gayle, who now had to postpone her singing auditions to support him; arrange hospital stays and visits; and provide more help in turning his memoirs into an autobiography. To this end, she moved them back to Lago di Vico, in the Lazio region, some 40 miles from Rome. Subsequently, they moved several more times, including to Grasse, near Cannes, on the French Riviera, so he could get specialist hospital treatment. He now had great difficulty in speaking and writing and needed the services of a speech therapist and neurologist. He finally had to abandon his Pinocchio project,[26] while the difficult task of putting together the chapters for his autobiography was taken on by Gayle, under his supervision; Ronnie Challoner and Alec would contribute after John's death.

By early 1995, Gayle had decided that the best treatment for him was in Britain, and she found them a cottage to rent in Herefordshire. Despite his long-standing fears, there was now no question of him being arrested on entering the UK, and in April, accompanied by a nurse, he left the South of France for England. Gayle met him on arrival and drove him to the village of Longhope. Here, they continued with their work, surrounded by their dogs and with occasional visits from his family. In late August he suffered another stroke. In early September his first wife Gabi died after suffering a serious injury in a tragic accident, when she was caught in revolving doors on leaving the fashionable restaurant 192 Notting Hill. He had always accepted that because Gabi's pension and health benefits depended on their marriage, they would not be divorced. In sad circumstances, he now had the chance to provide

Gayle with some security, and on 8 September they were married at the registry office in Herefordshire. By now he was in a wheelchair. A month later, on 8 October, he died in his sleep. At his funeral, family and friends commemorated the nonconformist and free spirit through one of his original poems, which ended:

> Lastly, whatever be my creed,
> Free me from blind conformism's chains;
> (Intellectuals of the world unite!
> You have nothing to lose but your brains).[27]

Epilogue: Fact and fiction in the life of John Cairncross

If there had been a Churchillian party in 1936–39, I would have remained a struggling clerk, and would be remembered, if at all, by my Racine.

JOHN CAIRNCROSS, LETTER TO DECLAN WALTON,
17 NOVEMBER 1991

For many years John Cairncross's status as a Cambridge spy remained a mystery, known to only a few MI5 officials, their American equivalents and (after 1964) his brother Alec. Once additional facts about his life became available his story continued to be misrepresented in newspapers or by molehunters, while it was often smothered in fictional portraits of the Cambridge spies. In contrast to the others he has been neglected, often regarded as dull and lacking the glamour of the famous four. His identity as the 'Fifth Man' towards the end of his life brought more interest, and he even appeared on the front pages of national newspapers, while he remained frustrated in his own attempts to present his account. His autobiography, published two years after his death, suffers from the absence of his own editing hand. The final manuscript was based upon selections from different earlier versions (he never completed his original autobiography) and was aided by different editors – under the supervision of his widow – and had to survive a legal challenge over its authorship brought by the espionage expert Nigel West, otherwise known as Rupert Allason, formerly a Conservative MP. In his strongly worded ruling the judge rejected any claim that West had ghostwritten or held copyright over the book. There are significant omissions in the published version, notably on the detail and regularity of his meetings with Soviet controllers, as well as errors in dates, while it is overly defensive in places, reacting to the various claims against him without adding a detailed explanation of some of his actions, notably in the period after 1945. Although it added significant background to his life and character, it understated the two essential factors most helpful to explain his motivations. First, the 'Fifth Man' claims halted his intended book on the appeasement crisis, without which it is impossible to fully understand his motivations. Second, the influence of the Italian anti-fascist exiles he met in Paris and those he knew later in Rome is as fundamental to an understanding of the choices he made as his holidays in Austria and Germany: 'Cambridge communism' pales by comparison. Cairncross's life after espionage has barely been discussed in any detail, his significant scholarship largely ignored; yet both are crucial to get a rounded picture of the man. His dedication to Molière was not merely academic; it is important in helping to understand his own character, his principles and his outlook on life.

For researchers of the Cambridge spies, there is inevitably a sharp difference between the quality of the research produced before and after the fall of the Berlin Wall. During the Cold War, because of the difficulty of gaining access to vital sources much attention was given to evidence provided by former FO officials or those members of the security services who were prepared to talk anonymously to persistent espionage writers and 'molehunters' like Chapman Pincher. Pincher provided a sympathetic ear to the grievances of Peter Wright and used material given to him by Wright as the basis for several books, as well as an investigation into the activities of Sir Roger Hollis, the former director general of MI5, whom he suspected of being a 'super spy' (a claim Cairncross himself briefly considered). After Andrew Boyle missed Cairncross entirely and made no mention of him in *The Climate of Treason*, Pincher, in 1981, drawing on conversations with Peter Wright and others, published what he called 'The Truth About John Cairncross'. Wright's information helped him to go a bit further than Penrose and Leitch in identifying Klugmann as his recruiter and explaining the nature of Caincross's work for the Soviets at Bletchley and in MI6. However, there were significant inaccuracies in his account which gave a misleading impression of Cairncross's motivations. Cairncross, according to Pincher, 'had experienced poverty and had concluded that Soviet-style communism was the only way of securing social justice'. Pincher also suggests, improbably, that

Cairncross, an intellectually self-confident Cambridge undergraduate, was indoctrinated with communist ideas by his Marxist superiors. Pincher is the initiator of some of the most common myths attached to Cairncross – that in 1936, on the instructions of 'Otto' (somebody he never met until 1937), he quit the 'Communist Party' (a party he never joined), abandoned a promising Cambridge academic career (one that was never offered to him), in order to join the FO. By now embellishing Wright's conversations with his own speculative theories, Pincher also claimed erroneously that Cairncross moved from the FO to the Treasury in 1938 on Moscow's instructions, whereas he was transferred because his FO superiors thought him unsuitable for 'representation'.[1]

The end of the Cold War enabled the publication of memoirs and testimonies from former KGB agents and access to Soviet archives, which was followed shortly after by the release of MI5's personal files on several spies and suspects (though they have yet to release Cairncross's own files). These provided whole new insight on the identities of spies and agents, the nature of the material they provided and the circumstances of their recruitment. When used judiciously the new material provides rich insight on the lives of individuals drawn to communism, while closing some loopholes. Inevitably they fuelled more speculation on the Cambridge spies, including more on the elusive 'Fifth Man'. Christopher Andrew is surely correct to point out that it was the KGB that decided the composition of the five. The problem for Cairncross – the last of the five to be recruited and the last to be exposed – was that his membership of the 'Cambridge Five' assumed a whole set of commonly shared characteristics that were not applicable to him.

This is partly because of the mythical nature of the Cambridge spies' story that has been glamorized in numerous films, novels and newspaper articles. The image of the Cambridge spies, now immortalized in the national memory, evokes a darker side to popular representations contained in fictional productions like *Brideshead Revisited* and *Downton Abbey*. These are inaccurate portrayals – none of the spies are aristocrats and the spying takes place well away from Cambridge quads. In Cairncross's case, however, these images are even more misleading and merely perpetuate the myth that he was a close associate of the other four.

He was neither an uncompromising Stalinist ideologue nor another victim of the 'God that Failed', those intellectuals of the 1930s who had put their faith in communism only to provide a full recantation of those principles in the 1940s. Cairncross always maintained that his decision to spy was a strategic choice, and he never subscribed to the more rigid doctrines of Marxism or believed in the 'Red Paradise', as he derided the Soviet Union. Moving to Russia, a country he had never visited, was not an option for him; such a move would not have been an escape, but a final defeat. In the decades when three of the other spies were adjusting uncomfortably to their new lives in the Soviet Union without any of the freedoms, status or intellectual stimulation they had found in Britain (though Maclean eventually produced a thoughtful analysis of British foreign policy), Cairncross enjoyed an intellectual renaissance, as well as personal liberation. Unlike the others, he did not turn to drink and had an uneventful personal life by comparison. His identification as the 'Fifth Man' obscured these differences, and the same psychological profile attached to the others was attributed to him; if he was not gay, then he was an intellectual of sorts, a category which in Britain carries connotations of unreliability and is often a cause for suspicion.

John Cairncross does not fit easily into the caricature of the 'Cambridge spy'. Previous accounts of his role as a spy have omitted the more nuanced details of his character. His aversion to what he regarded as the peculiarly English class hierarchies of Cambridge University and the FO did not amount to a Marxist endorsement of class conflict (he had little interest in workers' struggles). His appreciation of Marxism as a useful explanatory framework for some aspects of French literature was not indicative of a dogmatic ideologue. Belief in the merits of the Soviet Union as a wartime ally was not built upon the rigid principles of a Stalinist apparatchik. It was his lifelong interest in the history of religion and the origins of modern bourgeois societies that stimulated his research on polygamy and not the obsessions of an over-sexed philanderer. Politically, by today's standards (according to his niece), he would have been a supporter of the Scottish National Party, though critical of its intellectual limitations.[2]

One of the legacies of the Cambridge spy story, as Richard Davenport-Hines has argued, is its role in exaggerating the notion of an establishment engaged in cover-ups to defend its own people. That they were implicit in treachery, helping 'traitors' escape from justice. 'Establishment' cover-up was even less applicable in Cairncross's case, as someone who from his time in the FO and civil service through to his interrogation and later treatment by MI5 (in not offering him the same immunity given to Blunt) was always regarded as an outsider. Guy Liddell's diaries confirm the contrasting attitudes towards him and the others. Guy Burgess attributed his ability to get away with outrageous misdemeanours for so long to the 'class blinkers' that pervaded Whitehall: that he was protected because of his background. When cabinet papers revealed that after Cairncross's confession in 1964 the government was concerned about possible ramifications for his brother Alec, the government's chief economic adviser, following any prosecution, it was assumed that Cairncross had benefited from his 'establishment' connections and had been given immunity from prosecution. The reality was different: he had been assured in Cleveland that any confession would not be used as admissible evidence, and he had never been given immunity from prosecution. He felt that he had himself been a victim of the establishment and 'thrown to the wolves' by MI5. The perception that he had been protected in high places persisted, however. Following his public exposure in 1979 and later in 1990, questions were asked in parliament about his status and whether he had immunity, with the clear implication that he was the beneficiary of a cover-up. In fact – as we now know – there was no evidence admissible in a British court that could have led to a successful prosecution.

Cairncross was aggrieved that Blunt was protected by influential friends and unhappy that he had been unfairly placed in the same category. After his exposure, Blunt also received staunch support from what might be called the academic establishment, who resisted attempts to expel him from the British Academy, or even censure him for his conduct (of a non-academic nature). His case was supported by academics who held very different political views, from Lord Dacre (Hugh Trevor-Roper) to Eric Hobsbawm and A. J. P. Taylor. This was sufficiently robust to defeat the motions, though Blunt later resigned from the British Academy. Cairncross, despite his many friendships with international scholars, could not have expected such a demonstration of support.[3]

We might also wonder about the usefulness of the term 'traitor' as applied to John Cairncross. A term that has ancient origins, it is an easy label to apply at times of political crisis in Britain – for example, from appeasement in the 1930s, through the Cold War to the Brexit crisis – and the more difficult to define. Its meaning and application have been subject to the historical shifts in loyalties and the realignment of allies and enemies. 'Traitors' and 'Treachery' depend upon particular notions of loyalty (to nation or class) and often accompanied by associations with cover-ups and conspiracy. In the 1930s, it was a familiar cry primarily directed at Ramsay MacDonald for abandoning the Labour Party to lead a National Government with the Conservatives or at Neville Chamberlain for betraying Czechoslovakia and appeasing fascism in 1938; as war with Germany began, fascist apologists (and Italian Immigrants) were also targeted. As the Cold War intensified and the activities of the Cambridge spies and others were revealed, it assumed a particular association with communists. The end of the Cold War opened up the question once more, when the release of the security service files of former communists was closely followed by those of fascists and a stream of publications about their treachery. At the time of Cairncross's exposure, the most vocal parliamentarians denouncing his treachery were those on the Labour left, who believed that he had benefited from some class-based conspiracy in Whitehall and pushed for his extradition from France.

He always rejected claims that he was a traitor or involved in treachery, which he attributed to a misreading of the history of the 1930s and the legacy of the Cold War. Certainly, he betrayed the trust of FO and civil service colleagues like Lord Hankey (with whom he always enjoyed warm relations), William Strang and others. It must have tested his resolve to continue deceiving colleagues, smuggling documents, holding secretive meetings and withholding such a significant part of his life from family and friends. The post-war period, when he continued to pass documents to the Russians, was particularly hard. Hoping to be free of Moscow by the end of the war, he felt obliged to carry on for reasons of self-preservation, despite being aware of the deteriorating situation in Eastern Europe as the Cold War developed. It meant that whatever his earlier motivations, he could not substantiate the claim that he was entirely an 'agent for the duration'. In 2008, in a BBC Radio 4 interview with Stella Rimington, MI5's former director general, Frances Cairncross said she found her uncle's continued espionage in the late 1940s 'absolutely indefensible'. At the same time, she found Rimington's suggestion that more recent Islamic terrorists were motivated by similar idealism 'distasteful'. Her uncle, she reminded Rimington, never had any intention of 'destroying the society he lived in'.

This leads to one other explanation for why the story of John Cairncross – a complex and intriguing figure – has been so difficult to understand. It can be attributed to something he did share with the other spies – and, indeed, with all spies. This was the way he compartmentalized his life. After his confession in 1964, he still refused to talk about it with family or friends for a long while. 'Of course he never mentioned his other life, even when it came out in the press,' Silvia Balit, one of Cairncross's FAO lunch companions, recalled. Declan Walton believed Cairncross 'made an agreement with himself, that he would not talk, even to his friends about it'. 'He was a great obfuscator,' according to his nephew David Cairncross, though his aversion to forthright exposition was often down to his scholastic mannerisms.[4] The last time Alec Cairncross met his younger brother, at a family lunch in France, he left feeling that he had still to receive a full explanation for John's decision to spy.

Gayle Brinkerhoff regarded his espionage as belonging to a different life, a different world even. Nor did the stories of his 'prickly' nature, his intellectual arrogance or unwillingness to admit he was wrong fit the John Cairncross she knew: 'He helped me to see the world in a humanistic way. He opened the door for me intellectually.'[5] Rather than devious or secretive, let alone treacherous, she found him, from their first meeting, empathetic and light-hearted. Other friends and family talked of his 'engaging' and 'vivacious' nature and 'attractive personality'. Italy had mellowed him. In breaks from his translations he would often turn to P. G. Wodehouse, one of his favourite authors, for lighter amusement, and it is tempting to think that in later years he laughed at the latter's observation that 'it is never difficult to distinguish between a Scotsman with a grievance and a ray of sunshine'. One of the extraordinary aspects of John Cairncross's life is the way he managed these different compartments: his spying, his private life and his scholarship.

One consequence of the collective legacy of the perennial 'mole hunt', the odour of conspiracy and the Cold War hangover, has been the tendency to disregard the choices that faced young people of John Cairncross's generation. He and his friends felt that his original motivations had been obscured and distorted; mistakes and poor judgement aside, he never sought to harm the interests of his country. As he was working on his unfinished autobiography in the frenetic period after the 'Fifth Man' furore, he was, in his own words, 'still naïve enough to believe' that the 'reader will, I trust, go back with me to my early days'.[6]

Notes

Prologue

1 David Leitch and Barrie Penrose, 'I Was Spy for Soviets', *Sunday Times*, 23/12/1979.
2 Graham Greene to John Cairncross 22/2/1980, MS. 1995.003 Box 13, Folder 33, Graham Greene papers, John J. Burns Library, Boston College.
3 David Leitch, 'Introduction', in Yuri Modin, *My Five Cambridge Friends* (Headline, 1994), p. 5.
4 Marjorie Wallace, 'The Spy Who Nearly Loved Me', *The Sunday Telegraph*, 21 October 1990.
5 Christopher Andrew and Oleg Gordievsky, *KGB: The Inside Story* (Harper Collins, 1990).
6 Alan Coren, '… and Moreover', *The Times*, 19 October 1990.
7 John Costello, *Mask of Treachery: Spies, Lies, Buggery and Betrayal* (Atlantic, 1988), p. 410.
8 Ibid., p. 412.

Chapter 1

1 John Cairncross, *The Enigma Spy: An Autobiography* (Century Random House, 1997), p. 24.
2 Alan Bold, *Hugh MacDiarmid: The Terrible Crystal* (Routledge and Kegan Paul, 1983), pp. 22–3.
3 Alec Cairncross, *Living with the Century* (lynx, 1998), p. 15. In another version told to him by his eldest sister Elsie, they met after his mother disembarked from a horse-drawn brake outside his shop.

4 Frances Cairncross, interview with author.

5 CULMC, Add. 10042 Box 1. All John Cairncross's papers are held at Cambridge University Manuscripts Collection (CULMC) under ref. Add.10042.

6 Cairncross, *The Enigma Spy*, p. 26.

7 Cairncross, *Living with the Century*, pp. 14–15; Cairncross, *The Enigma Spy*, p. 23.

8 Cairncross, *The Enigma Spy*, p. 25.

9 Cairncross, *Living with the Century*, p. 16.

10 Cairncross, *The Enigma Spy*, p. 24.

11 As a fifteen-year-old schoolboy he offered advice on chess moves in The *Glasgow Herald* 19/6/1926. I am grateful to Alan McGowan for this reference.

12 Cairncross, *Living with the Century*, p. 21.

13 CULMC, Add. 10042 Box 1.

14 Graham Greene (ed.), *The Old School* (Jonathan Cape, 1934).

15 Andrew Lownie, *Stalin's Englishman: The Lives of Guy Burgess* (Hodder and Stoughton, 2015), p. 8.

16 Phillip Knightley, *Kim Philby K.G.B.Masterspy* (Guild Publishing, 1988), p. 26.

17 Knightley, *Kim Philby K.G.B.Masterspy*, p. 33.

Chapter 2

1 Cairncross, *Living with the Century*, p. 33.

2 Ibid., p. 35.

3 Alec Cairncross papers, University of Glasgow Archive (UGA) SEN 10/73.

4 CULMC, Add. 10042 Box 1.

5 UGA, SEN 10/74.

6 The Rationalist Press Association Glasgow District. Public Lectures 1931.

7 Ian Smith to Alec Cairncross, 24/3/1931 UGA, DC106 Add. 84/1/125: A. Cairncross, *Living With the Century*, pp. 33–4.

8 UGA, SEN 10/73; SEN 10/74.

9 UGA, DC106 Add. 87/9.

10 John Cairncross's diary is held at CULMC, Add. 10042 3/3 C110.

11 He calls it 'Polchington' in his diary.

Chapter 3

1 G. Borovik, *The Philby Files*, ed. Philip Knightley (Warner Book, 1995).

2 Roland Philipps, *A Spy Named Orphan: The Enigma of Donald Maclean* (The Bodley Head, 2018), p. 37.

3 Lownie, *Stalin's Englishman*, pp. 31–7.

4 Miranda Carter, *Anthony Blunt: His Lives* (Macmillan, 2001), p. 109.

5 Julia Boyd, *Travellers in the Third Reich* (Elliott and Thompson, 2017), p. 373.

6 John Colville, *Footprints in Time* (Michael Russell, 1984), p. 45.

7 Ibid.

8 Ibid., p. 46.

9 Ibid.

10 Ibid.

11 Ibid., p. 49.

12 Ibid., p. 51.

13 CULMC, Add. 10042 Box 9.

14 Cairncross, *The Enigma Spy*, p. 31.

15 Molière, 'Don Juan' from *The Miser and Other Plays*, trans. John Wood and David Coward (Penguin Classics, 2004).

16 Cairncross, *The Enigma Spy*, p. 30.

17 Walter Salant, letter to Alec Cairncross 28/11/1995. UGA, DC106 Add. 80/1.

18 Cairncross, *The Enigma Spy*, pp. 31–2.

19 Cairncross, *The Enigma Spy*. Cairncross erroneously states that Thalmann was released; in fact, he was held for eleven years and was shot in 1944.

20 CULMC, Add. 10042 Box 1.

21 For an excellent account of these groups, see Caroline Moorehead's *A Bold and Dangerous Family: The Rossellis and the Fight against Mussolini* (Chatto and Windus, 2017).

22 Cairncross, *The Enigma Spy*, p. 34.

Chapter 4

1   Cairncross, *Living with the Century*, p. 42.

2   Cited in Richard J. Evans, *Eric Hobsbawm: A Life in History* (Little, Brown, 2019), pp. 54–5.

3   Victor Kiernan, 'Herbert Norman's Cambridge', in Roger W. Bowen (ed.), *E. H. Norman: His Life and Scholarship* (University of Toronto Press, 1984), p. 27.

4   Kiernan, 'Herbert Norman's Cambridge', p. 28.

5   Cairncross, *Living with the Century*, p. 41.

6   McDaly to Alec Cairncross 19/10/35. UGA, DC106 Add. 86/1/13.

7   CULMC, Add. 10042 Box 1.

8   Ibid.

9   Ibid.

10   Henry Ashton, *A Preface to Moliere* (Longmans, 1927), p. 11.

11   Ashton, *A Preface to Moliere*, p. 10.

12   Douglas Parmée to John Cairncross 12/11/1991. CULMC, Add. 10042 Box 1.

13   Carter, *Anthony Blunt: His Lives*, p. 83.

14   Anthony Blunt, 'Biographical Memoir', *British Library*, MS 88902/1, p. 17.

15   Carter, *Anthony Blunt: His Lives,* p. 82.

16   Ibid., p. 189.

17   Anthony Blunt, 'Art under Capitalism and Socialism', in C. Day Lewis (ed.), *The Mind in Chains: Socialism and the Cultural Revolution* (Frederick Miller Ltd., 1937), p. 113.

18   CULMC, Add. 10042 Box 1.

19   Ibid.

20   Ibid.

21   McDaly to Alec Cairncross 10/12/1935 UGA, DC106 Add. 86/1/13.

22   Moliere, *Don Juan and Other Plays*, trans. George Graveley and Ian Maclean (Oxford University Press, 1989), p. 19.

23   Louis MacNeice, *The Strings are False: An Unfinished Autobiography,* p. 133. Cited in Carter, *Anthony Blunt*, p. 96.

24   Carter, *Anthony Blunt*, p. 96.

25   Information on Green's earlier life is scarce, but some background has been provided by his family and is available through public genealogy records.

26   Cairncross, *The Enigma Spy*, p. 39.

27   McDaly to Alec Cairncross, 19/10/1935 UGA, DC106 Add. 86/1/13.

28 Michael Straight, *After Long Silence* (W.W. Norton, 1983), p. 61. Straight is a little more reliable on this than on the question of his own espionage.

29 Geoff Andrews, *The Shadow Man* (I.B. Tauris, 2015).

30 *Trinity Magazine* Easter 1935 and June 1936. Wren Library, Trinity College, Cambridge.

31 *Communist Review*, September 1932.

Chapter 5

1 CULMC, Add. 10042 Box 1.

2 Ian Smith to Alec Cairncross 13/7/1931. UGA, DC106 Add. 86/1/11.

3 Declan Walton, written communication with author. Walton was a friend of both Cairncross and Singer, who recounted the story to him when they worked together at the United Nations in New York.

4 Alec Cairncross, 'Appendix', in *Living with the Century* (lynx, 1998), p. 300.

5 Cairncross, *The Enigma Spy*, p. 49.

6 Ibid., p. 50.

7 For discussion of Vansittart's attitude to Hitler, see B. J. C. McCarcher, 'The Foreign Office 1930-39: Strategy, Permanent Interests and National Security', *Contemporary British History* 18, no. 3 (Autumn 2004).

8 McCarcher, 'The Foreign Office 1930-39: Strategy, Permanent Interests and National Security'.

9 The National Archives (TNA) FCO 158/129.

10 CULMC, Add. 10042 Box 1.

11 Philipps, *A Spy Named Orphan: The Enigma of Donald Maclean*.

12 TNA, FO 371.

13 TNA, FO 371.

14 TNA, FO 371.

15 Arthur Koestler, *The Invisible Writing* (Vintage, 2005), p. 383.

16 Ibid., p. 395.

17 Arthur Koestler, 'Dialogue with Death', in *Spanish Testament* (Victor Gollancz, 1937), p. 285.

18 Ibid., p. 287.

19 Ibid., p. 367.

20 Cairncross, *The Enigma Spy*, p. 56.

21 'Extract from statement by John Cairncross re Burgess and mentioning Nicolson', 2/4/1952. TNA, KV 2/4364.

22 Sir Vernon Kell to Major Goldsmith 14/9/1937, TNA, KV 2/1273. An earlier memo, dated three days after Koestler's release in response to a Home Office enquiry, states that 'we do not appear to have any special information either for or against him'.

23 Arthur Koestler, *Spanish Testament* (Victor Gollancz, 1937), p. 18.

24 The Duchess of Atholl 'Foreword' to *Spanish Testament*, p. 5.

Chapter 6

1 From 1937 it added its own bar (the 'Isobar') and restaurant (the 'Half Hundred Club'). For more discussion of the Isokon building and its residents, see Jill Pearlman, 'The Spies Who Came into the Modernist Fold; The Covert Life of Hampstead's Lawn Road Flats', *Journal of the Society of Architectural Historians* 72, no. 3 (September 2013): 358–81;David Burke, *The Lawn Road Flats: Spies, Writers and Artists* (The Boydell Press, 2014).

2 Straight, *After Long Silence*, pp. 101–2; Carter, *Anthony Blunt: His Lives*, 184–5.

3 Nigel West and Oleg Tsarev, *The Crown Jewels* (Harper Collins, 1999), pp. 204–5.

4 Ibid., p. 204.

5 Ibid., p. 206.

6 Cairncross, *The Enigma Spy*, pp. 54–5.

7 West and Tsarev, *The Crown Jewels*, p. 210.

8 CULMC, Add. 10042 Box 1.

9 West and Tsarev, *The Crown Jewels*, p. 209.

10 John Cairncross confirmed this. CULMC, Add. 10042 Box 1.

11 TNA, KV 2/1009. One of the two MI5 files on Maly, released under 'Paul Hardt', one of his pseudonyms.

12 CULMC, Add. 10042 Box 1.

13 Mann file No 9705, p. 239, cited in West and Tsarev, *The Crown Jewels*, p. 121.

14 TNA, FCO 158/129. 'Memo of 28 December 1979', referring to note on Cairncross's probation report of January 1938.

Chapter 7

1 Tim Bouverie, *Appeasing Hitler* (The Bodley Head, 2019), p. 157.

2 Paul Willetts, *Rendezvous at the Russian Tea Rooms* (Constable, 2015), p. 14.

3 Lownie, *Stalin's Englishman*, p. 61.

4 Kim Philby, *My Silent War* (The Modern Library, 2002), p. xxvii.

5 Boyd, *Travellers in the Third Reich*, p. 262.

6 Ibid., p. 263.

7 Ibid., p. 265.

8 Cairncross, *The Enigma Spy*, pp. 66–7.

9 Lord Strang, *Home and Abroad* (Andre Deutsch, 1956), p. 21.

10 Ibid., p. 22.

11 Ibid., p. 29.

12 Ibid., p. 37.

13 Ibid., p. 50.

14 Gill Bennett, *The Zinoviev Letter: The Conspiracy that Never Dies* (Oxford University Press, 2018), p. 253.

15 Strang, *Home and Abroad*, p. 65.

16 Details of the Travellers Club membership are held at London Metropolitan Archives (LMA/4519/B/02). Cairncross was formally accepted at a meeting of 25 November 1939. He was evidently a regular visitor, as a guest, before his membership was officially confirmed.

17 I am grateful to David Broadhead, the secretary of the Traveller's Club, for this information.

18 CULMC, Add. 10042 Box 1.

19 Strang, *Home and Abroad*, p. 122.

20 Ibid., pp. 125–6.

21 Ibid., p. 126.

22 Ibid., p. 137.

23 Ibid.

24 Ibid., p. 139.

25 Ibid.

26 Ibid., p. 140.

27 Ibid., p. 145.

28 Ibid., p. 148.

29 Hansard 3/10/1938 Vol. 339 has the speeches of this long-running debate.

30 Eric Hobsbawm, *Age of Extremes: The Short Twentieth Century* (Michael Joseph, 1994), p. 145.

31 Denis Healey, *The Time of My Life* (Penguin Books, 1990), p. 37.

32 TNA, PREM 19/3942.

33 Cairncross, *The Enigma Spy*, p. 73.

Chapter 8

1   David Rubin, email to author.

2   CULMC, Add. 10042 Box 1.

3   Frances Cairncross, interview with author.

4   Moscow was aware of this. West and Tsarev, *The Crown Jewels*, p. 209.

5   CULMC, Add. 10042 Box 1.

6   CULMC, Add. 10042 Box 2.

7   West and Tsarev, *The Crown Jewels*, p. 209.

8   Cairncross, *The Enigma Spy*, p. 80.

9   Gabriel Gorodetsky (ed.), *The Maisky Diaries* (Yale University Press, 2015), p. 173.

10 Foreign Policy Committee, cited in Gorodetsky, *The Maisky Diaries*, p. 182.

11 Gorodetsky, *The Maisky Diaries*, pp. 182–3.

12 William Strang, *Documents on British Foreign Policy 1919–1939*, Third Series, Vol. VI 20/7/1939, no. 376. Cited in Bouverie, *Appeasing Hitler*, p. 354.

13 Cairncross, *The Enigma Spy*, pp. 79–80.

14 TNA, FCO 158/129.

15 *War on the USSR?* was a sixteen-page pamphlet produced by the University Socialist Club and published by the University Labour Federation.

16 Ibid.

17 Henry Hemming, *M: Maxwell Knight, MI5's Greatest Spymaster* (Preface, 2017), p. 231.

18 Willetts, *Rendezvous at the Russian Tea Rooms*, p. 63. See also Tim Tate, *Hitler's British Traitors* (Icon, 2018). The list of Right Club members passed to MI5 is held at TNA, KV 2/677.

19 Philipps, *A Spy Named Orphan*, pp. 116–17.

20 Cairncross, *The Enigma Spy*, p. 83.

21 West and Tsarev, *The Crown Jewels*, p. 216.

22 Michael Smith, *The Anatomy of a Traitor* (Aurum Press, 2017), p. 239.

23 West and Tsarev, *The Crown Jewels*, p. 215. Richard Davenport-Hines, *Enemies Within: Communists, The Cambridge Spies and the Making of Modern Britain* (William Collins, 2018), p. 328.

24 West and Tsarev, *The Crown Jewels*, p. 204.

Chapter 9

1 Michael Smith, *The Secrets of Station X* (Biteback, 2011), p. 235.

2 West and Tsarev, *The Crown Jewels*, p. 218.

3 Cairncross, *The Enigma Spy*, p. 97.

4 William Millward, 'Life In and Out of Hut 3', in F. H. Hinsley and Alan Stripp, *Codebreakers: The Inside Story of Bletchley Park* (Oxford University Press, 1993), p. 17.

5 Irene Young, *Enigma Variations: A Memoir of Love and War* (Mainstream Publishing, 1990), p. 73.

6 Millward, 'Life In and Out of Hut 3', p. 20.

7 Cairncross, *The Enigma Spy*, p. 100.

8 Ibid., p. 99.

9 Ibid., p. 103.

10 Richard J. Aldrich, *GCHQ: The Uncensored Story of Britain's Most Secret Intelligence Agency* (Harper Press, 2010), pp. 36–7.

11 Yuri Modin, *My Five Cambridge Friends* (Headline Books, 1994), p. 113.

12 Ibid., p. 114.

13 Ibid.

14 Henry Dryden, 'Recollections of Bletchley Park, France and Cairo', in *Codebreakers: The Inside Story of Bletchley Park*, eds. F. H. Hinsley and Alan Stripp (Oxford University, Press, 2001), p. 208.

15 TNA, KV 2/980.

16 John Cairncross to Douglas Parmée 25/4/1992. Correspondence provided by Nick Parmée.

Chapter 10

1 Hugh Trevor-Roper, *The Secret World* (I.B. Tauris, 2014), p. 42.

2 Gorsky's report to Moscow, cited in West and Tsarev, *Crown Jewels*, p. 219.

3 West and Tsarev, *Crown Jewels*, p. 220.

4 Cairncross, *The Enigma Spy*, p. 114.

5 Lownie, *Stalin's Englishman*, p. 87.

6 Chapman Pincher, *Too Secret Too Long* (St. Martin's Press, 1984), p. 397; Christopher Andrew and Vasili Mitrokhin, *The Sword and the Shield* (Basic Books, 1999), p. 126.

7 Tim Milne, *Kim Philby* (Biteback, 2014), p. 69.

8 Ibid., p. 84.

9 Malcolm Muggeridge, *Chronicles of Wasted Time, Volume 2: The Infernal Grove* (William Collins, 1973), p. 124.

10 Ibid., pp. 125–6.

11 Cairncross, *The Enigma Spy*, p. 115.

12 Graham Greene, *Ways of Escape* (The Bodley Head, 1980), p. 34.

13 West and Tsarev *The Crown Jewels*, p. 221.

14 Ibid., pp. 220–1.

15 Philipps, *A Spy Named Orphan: The Enigma of Donald Maclean*, p. 167.

16 Davenport-Hines, *Enemies Within*, p. 331.

17 Cairncross, *The Enigma Spy*, p. 127.

18 Lord Vansittart, 'Communists in the Public Service', *Hansard*, 29 March 1950.

19 They were published in *The Penguin New Writing*, numbers 39 and 40 (its final edition) in 1950.

20 Cairncross, *The Enigma Spy*, p. 125.

Chapter 11

1 Modin, *My Five Cambridge Friends*, p. 45.

2 Cited in Evans, *Eric Hobsbawm: A Life in History*, p. 263.

3 Evans, *Eric Hobsbawm: A Life in History*, pp. 263–4.

4 BBC Written Archives (BBC WA) John Cairncross Talks: File 1.

5 Cairncross, *The Enigma Spy*, p. 127.

6 West and Tsarev, *The Crown Jewels*, p. 223.

7 Modin, *My Five Cambridge Friends*, p. 170.

8 West and Tsarev, *The Crown Jewels*, p. 223.

9 Aldrich, *GCHQ: The Uncensored Story of Britain's Most Secret Intelligence Agency*.

10 Roland Philipps, *A Spy Named Orphan*, pp. 285–9.

11 Guy Liddell Diaries 27/6/1951 TNA, KV 4/473, p. 83.

12 Guy Liddell Diaries 10/7/1951 TNA, KV 4/473.

13 Guy Liddell Diaries 3/11/1951 TNA, KV 4/473.

14 Guy Liddell Diaries 14/11/1951 TNA, KV 4/473.

15 Guy Liddell Diaries 4/3/1952 TNA, KV 4/474.

16 Details of Cairncross's interviews with the Security Service in 1951 can be found in Guy Burgess's MI5 file. TNA, KV 2/4108.

17 Jim Skardon, 'Interview with John Cairncross on 31.3.52'. TNA, KV 2/4108.

18 Ibid.

19 Guy Liddell Diaries 1/4/1952. TNA, KV 4/474.

20 Jim Skardon, 'Interview with John Cairncross on 2/4/1952'. TNA, KV 2/4108.

21 Guy Liddell Diaries 3/4/1952 TNA, KV 4/474.

22 Cairncross, *The Enigma Spy*, p. 131.

23 Christopher Andrew, *The Defence of the Realm* (Allen Lane, 2009), p. 428; CULMC Add. 10042 Box 1.

24 Nigel West, *Cold War Spymaster*, Frontline Books (Barnsley, 2018), p. 195.

25 Modin, *My Five Cambridge Friends*, p. 217.

26 'A Civil Service Love Song', in John Cairncross, *By a Lonely Sea* (Hong Kong University Press/Oxford University Press, 1959), p. 92; emphasis in original.

Chapter 12

1 Lord Hankey to John Cairncross 5/6/1952, CULMC Add. 10042 Box 5.

2 'An Economist Looks Round Moscow', *The Listener* 29/5/1952.

3 Cairncross, *Living with the Century*, p. 165.

4 Helena Wood memo no date but 1951. BBC WA. John Cairncross Scriptwriter File 1 1951-1962.

5 Rayner Heppenstall to John Cairncross, 27/10/1952. BBC WA. John Cairncross Scriptwriter File 1 1951-1962.

6 CULMC, Add. 10042 Box 10.

7 Frances Cairncross, interview with author.

8 CULMC, Add. 10042 Box 10.

9 Giulia Cerquetti, 'La Stampa antifascista a Boston fra 1939 e il 1945', *La Stampa Italiano all'estero* July–December 2007.

10 Silva Balit (Enzo Tagliacozzo's daughter), interview with author.

11 Stephen Gundle, *Death and the Dolce Vita* (Canongate, 2011), p. 7.

12 CULMC, Add. 10042 Box 4.

13 Andrew Boyd to John Cairncross 19/8/1955 CULMC, Add. 10042 Box 4.

14 John Cairncross to Andrew Boyd 27/8/1955 CULMC, Add. 10042 Box 4.

15 He recalled this in a letter to his sister Elsie Cairncross, 25/5/1977. UGA, DC106 Add. 87/8.

16 John Cairncross, *The Enigma Spy*, p. 135; John Cairncross, 'Madonna Weeps in Italian Town', *Boston Globe* 6/6/1954.

17 Young's 'Table Talk' column in *The Observer* 15/8/1954 confirms his interest in such circles.

18 M. Salvadori review of Antifascismo e della Resistenza, in *The Journal of Modern History* 42, no. 3 (September 1970).

19 Gabi Cairncross to Mary Cairncross 15/5/1955. UGA, DC106 Add. 87/8.

20 John Cairncross to Alec Cairncross 28/5/1955. UGA, DC106 Add. 87/8.

21 Declan Walton, interview with author.

22 Ibid.

Chapter 13

1 CULMC, Add. 10042 Box 2.

2 *Times Literary Supplement*, 11/1/1957.

3 CULMC, Add. 10042 Box 10.

4 A.F. Maddocks memo to J. Street 26/8/1964. TNA, FCO 158/129.

5 Cairncross, *The Enigma Spy*, p. 136.

6 John Weightman (BBC Talks Dept) to John Cairncross 5/6/1957. BBC WA, John Cairncross Scriptwriter File 1 1951-1962.

7 *Times Literary Supplement*, 12/9/1958.

8 Declan Walton, interview with author.

9 *Times Literary Supplement*, 12/9/1958.

10 John Cairncross to Alec Cairncross 4/11/1958. UGA, DC106. Add. 87/8.

11 John Cairncross to Alec Cairncross 1/12/1958. UGA, DC106. Add. 87/8.

12 John Cairncross, *By a Lonely Sea* (Hong Kong University Press, 1958).

13 John Cairncross to Alec Cairncross 4/11/1958. UGA, DC106. Add. 87/8.

14 John Cairncross to Alec Cairncross 1/3/1961. UGA DC106. Add. 87/8.

15 John Cairncross to Alec Cairncross 1/3/1961. UGA DC106. Add. 87/8.

16 Jeannette Walton, interview with author.

17 John Cairncross to Alec Cairncross 11/1/1962. UGA DC106. Add. 87/8.

18 John Cairncross to Graham Greene 4/8/1963. MS. 1995.003 Box 13, Folder 32.

19 Graham Greene to Dr Lester Crocker 26/8/1963. MS. 1995.003 Box 13, Folder 32.

20 Cyril Connolly, *Enemies of Promise* (Penguin Books, 1961), p. 126.

21 Gabi Cairncross to Alec Cairncross 30/1/1964. CULMC, Add. 10042 Box 10.

22 Connolly, *Enemies of Promise*, p. 127.

23 Gabi to Alec 30/1/1964. CULMC, Add. 10042 Box 10.

24 CULMC Add. 10042 Box 11. FBI file 65-68525. The FBI file was released after request made by Richard Norton-Taylor.

25 Donald Davie, 'Unsettling Restraint', *New Statesman*, 3/1/1964.

26 *Times Literary Supplement*, 23/4/1964.

27 Letters, *Times Literary Supplement*, 25/6/1964.

Chapter 14

1 Richard Norton-Taylor, 'MI5 and MI 6 Cover-Up of Cambridge Spy Ring Laid Bare', *The Guardian*, 23/10/2015.

2 For the circumstances of Philby's defection see Ben Macintyre's brilliant account in *A Spy Among Friends* (Bloomsbury, 2014).

3 *The Enigma Spy* dates the first meeting in mid-April, but FO records confirm the February date TNA, FCO 158/129.

4 Cairncross, *The Enigma Spy*, p. 142.

5 Carter, *Anthony Blunt: His Lives*, p. 436.

6 Andrew, *The Defence of the Realm*, p. 437.

7 Minutes of meeting held at 10 Downing St. 5.00 pm Thursday 20 February 1964 TNA, FCO 158/129.

8 Ibid.

9 This and other ongoing correspondence between Burke Trend, the prime minister and Roger Hollis on the Cairncross case can be found at TNA, FCO 158/129.

10 Burke Trend, memo to PM 6/3/1964 TNA, FCO 158/129.

11   Cairncross, *Living with the Century*, p. 302.

12   Frances Cairncross, interview with author.

13   Lester Crocker to John Cairncross 21/7/1964. CULMC, Add. 10042 Box 10.

14   Lester Crocker to John Cairncross 14/9/1964. CULMC, Add. 10042 Box 10.

15   Gabi Cairncross to Alec Cairncross 20/10/1964. CULMC, Add. 10042 Box 10.

16   Martin Esslin to John Cairncross 5/6/1964. John Cairncross Scriptwriter File II BBC WA.

17   John Cairncross to Martin Esslin 9/6/1964. John Cairncross Scriptwriter File II BBC WA. Emphasis in original.

18   John Cairncross Scriptwriter File II. BBC WA.

19   John Cairncross Scriptwriter File IV. Drama department memo. BBC WA.

Chapter 15

1   This is John Cairncross's translation from *By a Lonely Sea* (Hong Kong University Press, 1959), p. 78.

2   Richard Davenport-Hines has detailed the response of Dick White and MI6 colleagues in *Enemies Within*, pp. 498–504.

3   Graham Greene's 'Foreword' to Kim Philby, *My Silent War* (McGibbon and Kee, 1968).

4   This is the view of Martin Pearce, Oldfield's nephew, in *Spymaster* (Bantam Press, 2016), pp. 300–1 and Phillip Knightley in his introduction to the 2002 edition of *My Silent War* (Modern Library Paperback).

5   Davenport-Hines, *Enemies Within*, p. 505.

6   TNA, PREM 19/3942. W.C. Beckett memo.

7   TNA, PREM 19/3942.

8   David Cairncross, interview with author. David Cairncross was a regular participant in such meetings and would occasionally meet Gabi.

9   TNA, PREM 19/3942.

10   Andrews, *The Shadow Man*.

11   Cairncross, *The Enigma Spy*, p. 145.

12   David Rubin, correspondence with author.

13   Stella Rimington, *Open Secret* (Hutchinson, 2001), p. 117.

14   Rimington, *Open Secret*, p. 120.

15 Cairncross, *The Enigma Spy*, p. 148.

16 Ibid., p. 149.

17 Rimington, *Open Secret*, p. 120.

18 John Cairncross, *After Polygamy Was Made a Sin* (Routledge and Kegan Paul, 1974), pp. 204–5.

19 Cyril Connolly, 'How Many Wives at a Time?' *Sunday Times*, 26/5/1974.

20 Freddie Ayer to John Cairncross 30/1/1977. CULMC, Add. 10042 Box 10.

21 Graham Greene to John Cairncross 23/1/1975 and 7/4/1975. MS. 1995.003 Box 13, Folder 31.

22 John Cairncross to Graham Greene 15/2/1977. MS. 1995.003 Box 13, Folder 31.

23 Vikram Shah, interview with author.

24 John Cairncross to Alec Cairncross 15/5/1977 UGA, DC106 Add. 87/8.

25 John Cairncross to Elsie Cairncross 28/5/1977 UGA, DC106 Add. 87/8.

26 John Cairncross to Elsie Cairncross 28/5/1977 UGA, DC106 Add. 87/8.

27 John Cairncross to Allan Evans 20/11/1979. Correspondence made available to author.

28 Allan Evans 'Memories of John Cairncross', private document passed to author.

Chapter 16

1   David Rubin, email communication with author.

2   All contributions to the debate can be found in Hansard 21/11/1979 Vol. 974 cc. 402–520.

3   Richard Davenport-Hines captures the atmosphere of the times well in *Enemies Within*, pp. 525–34.

4   Hansard op. cit.

5   Reported in *The Guardian*, 24/12/1979.

6   *The Sunday Times*, 23/12/1979.

7   'Sir Alec "astonished" by confession', *The Guardian*, 24/12/1979.

8   *The Scotsman*, 24/12/1979.

9   Hansard Vol. 976 c817W 17/1/1980.

10 David Cairncross, interview with author.

11 Declan Walton, interview with author.

12 John Cairncross to David Rubin 10/2/1980. CULMC Add. 10042 Box 4.

13   Graham Greene to John Cairncross 28/7/1980. MS. 1995.003 Box 13, Folder 33.

14   Silvia Balit, interview with author.

15   John Cairncross to Graham Greene 3/7/1982. MS. 1995.003 Box 13, Folder 34.

16   Graham Greene to John Cairncross 16/7/1982 MS. 1995.003 Box 13, Folder 33.

17   John Cairncross to Alec Cairncross 15/11/1984 CULMC, Add. 10042 Box 10.

18   Kay Killingsworth, interview with author.

19   David Cahn, correspondence with author.

20   Gayle Brinkerhoff/David Gow interview.

21   Gayle Brinkerhoff, interview with author.

22   John Cairncross to David Rubin 9/7/1985. CULMC, Add. 10042 Box 4.

23   Marco Zatterin, 'John Cairncross: La Dolce Vita del Quinto Uomo', *La Stampa*, 14/5/2018.

24   Fiorenzo Niccoli, interview with author.

25   John Cairncross to David Rubin 14/3/1987. CULMC, Add. 10042 Box 4.

Chapter 17

1   Allan Evans, 'Memories of John Cairncross'.

2   CULMC, Add. 10042 Box 1.

3   John Cairncross to David Rubin 14/3/1987. CULMC, Add. 10042 Box 4.

4   Hugh Trevor-Roper, 'The Real Harm Done by the Fifth Man', *Sunday Telegraph*, 21/10/1990.

5   Phillip Knightley, 'The Don and the Defector', *The Spectator*, 3/11/1990.

6   For an impressive demolition of Gordievsky's claims about Michael Foot, see Francis Wheen 'When the Boot Was on the Other Foot', *The Guardian*, 22/2/1995. The Gordievsky claim was repeated in Ben Macintyre's *The Spy and the Traitor* (Viking, 2018).

7   Knightley, 'The Don and the Defector'.

8   Macintyre, *The Spy and the Traitor*, pp. 120–1.

9   Richard Norton-Taylor 'So Many Faces Went So Many Tales', *The Guardian*, 17/12/1994.

10   Francis Wheen, *Independent on Sunday*, 14/11/1990.

11 'Lesmahagow man named as "fifth" spy', *Hamilton Advertiser*, 9 October 1990. His sister Margaret refused to talk to the paper.

12 David Cairncross, interview with author.

13 CULMC, Add. 10042 Box 10.

14 Gayle Brinkerhoff, interview with author.

15 Ibid.

16 Graham Greene, *The Virtue of Disloyalty* (University of Hamburg, 1969).

17 'Thoughts in a Greene Shade'. CULMC, Add. 10042 Box 1.

18 CULMC, Add. 10042 Box 1.

19 Gayle Brinkerhoff, interview with author.

20 CULMC, Add. 10042 Box 1.

21 John Cairncross to Alec Cairncross 21/8/1991. CULMC. Add. 10042 Box 9.

22 John Cairncross to Alec Cairncross 1/8/1993. CULMC. Add. 10042 Box 9.

23 David Rubin, communication with author.

24 *The Guardian*, 25/5/1982.

25 John Cairncross to Judith Luna (OUP editor) 6/9/1993. CULMC, Add. 10042 Box 2.

26 His intended project was passed on to Ann Lawson Lucas, whose translation of *The Adventures of Pinocchio* was published by OUP in 1996.

27 John Cairncross, 'Prayer' from *By a Lonely Sea* (Hong Kong University Press/Oxford University Press, 1959).

Epilogue

1 Chapman Pincher, *Their Trade is Treachery*, (Sidgwick and Jackson, 1981), pp. 153–9.

2 Frances Cairncross, interview with author.

3 See Richard J. Evans discussion of support for Blunt in *Eric Hobsbawm: A Life in History*, pp. 482–5.

4 Declan Walton, Silvia Balit and David Cairncross, interviews with author.

5 Gayle Brinkerhoff, interview with author.

6 CULM, Add. 10042 Box 1.

Select Bibliography

Aldrich, R. J., *GCHQ* (London: Harper Press, 2010).

Andrew, C., *The Defence of the Realm* (London: Allen Lane, 2009).

Andrew, C. and O. Gordievsky, *KGB: The Inside Story* (London: Harper Collins, 1990).

Andrew, C. and V. Mitrokhin, *The Sword and the Shield* (New York: Basic Books, 1999).

Andrews, G., *The Shadow Man* (London: I.B. Tauris, 2015).

Ashton, H., *A Preface to Molière* (London: Longmans, 1927).

Bailey, R., 'Communist in SOE: Explaining James Klugmann's Recruitment and Retention', *Intelligence and National Security* xx/1 (2005): 72–97.

Borovik, G., *The Philby Files*, ed. P. Knightley (London: Warner Books, 1995).

Bouverie, T., *Appeasing Hitler* (London: Bodley Head, 2019).

Bower, T., *The Perfect English Spy: Dick White and the Secret War 1935–1990* (London: Heinemann, 1995).

Boyd, J., *Travellers in the Third Reich* (London: Elliott and Thompson, 2017).

Boyle, A., *The Climate of Treason* (London: Hutchinson, 1979).

Burke, D., *The Lawn Road Flats: Spies, Writers and Artists* (Martlesham: Boydell Press, 2014).

Cairncross, A., *Living with the Century* (Fife: lynx, 1998).

Cairncross, J., *The Enigma Spy: An Autobiography* (London: Century Random House, 1997).

Carter, M., *Anthony Blunt: His Lives* (London: Macmillan, 2001).

Cecil, R., *A Divided Life: A Personal Portrait of the Spy Donald Maclean* (New York: William Morrow, 1989).

Colville, J., *Footprints in Time: Memories* (London: Michael Russell, 1984).

Connolly, C., *Enemies of Promise* (Harmondsworth: Penguin 1961).

Conradi, P. J., *Iris Murdoch: A Life* (London, Harper Collins, 2001).

Davenport-Hines, R., *Enemies Within: Communists, The Cambridge Spies and the Making of Modern Britain* (William Collins: London, 2018).

Davenport-Hines, R., *John Cairncross* (Oxford: Oxford Dictionary of National Biography, 2009).

Davenport-Hines, R. and A. Sisman (eds), *One Hundred Letters from Hugh Trevor-Roper* (Oxford: Oxford University Press, 2015).

Driberg, T., *Guy Burgess: A Portrait with Background* (London: Weidenfeld and Nicolson, 1956).

Evans, Richard J., *Eric Hobsbawm: A Life in History* (London: Little, Brown, 2019).

Greene, G., *Ways of Escape* (London: The Bodley Head, 1980).

Gundle, S., *Death and the Dolce Vita* (Edinburgh: Canongate, 2011).

Haden Guest, C., *David Guest: A Scientist Fights for Freedom* (London: Lawrence and Wishart, 1939).

Hart, J., *Ask Me No More: An Autobiography* (London: Peter Halban, 1998).

Hazzard, S., *Greene on Capri* (London: Virago, 2001).

Healey, D., *The Time of My Life* (London: Penguin, 1990).

Hemming, H., *M: Maxwell Knight, MI5's Greatest Spymaster* (London: Preface Publishing, 2017).

Hinsley, F. H. and A. Stripp, *Codebreakers: The Inside Story of Bletchley Park* (Oxford: Oxford University Press, 1994).

Hobsbawm, E., *Interesting Times* (London: Allen Lane, 2002).

Howarth, T. E. B., *Cambridge between the Wars* (London: Collins, 1978).

Hyde, D., *I Believed* (London: William Heinemann, 1951).

Ireland, J., *The Traitors* (London: John Murray, 2017).

Jackson, J., *The Popular Front in France: Defending Democracy 1934–1938* (Cambridge: Cambridge University Press, 1988).

Kiernan, V., 'On Treason', *London Review of Books* ix/12 (25 June 1987).

Kiernan, V., 'The Unrewarded End', *London Review of Books* xx/18 (17 September 1998).

Kingsford, P., *The Hunger Marchers in Britain 1920–1940* (London: Lawrence and Wishart, 1982).

Klugmann, J., *From Trotsky to Tito* (London: Lawrence and Wishart, 1951).

Koestler, A., *The Invisible Writing* (London: Vintage 2005).

Krivitsky, W., *I Was Stalin's Agent* (London: Hamish Hamilton, 1939).

Lewis, J., *Shades of Greene* (London: Jonathan Cape, 2010).

Lownie, A., *Stalin's Englishman: The Lives of Guy Burgess* (London: Hodder and Stoughton, 2015).

MacGibbon, H., *Maverick Spy: Stalin's Super-Agent in World War II* (London: I.B. Tauris, 2017).

Macintyre, B., *A Spy Among Friends* (London: Bloomsbury, 2014).

Macintyre, B., *The Spy and the Traitor* (London: Viking, 2018).

Macleod, A., *The Death of Uncle Joe* (London: Merlin Press, 1997).

McKay, S., *The Secret Life of Bletchley Park* (London: Aurum, 2011).

McMeekin, S., *The Red Millionaire: A Political Biography of Willi Munzenberg* (New Haven, CT: Yale University Press, 2003).

McNeish, J., *The Sixth Man: The Extraordinary Life of Paddy Costello* (London: Quartet Books, 2008).

Miles, J., *The Nine Lives of Otto Katz* (London: Bantam Books, 2010).

Modin, Y., *My Five Cambridge Friends* (London: Headline, 1994).

Moorehead, C., *A Bold and Dangerous Family: The Rossellis and the Fight Against Mussolini* (London: Chatto and Windus, 2017).

Morgan, K., *Against War and Fascism* (Manchester: Manchester University Press, 1989).

Orwell, G., *The Road to Wigan Pier* (London: Penguin Books, 2014 (1937)).

Page, B., D. Leitch and P. Knightley, *Philby: The Spy Who Betrayed a Generation* (London: Sphere Books, 1977).

Pearce, M., *Spymaster* (London: Bantam Press, 2016).

Philby, K., *My Silent War* (London: MacGibbon and Kee, 1968).

Philipps, R., *A Spy Named Orphan: The Enigma of Donald Maclean* (London: The Bodley Head, 2018).

Pincher, C., *Their Trade Is Treachery* (London: Sidgwick and Jackson, 1981).

Pugliese, S., *Carlo Rosselli* (London: Harvard, 1999).

Rees, G., *A Chapter of Accidents* (London: Chatto and Windus, 1972).

Rimington, S., *Open Secret* (London: Hutchinson, 2001).

Rycroft, C., 'Memoirs of an Old Bolshevik', in P. Fuller (ed.), *Psychoanalysis and Beyond* (London: Hogarth Press, 1991).

Samuel, R., *The Lost World of British Communism* (London: Verso, 2006).

Schlogel, K., *Moscow 1937* (Cambridge: Polity, 2012).

Seale, P. and M. McConville, *Philby: The Long Road to Moscow* (London: Hamish Hamilton, 1973).

Sherry, N., *The Life of Graham Greene Volume 2: 1939–1955* (London, Jonathan Cape, 2004).

Smith, M., *The Secrets of Station X* (London: Biteback, 2011).

Straight, M., *After Long Silence* (New York: W.W. Norton, 1983).

Strang, W., *Home and Abroad* (London: Andre Deutsch, 1956).

Tate, T., *Hitler's British Traitors* (London: Icon, 2018).

Trevor-Roper, H., *The Secret World*, ed. E. Harrison (London: I.B. Tauris, 2014).

West, N., *Cold War Spymaster* (Barnsley: Frontline, 2018).

West, N., *MASK: MI5's Penetration of the Communist Party of Great Britain* (London: Routledge, 2005).

West, N. and O. Tsarev, *The Crown Jewels* (London: Harper Collins, 1999).

Willetts, P., *Rendezvous at the Russian Tea Rooms* (London: Constable, 2015).

Wood, N., *Communism and British Intellectuals* (London: Victor Gollancz, 1959).

Wright, P., *Spycatcher* (New York: Viking Penguin, 1987).

Young, I., *Enigma Variations* (Edinburgh: Mainstream, 1990).

Young, W., 'Table Talk', *The Observer* 15 August 1954.

John Cairncross's Publications

New Light on Molière (Librairie Droz, 1956).
By a Lonely Sea (Hong Kong University Press/OUP, 1959).
Molière: Bourgeois et Libertin (Nizet, 1963).
After Polygamy Was Made a Sin (Routledge, 1974).
L'Humanite de Molière (Nizet, 1988).
The Enigma Spy (Century, 1997).

Translations

Phaedra (Racine, Droz, 1958).
Iphigenia; Phaedra; Athaliah (Racine, Penguin Classics, 1963).
Andromache; Britannicus; Berenice (Racine, Penguin Classics, 1967).
The Cid; Cinna; The Theatrical Illusion (Corneille, Penguin Classics, 1975).
Polyeuctus; The Liar; The Nicomedes (Corneille, Penguin Classics, 1980).
La Fontaine Fables and Other Poems (Colin Smythe, 1982).
Picard, Raymond. *Two Centuries of French Literature. 1600 – 1800.*
　(Translated by John Cairncross, World University Library, 1969).

Index